THE SELF IN TIME

Developmental Perspectives

THE SELF IN TIME

Developmental Perspectives

Edited by

Chris Moore
Karen Lemmon
Dalhousie University

 LAWRENCE ERLBAUM ASSOCIATES, PUBLISHERS

2001   Mahwah, New Jersey   London

The final camera copy for this work was supplied by the editors.

Lawrence Erlbaum Associates, Inc., Publishers
10 Industrial Avenue
Mahwah, NJ 07430

Cover design by Kathryn Houghtaling Lacey

Library of Congress Cataloging-in-Publication Data

The self in time : developmental perspectives / edited by Chris Moore & Karen Lemmon.
   p. cm.
   Includes bibliographical references and indexes.
ISBN 0-8058-3455-9 (hardcover : alk. paper)
1. Self–Congresses. 2. Self in children–Congresses. 3. Time–Psychological aspects–Congresses. I. Moore, Chris, 1958- II. Lemmon, Karen.
BF697 .S4375 2001
126—dc21   00-067720
                                                CIP

Books published by Lawrence Erlbaum Associates are printed on acid-free paper, and their bindings are chosen for strength and durability.

Printed in the United States of America
10 9 8 7 6 5 4 3 2 1

Contents

Preface

As the chapters in this volume will attest, there are a variety of routes to an interest in the idea of the self in time. We first became interested in the topic in considering the function of theory of mind. Having a theory of mind had always been supposed to be useful in the organization of social behavior. However, it also seemed to us to be an essential component of the organization of one's own future behavior. In other words, to show adaptive future behavior, the child must come to grips with the idea that his or her own immediate mental states are connected to his or her own future mental states. Meanwhile, in the memory literature, research on episodic and autobiographical memory seemed to require the notion of an extended self. In particular, the developmentalists working on early memory were forced to tackle head on the relations between autobiographical memory and self-development. And then there were those with perhaps a more direct interest in self-development faced with the idea that mirror self-recognition did not seem to capture all that was entailed by having an understanding of self. This convergence of a variety of research interests around the notion of the temporally extended self called out for an attempt at integration, and so, in 1997, we organized a symposium at the meeting of the Society for Research in Child Development in Washington, DC. This volume is an expanded version of that symposium. We are grateful to Judi Amsel for her faith in the project and for her encouragement. Judi was a great ally for developmental psychology during her time with Lawrence Erlbaum Associates. We are also most grateful to Bonita D'Amil and Sarah Wahlert of Lawrence Erlbaum Associates for their excellent editorial work.

- Chris Moore
- Karen Lemmon

1

The Nature and Utility of the Temporally Extended Self

Chris Moore
Karen Lemmon
Dalhousie University

What would it take to have the foresight to send a letter to one's future self (Fig. 1.1)? And what would it take for someone, on receiving such a letter, to feel sorrow for the sender? Because the persistence of personal identity through time is such a fundamental feature of our self-concepts, it is likely that these questions rarely enter into our day-to-day thinking. However, they are significant questions because, in a very real sense, Hobbes is correct: None of us *is* the same either as we were in the

FIG. 1.1. Calvin and Hobbes © Watterson. Reprinted with permission of Universal Press Syndicate. All rights reserved.

past or as we will be in the future. If the self in the past is indeed a different person, how is it that we assume a special attachment to that particular person? More provocatively, what gives any one of us the right to make decisions now that will affect the future circumstances of the person whom we will become? Answers to these questions require an analysis of what constitutes a notion of self spanning past, present, and future. A developmental approach to these issues attempts to answer the further question: When and how do children acquire such a notion? The chapters in this volume attempt in various ways to address these issues.

THE NATURE OF THE TEMPORALLY EXTENDED SELF

At least since the time of William James (1890/1950), numerous authors have identified many forms of self (see Mitchell, 1994, for a good accounting; see also Nelson, chap. 2, this volume). The recent study within psychology of the "self in time" started with Neisser (1988) who distinguished the "extended self" as one of his "five kinds of self-knowledge." More common these days is that the modifier *temporally* is added to Neisser's term to denote the critical aspect of this kind of self—that it is a self with a past and a future not just a present. The incorporation of *temporally* also distinguishes this kind of self from other forms of extension (e.g., Mitchell, 1994) whereby the self is thought to extend beyond the individual mind-body to include other entities, such as possessions. In what follows we adopt for convenience the term *temporally extended self* (TES).

Authors who have explicitly addressed the idea of the TES have recognized that the TES covers past, present, and future (e.g., Neisser, 1988; Povinelli, 1995; Suddendorf, 1999). As Neisser (1988, p. 46) put it, "The extended self is the self as it was in the past and as we expect it to be in the future, known primarily on the basis of memory." However, it is fair to say that the bulk of the work on the TES has concentrated on its role in personal forms of memory: Episodic and autobiographical memory. Indeed, there are other collections on the role of the self in memory (e.g., Neisser & Fivush, 1994). More recently, interest in future-oriented thinking has started to grow (e.g., Haith, Benson, Roberts, & Pennington, 1994; Thompson, Barresi, & Moore, 1997). The time seems right to try to connect these two bodies of work and to try to reach some consensus on the way in which the self can be understood to span past, present, and future.

For most of the authors in this volume, having a TES amounts to possessing a kind of representation of self. *Self* is understood to be a person with continuous existence through time. Thus the person who performed certain activities and had certain experiences at particular moments in the past is understood to be, in an essential way, identical with the person who is now acting or experiencing. Furthermore, this person will continue to be essentially identical to a person who will act and experience things in the future. This kind of understanding is premised on the self as experiencer (the "I"), and the recognition of self as an object (the "me"; Harley & Reese, 1999; Howe & Courage, 1997; Nelson, chap. 2, this volume).

There are a number of points to stress in this type of account. First, a key idea here is that of identity. A TES entails an identity between self-representations from different moments in time. In a sense, the self provides a common semantic thread for the interpretation of memory information. Neisser (1988, p. 47), wrote: "The extended self can be thought of as a kind of cumulated total ... of the things that I remember having done and the things I think of myself as doing regularly." Thus, particular events can be coded in terms of whether they were personally experienced and scripts coded in terms of whether they involve the self. However, recognizing an identity relation between any two moments in time involving the self is not enough. So, second, the identity relation must be between one or more noncurrent self-representations—for example, the self that went to the University each day this week—and a current self-representation—for example, the self that is right now staying home on Saturday and writing. Merely recognizing an identity between two noncurrent self-representations—for example, memories of the particular person that went to work on Monday of this week and Friday of this week—would not constitute a TES if those representations were not also recognized to be identical with the current self.

Third, a TES entails more than just a simple identity relation involving the current self and one or more noncurrent self states. Certainly, we are able to say that the "I" that went to work on Friday is the same as the "I" that stayed home on Saturday. However, we are able to connect these self-representations in richer ways. There may be different ways in which the ordering of events is represented. At the simplest level, perhaps, self-representations can be *contingently* ordered in the sense that it is understood that one event involving the self preceded another event involving the self. Most obviously, remembered self-related events precede the current situation. Such events may also be *temporally* ordered in the sense that the events can be ordered not only in relation to each other but also in relation to an ordering of independent events. The existence of a system of temporal units—seconds, minutes, hours, days, weeks, and so on—provides a standardized method for providing such a temporal ordering (see also McCormack & Hoerl, chap.11, this volume; Zelazo & Sommerville, chap. 12, this volume). Furthermore, events can be *causally* ordered in the sense that certain earlier self-related events are understood to be necessary for certain later self-related events (e.g., Povinelli, 1995; chap. 5, this volume).

A further characteristic of the TES is that it has both an objective, or third-person dimension and a subjective, or first-person dimension. Just as a distinction may be drawn between the experiencing "I" and the objective "me" at the earlier stage of self development during the second year of life (see, e.g., Nelson, chap. 2, this volume), so one can distinguish between the temporally extended "I" and the temporally extended "me" represented by about 4 years of age. At both developmental points the "me" captures the idea that the self is an objective entity that is available to the experience of others. In the temporally extended case the "me" entails the recognition that the objective self has continuous existence through time even though some of its properties may change with time.

Also at both developmental points, the "I" captures the idea that the self is an agent that acts, that has intentions, and that experiences objects and events. In the temporally extended case it entails a re-experiencing in the current situation of the subjectivity of the noncurrent self (see also Wheeler, Stuss, & Tulving, 1997). In short, the representation of noncurrent self states occurs at least in part from a first-person perspective. Events from one's past are remembered as experiences, involving the full range of phenomenology available to one in the present, even if the intensity of that phenomenology is attenuated over time. Imagined future events involving the self are correspondingly represented at least in part from a subjective point of view.

The consideration of the subjective dimension of the TES points us to a different approach to the TES. In this approach the TES is not just a kind of representation, it is also intricately tied to a way of processing information so that that information has particular properties. The strongest statement of this position is that of Tulving and his colleagues (e.g., Tulving, 1985; Wheeler et al., 1997). These authors claim that a particular kind of consciousness (autonoetic consciousness), dependent on the prefrontal cortex, is what makes possible the TES. Wheeler et al. (1997) claimed that

> the prefrontal cortex, in conjunction with its reciprocal connections with other cortical and subcortical structures, empowers healthy human adults with the capacity to consider the self's extended existence throughout time. The most complete expression of this capacity, autonoetic consciousness, occurs whenever one consciously recollects or re-experiences a happening from a specific time in the past, attends directly to one's present or on-line experience, or contemplates one's existence and conduct at a time in the future. (p. 350)

We contend that a critical property of the TES is that personally relevant events are connected through first-person experience (see also chaps. 8 by Barresi, 3 by Fivush, 9 by Lemmon & Moore, and 6 by Welch-Ross, this volume). First-person experience endows self-related representations with a phenomenology, both perceptual and emotional, that sets them apart from other kinds of representations. For example, when one recalls personally related events from one's past, one can feel again the pride of a hard-gained achievement or the sorrow of a loss. Similarly, when one imagines one's future that may result from one's plans one can feel similar emotions depending upon the imagined success or failure of one's plans. Thus, the representation of noncurrent (past or future) states of self leads to a direct first-person experience of those states. We argue later that it is this sharing of phenomenology across temporally separated self states that provides the TES with its functionality.

In sum, the TES involves a recognition of identity between self states in time, spanning past, present, and future. These self states are recognized to have an order that can be measured against external or non-self related events, and that order is necessary in that earlier states result in later states. Finally, there is not only a recognition of an identity across time but also an identification across time in that the representation of noncurrent self states yields immediate first-person experience of those states.

THE CURRENT VOLUME

The chapters in this volume represent a range of contemporary approaches to understanding the development of the TES. The first three chapters present accounts that place the developing TES within a linguistic and discursive structure.[1] The general theme here is that young children come to recognize the extended nature of self by participating in conversations about noncurrent events involving the self. The social world plays a crucial role in the creation of the temporally extended self in that personal narratives are created, in part, through the reliving of these events in discourses with others, notably family members in early childhood. In chapter 2, Katherine Nelson shows how narrativizing talk between children and their parents moves the child beyond the sense of "I" and "me" in the here and now and facilitates the construction of the

---

[1] It is worth noting that the idea of the TES overlaps with what is denoted by another commonly used term, the *narrative self*. By *narrative self* is usually meant the self as constituted in the various stories, spanning past, present, and future, told about oneself. The narrative self occupies a prominent position in modern philosophy (e.g., Dennett, 1991; see Gallagher, 2000) as well as psychology (e.g., Neisser & Fivush, 1994). Our interest in this book, however, is more generally in the various ways that children may consider the connection of self states over time and therefore includes, but is not limited to, narrative approaches.

TES. Social discourse provides the means by which children become able to gain a metaperspective on their self-related representations. These representations can be reflected on through discourse, and this reflection yields metarepresentation.

Linguistic devices provide the means by which this reflection can occur. For example, Robyn Fivush shows in chapter 3 how evaluative remarks move the child beyond a mere recounting of an event to a perspective on that event. Fivush argues that very young children have episodic memory in the sense that they can recall events that were personally experienced. These events, however, are not recalled *as* personally experienced, and as a result they are not integrated into autobiographical memory. The negotiation of the representation of past events in discourse provides the mechanism whereby episodic memories are transformed into an autobiographical memory that incorporates a TES. For Fivush, it is the elicitation of the subjective perspective by evaluative remarks that achieves this transformation.

In chapter 4 Judith A. Hudson extrapolates this idea to children's future orientation. She argues that language allows future reference to be established, and again such reference likely occurs initially in the context of discourse. Conversations between mothers and children about things that are going to happen provide the context within which the children become able to extend their selves into the future.

In Daniel J. Povinelli's chapter, consideration turns to more individually based developmental changes. Povinelli reviews his innovative experiments on delayed self-recognition that show how the understanding of the causal connection between previous and present self states develops at about 4 years of age, considerably later than simple mirror self-recognition. Before the development of what Povinelli calls the *proper self*, noncurrent self states are dissociated from the current self such that, whereas a simple identity may be recognized, it has none of the richer forms of linkage that characterize a TES. Povinelli suggests that being able to link separate and potentially conflicting self-representations across time may depend upon the general ability to handle conflicting representations.

In chapter 6 Melissa Welch-Ross goes further in detailing how the social construction of autobiographical memory and the TES may interact with other aspects of cognitive development. She presents an integrative model of how these different aspects of development may conspire to yield a temporally extended self. In particular, she presents evidence that having a subjective perspective, being able to connect events in a temporal-causal sequence, and understanding the representational nature of knowledge may all influence autobiographical recall. However, these components probably all depend critically on the manner of mother-child discourse surrounding personally experienced events.

The next three chapters address the role of the future self. Cristina M. Atance and Daniela K. O'Neill approach this issue in chapter 7 by examining simple planning abilities in preschoolers. They start from the position that planning may reflect the existence of a notion of the future self, and they devise simple one-step planning tasks in which young children must suggest a novel action that would be appropriate for them to achieve a goal. Their results indicate that young children are able to provide simple plans in these tasks. However, as Atance and O'Neill argue, it is in fact not necessarily the case that such tasks require children to actually look into the future and imagine the self's activity. Nevertheless, this work represents a potentially very fruitful approach to the difficult problem of how to measure the role of the future self.

In chapter 8 John Barresi locates contemporary issues in the development of the TES in a philosophical heritage going back to Locke and Hazlitt. In particular, it was Hazlitt who first wrestled with the problem of why one might be interested in one's future self. After reviewing recent experiments on future-oriented prudence and altruism, Barresi proposes a developmental transition in future orientation that assigns significant roles to the TES and the ability to assume some psychological distance from one's immediate state.

Our chapter, 9, addresses the common claim that the TES spans past, present, and future. Despite this claim, no research has directly assessed whether the development of the self extending into the past (as measured, e.g., by delayed self-recognition) co-occurs with the ability to extend the self into the future. We report the first evidence that indeed children's performance on tasks assessing the past self is correlated with performance on tasks assessing the future self. This association supports the idea that, when it is first acquired, the TES does range across past, present, and future. We argue further that this association supports the idea that a common psychological mechanism is at work here. On the basis of correlations with children's performance on memory tasks, we suggest that the development of autonoetic consciousness may play an important role.

This volume ends with three chapters that provide more theoretical analyses of the nature of the TES. Recent work on the TES has largely developed out of the study of episodic and autobiographical memory. Ever since Tulving (1972) suggested the distinction between episodic and semantic memory, memories for personally experienced events have been granted special status in the study of memory. In the years since Tulving originally presented the episodic-semantic distinction there has been continual refinement in theorizing on the nature of personal memory. The fact that these forms of memory are inherently self-related indicates a fundamental connection between personal memory and the self. The nature of this connection is still at issue and is addressed in a number of the chapters in this volume.

In chapters 10 and 11, Josef Perner and Teresa McCormack and Christoph Hoerl address two questions: What counts as episodic memory, and what is the relation between episodic memory and self-consciousness? Perner draws out a number of distinctions in order to clarify what counts as episodic memory. This analytic approach leads him to make relatively strong claims about the relations between episodic memory and self-consciousness. In particular, for Perner, episodic memory is inherently self-referential in that such memories are distinguished on the basis of the self's role in remembering.

McCormack and Hoerl, in contrast, argue that episodic memory is not self-referential as such but may well depend on self-consciousness in a developmental sense. For McCormack and Hoerl, episodic remembering involves the understanding that events occur in a nonrepeatable sequence and is linked to the representation of these events in terms of independent temporal sequences. This understanding, they claim further, requires temporal perspective taking. Finally, they suggest that the TES may be implicated in the development of these capacities. Thus, thinking of one's current perspective as one of many perspectives in a temporal sequence requires the ability to think of oneself as an entity that persists through time.

Although in chapter 12 they start with a different developmental approach, Philip David Zelazo and Jessica A. Sommerville end up making some claims similar to those of McCormack and Hoerl. Zelazo and Sommerville present a levels-of-consciousness account of the development of the TES. The levels-of-consciousness account assigns different developmental achievements to increasing degrees of representational recursion in consciousness. This account leads the authors to suggest developmental stages in the acquisition of the TES. First, Zelazo and Sommerville claim that the child can be said to have a temporally extended "I" before a temporally extended "me." Second, the TES may be understood in an ahistorical sense before it is linked to the sequence of independent events that characterizes the flow of time (cf., chap. 11 by McCormack & Hoerl). The levels-of-consciousness approach provides an analysis of development that is broadly consistent with the claims of other authors in this volume who argue for the dependence of the TES on the achievement of some kind of psychological distance from the present self (e.g., chaps. 8 by Barresi, 9 by Lemmon & Moore, and 11 by McCormack & Hoerl). It is worth noting that their account is also consistent with those of authors who advocate a discursive approach to the TES in that discourse may be read as providing a social mechanism for Zelazo and Sommerville's levels-of-consciousness approach (chaps. 2 by Nelson, 3 by Fivush, 4 by Hudson, 6 by Welch-Ross).

THE UTILITY OF THE TES

We end this chapter by speculating on the utility of the TES. A relatively common theme in writings on the TES has been the suggestion that discourse surrounding personally experienced events serves to solidify social connections at the more local family level and at the broader cultural level (e.g., Farrant & Reese, 2000; Neisser, 1988). For example, in his writing on the extended self, Neisser (1988, p. 48) wrote, "The most important adaptive function of memory may be that it makes permanent interpersonal relations possible, and thus vastly strengthens the coherence of human groups."

In contrast to the social cohesion hypothesis, it is possible that the organization of future behavior provides the bottom line against which the function of the TES should be assessed, and it is this line of thinking that we explore in more detail here. From a general functional point of view, the ultimate purpose of psychological processes must be to produce adaptive behavior. We take it as given that humans, at least, are able to produce adaptive behavior by imagining possible futures and planning action designed to bring about one of those possible futures (Dennett, 1995, 1996). This is not to say that other forms of adaptive behavioral control are absent in the human repertoire. Some behavior obviously is produced reflexively, instinctively, or through conditioning. However, human behavioral control depends significantly on imagination and planning. How do imagination and planning serve to produce adaptive behavior?

As with other forms of adaptive behavioral control, Dennett (1995) suggested that planning involves a two-stage process of generation of variability and selection. The initial step is to generate a variety of possible actions through simulation in imagination. Selection then occurs through comparison of the emotional consequences of the simulated plans. In this way the individual does not actually have to produce behavior for adaptive actions to be selected; rather, different action plans can be tried out in imagination. These imagined actions lead to differing emotional consequences, and the imagined action that leads to the most positive or least negative emotional consequence is translated into actual behavior. Notice that a sophisticated version of this kind of planning might involve multiple cycles of plan generation and selection in imagination. Thus, in determining a course of action, the organism may first generate a variety of possible actions, select out one, generate a variety of next possible moves, select out one, and so on, leading ultimately to some final consequence or until mental resources have reached their limit. This pattern of plan generation and selection in imagination will be familiar to anyone who has played games such as chess.

A full account of how such planning is realized psychologically would include, at least, answers to how the inner environment is structured, how action plans are generated, and how the emotionally based selection decision is made and implemented. Such a full account is considerably beyond the scope of this chapter. Our concern is primarily in showing how the notion of a TES fits into this system.

For planning to work, there has to be a mechanism for the imagined consequences of plans of action to affect action in the here and now. Action plans would be so much mental thumb-twiddling if they were dissociated from the here and now and did not in fact influence the particular action implemented. Indeed, there is evidence from neuropsychology that is consistent with this claim. Damasio (e.g., 1994) and his colleagues have reported on a number of frontal lobe damaged patients who show impaired decision making, not because they cannot generate appropriate imagined action sequences or plans but because the generated plans do not appear to lead to differentiable emotional consequences and therefore no one plan can be selected and initiated.

How, then, can a particular simulated course of action be selected? In normal circumstances the relative emotional consequences of action plans are compared, and the winner (or most positive plan) is implemented. Now, if one were only ever concerned with estimating the value of a course of action carried out in a nonsocial environment, planning could be done entirely from a first-person point of view, and imagined emotional consequences of plans could automatically determine current action. In effect, imagined consequences could act just like real past consequences by increasing or decreasing the probability of behavior. This parallel between past and future consequences suggests that the same mechanisms of reinforcement could be involved in the control of action by imagined future consequences as are involved in the control of action by past consequences. All that would be needed would be an "as-if" trigger for the experience of reinforcement and punishment. There would be no more need to represent the self in the future than there is for a Skinnerian creature to represent the self in the past. The self could remain entirely implicit or *representationally silent*.

However, for individuals living in a highly interactive social world, one's own plans almost inevitably interact with those of others. In many situations, both competitive and cooperative, the achievement of one's own goals depends on others' action. Thus, action planning is typically done by simulating one's own future action in association with simulating the action plans of others. This basic idea provides a background theoretical rationale for the research on theory of mind (e.g., Moore & Frye, 1991) and Machiavellian intelligence (Byrne & Whiten, 1988; Whiten, 1991). Indeed, some have argued that a planning system of the type assumed to characterize human intelligence could not even have evolved in a solitary species (e.g., Humphrey, 1984). However, the question of the conditions for the evolution of complex planning is a separable issue that need not trouble us here.[2]

The significance of the social nature of planning is that it is plausible that the same cognitive machinery is involved in generating plans for others as in generating plans for self. Self and other are represented in the same way in humans (see Barresi & Moore, 1996). We know, for example, that understanding mental states of self and other develop together (for a thorough treatment, see Gopnik, 1993) and that the ability to act in one's own future interests and the future interests of others develops at about the same time (see Barresi, chap. 8, this volume). If an individual is to simulate plans for both self and others, then the problem of action plan selection becomes more difficult. Somehow a decision has to be made on whose future is deemed relevant for guiding current action. For the imagined consequences of plans to influence the current choice of action, the planner has to identify with an individual in the simulation so that the plan that turns out well for that individual is the one that is actually translated into action.

Identification involves representing the self separately from others in the simulation—literally recognizing an individual in the simulation as identical with the self. However, it involves more than just representing an identity between the self in the current situation and the self in the future situations. Not only must the self be represented separately from others, but also the motivation for current action has to be tied into the appropriate future plan. It is here that the notion of a TES of the kind detailed previously becomes relevant. As we noted earlier, the TES links the self across time in an experientially rich way. In short, we care about our imagined future selves. It is through this empathic connection that the consequences of planned action for the future self are deemed relevant for the current self.

It is worth pointing out that the scope of this empathic identification is probably not limited to the individual self. To the extent that one individual can identify and empathize with other individuals (e.g., kin, friends) or with a larger group (e.g., family, tribe), the future interests of those others may connect quite directly with the current self and simulated plans involving the future interests of others will motivate current action. The scope of empathic identification is almost certainly influenced ontogenetically. It may even be that the kinds of conversations around autobiographical events that commonly occur within families and other social groups establish the scope of identification. Here, then, is a possible adaptive role for discourse surrounding personal memories to which a number of authors (e.g.,

---

[2]The issue here is what provided the selection pressure for the evolution of planning. The social argument is an arms race argument, that is, a mental arms race provided forced selection on a complexity of planning considerably beyond anything achieved without social conditions (see, e.g., Moore, 1996).

Farrant & Reese, 2000; Neisser, 1988) have pointed. One identifies with those with whom one has shared past experiences, and this sharing is fixed through discourse on the nature of those experiences.

Our suggestion, then, is that the TES is a necessary component of an adaptive behavioral system that operates in a complex social environment by simulating future plans for self and others. Without it there would be no clear way that the imaginatively simulated plans of action of a variety of protagonists could be resolved into those that should motivate current action and those that should not.

CONCLUSION

Understanding the self in time involves recognizing the self as an entity with physical, psychological, and social continuity through time. As such, it is a core component of the developing cognitive system in the preschool child and a significant social attribute. It is intimately involved with the representation of past events, the generation of future-oriented behavior, and the negotiation of social relations. Without it, prior events involving the self are largely dissociated from the here and now, and behavior is directed at the fulfillment of immediate goals rather than the achievement of long-term personal and social satisfaction.

ACKNOWLEDGMENTS

Preparation of this chapter was supported by a grant from the Social Sciences and Humanities Research Council of Canada to Chris Moore.

REFERENCES

Barresi, J., & Moore, C. (1996). Intentional relations and social understanding. *Behavioral and Brain Sciences, 19*, 107-122.

Byrne, R., & Whiten, A. (1988). *Machiavellian intelligence: Social expertise and the evolution of intellect in monkeys, apes, and humans.* New York: Oxford University Press.

Damasio, A. (1994). *Descartes' error: Emotion, reason, and the human brain.* New York: Grosset/Putnam.

Dennett, D. C. (1991). *Consciousness explained.* Boston: Little, Brown.

Dennett, D. C. (1995). *Darwin's dangerous idea: Evolution and the meanings of life.* New York: Simon & Schuster.

Dennett, D. C. (1996). *Kinds of minds: Towards an understanding of consciousness.* New York: Basic Books.

Farrant, K., & Reese, E. (2000). Maternal style and children's participation in reminiscing: Stepping stones in children's autobiographical memory development. *Journal of Cognition and Development, 1*, 193-226.

Gallagher, S. (2000). Philosophical conceptions of the self: Implications for cognitive science. *Trends in Cognitive Sciences, 4*, 14-21.

Gopnik, A. (1993). How we know our own minds: The illusion of first-person knowledge of intentionality. *Behavioral and Brain Sciences, 16*, 1-14.

Haith, M. M., Benson, J. B., Roberts, R. J., & Pennington, B. F. (1994). *The development of future-oriented processes.* Chicago: University of Chicago Press.

Harley, K., & Reese, E. (1999). Origins of autobiographical memory. *Developmental Psychology, 35*, 1338-1348.

Howe, M. L., & Courage, M. (1997). The emergence and early development of autobiographical memory. *Psychological Review, 104*, 499-523.

Humphrey, N. (1984). *Consciousness regained.* Oxford, England: Oxford University Press

James, W. (1950). *The principles of psychology.* New York: Dover. (Original work published 1890)

Mitchell, R. (1994). Multiplicities of self. In S. Parker, R. Mitchell, & M. Boccia (Eds.), *Self-awareness in animals and humans: Developmental perspectives* (pp. 81-107). New York: Cambridge University Press.

Moore, C. (1996). Evolution and the modularity of mindreading. (Essay review of Mindblindness: An essay on autism and theory of mind. by Simon Baron-Cohen). *Cognitive Development, 11*, 605-621.

Moore, C. & Frye, D. (1991). The acquisition and utility of theories of mind. In D. Frye & C. Moore (Eds.), *Children's theories of mind: Mental states and social understanding* (pp. 1-14). Hillsdale, NJ: Lawrence Erlbaum Associates.

Neisser, U. (1988). Five kinds of self-knowledge. *Philosophical Psychology, 1*, 35-59.

Neisser, U. & Fivush, R. (1994). *The remembering self: Construction and accuracy in the self-narrative.* New York: Cambridge University Press.

Povinelli, D. J. (1995). The unduplicated self. In P. Rochat (Ed.), *The self in early infancy* (pp. 161-192). Amsterdam: Elsevier.

Suddendorf, T. (1999). The rise of the metamind. In M. C. Corballis & S. Lea (Eds.), *The descent of mind: Psychological perspectives on hominid evolution* (pp. 218-260). New York: Oxford University Press.

Thompson, C., Barresi, J., & Moore, C. (1997). The development of future-oriented prudence and altruism in preschoolers. *Cognitive Development, 12*, 199-212.

Tulving, E. (1972). Episodic and semantic memory. In E. Tulving & W. Donaldson (Eds.), *Organization of memory* (pp. 381-403). New York: Plenum.

Tulving, E. (1985). Memory and consciousness. *Canadian Psychology, 25*, 1-12.

Wheeler, M. A., Stuss, D. T., & Tulving, E. (1997). Toward a theory of episodic memory: The frontal lobes and autonoetic consciousness. *Psychological Bulletin, 121*, 331-354.

Whiten, A. (1991). *Natural theories of mind. Evolution, development, and simulation of everyday mindreading.* Oxford, England: Basil Blackwell.

2

Language and the Self: From the "Experiencing I" to the "Continuing Me"

Katherine Nelson
City University of New York Graduate Center

In this chapter I provide a framework for thinking about the development of a self-conscious self-concept from infancy to middle childhood. The framework is an experiential one, emphasizing that what needs to be explained is how the individual child comes to think of him- or herself as a unique individual among a world of persons with a past and a future, in a world that can be known only in part through direct experience. The framework begins with the emergence of the "Experiencing I" through exploratory actions and directed interactions in the context of immediate experience. For development beyond the Experiencing I - to the construction over time of the "Continuing Me" - the child must encounter and supplement direct experience with accounts of the unknown and unexperienced. Immediate interactions must be set into the framework established by representations of the past, the future, other places, other people, other worlds. In this sense the construction of self is but one aspect of the ongoing construction of world models, known and imagined.

The developmental process by which the self becomes extended in time and space with a self-consciousness that eventually situates the self in a specific cultural and historical space-time is the issue here. Essentially the problem can be phrased as follows: How does the child establish a sense of a continuing self that extends over time but that also changes over time and that is different in significant ways from others' selves? The problem, then, is twofold: First, the self must be recognized as continuous but also continually changing (experiencing, growing, learning). The challenge is to identify the psychological essence that continues and to distinguish it from what changes, as William James (1890/1950) noted. Second, the self must be recognized as unique and distinct from others, the same kind, but different in psychic essence, with separate and unique subjectivities. The challenge for the child here is to recognize that different people may have different attitudes and feelings about the same experience and that they may have different likes, dislikes, beliefs, and ideas that contrast with one's own.

The experiencing self is a self in the present. The Experiencing I incorporates the *ecological self* and the *interpersonal self* Neisser (1997) described in discussing the developmental origin of the concept of self. To the extent that Neisser's ecological and interpersonal selves can be distinguished, however, I suggest that they are distinguished by the psychologist and not by the experiencing person. At times the ecological may dominate, and at other times the interpersonal, but for the infant or toddler they are part of the same experiential reality. Thus they are incorporated here in the Experiencing I. However, a different consciousness of self is realized in terms of the projection of self in time - forward, backward, and ongoing. It is this continuing self, or autobiographical self, that is constitutive of a represented self that endures over a life span. The Continuing Me therefore is analogous to Neisser's (1988) concept of the extended self. These aspects of self must be explained in developmental terms after the infancy and toddler periods. It is not that the experiencing self, which emerges during infancy and includes a degree of self-awareness, is obliterated by or subsumed by an extended self, but rather that the latter develops as part of self-understanding and eventually is part of a multiple sense of self, as Neisser (1988) proposed.

The basic premise here is that the extended self is a specifically human collaborative construction, facilitated by the capacity to verbalize aspects of experience and related attitudes and emotions and to receive the reflections of these from others about oneself, resulting in a continuous, differentiated, changeable self. Locating oneself in time, not only in the present but in different times, is basic to the idea of the continuing self, which depends crucially on opportunities to talk about the experiences of others, both in shared activities and in activities that have taken place at a different time and in a different place from the self. Others' talk about their experiences includes as well attitudes, motivations, mental states, and emotions—what Bruner (1990) termed the *landscape of consciousness*. From these materials the self becomes a collaborative construction, constructed by the child him- or herself in collaboration with significant others whose subjectivities he or she can come to understand as like, but distinct from, his or her own.

The chapter unfolds as follows. I begin with a further explication of the Experiencing I and then move to the foundations of the Continuing Me in talk of there and then—the self in time—and of you and me—the self among others. These sections highlight the important part that narratives of personal experience play in the construction of a concept of a continuing self. At the end of the chapter, I briefly consider the self in culture, involving talk of other times, other places, other people, and with a forecast of the self in the future.

THE EXPERIENCING I

The foundations of an Experiencing I are established during the first few months of life in intimate interactions with caretakers, and these foundations grow stronger as perceptual and motor development enables greater contact with the world outside the boundaries of the body (Butterworth, 1990; Meltzoff, 1990; Stern, 1985). Toward the end of the first year a new level of interpersonal activity is observed that may signal the onset of an initial level of a distinctive self-awareness, characterized by four apparently related developments: shared attention with the adult to objects of interest by following the adult's gaze; social referencing, that is looking to the adult for clues to the meaning of novel events; disposition to imitate adult gestures (including verbal gestures) and actions; and wariness of strangers.

Levels of Representation

From a state of total dependency the infant at this age is moving into a state of mobility and exploration, where the adult provides a secure base (Bowlby, 1982) but where the infant takes more independent risks and thus must be more aware of him- or herself in his or her surroundings, both social and physical. For this reason I posit that a new level of representation of the experienced world comes into play; in the terms of attachment theorists, a level of *internal working models*, in cognitive terms, a level of *mental event representations* (MERs; Nelson, 1986, 1996). I suggest that the further development of self-understanding can be conceptualized at least in part in terms of the levels of representation that have been postulated as events, mimesis, and narrative (Donald, 1991; Nelson, 1996). The event level, as just suggested, seems to be the first level of self-awareness, but it is important that these different levels that emerge in development are not subsumed in one another; they all exist in what Donald (1991) calls the modern *hybrid* mind. However, the experience of events, including the self-awareness of the Experiencing I, is inevitably transformed as the more complex understandings of a wider social, cultural, and narrative world come into consciousness.

From this perspective, actions and activities constitute the knowledge content of the infant's first representations. What the child encounters in the world of experience is scaffolded and guided, and eventually linguistically labeled and redescribed, by other people who are critical to the child's very existence. In this sense the child's knowledge is from the beginning coconstructed with social others, and after a few years it is coconstructed explicitly much of the time through linguistic forms. The focus of the child's model of the social world is from the outset on activities and actors, of self and others. The self-awareness emerging during infancy comes, then, not just from being in the world but from being in the world with others.

MERs are vividly apparent in the everyday world of the infant who anticipates caretaking routines, such as feeding and bathing; attempts to take a role in the activity; and signals when it is time to end, by, for example, holding his or her arms out to be lifted out of the bath or the feeding chair. Such evidence indicates that the child's participation in the activity supports attention to, and leads to an organized model of, the usual routine. Outside of the routine itself the infant may give evidence of knowing the parts of his or her role in familiar activities by what Piaget (1962) called "recognitory gestures" such as stirring with a spoon or holding a cup to the lips. What the child knows at first, however, is his or her own part in the activity, not the activity as a whole. At this developmental point event representations in themselves are in this sense egocentric. It is important to emphasize that MERs are not specific to this stage but continue as important supports of understanding, interpretation, and action throughout life. Later in development, however, MERs need not be egocentric but may be broadly social and cultural as, for example, the restaurant script that Schank and Abelson (1977) considered prototypical of adult knowledge of this kind.

At the next level of the Experiencing I are mimetic representations (MMRs) that involve the replication of actions engaged in by others, for example, in action games; songs; and skills such as sweeping, hammering, and throwing a ball. This level for the infant can be demonstrated in terms of delayed imitation and recall of modeled actions beginning toward the end of the first year (Bauer, Hertsgaard, & Dow, 1994; McDonough & Mandler, 1994; Meltzoff, 1990). However, the full development of mimesis is realized later in symbolic play and practicing skills. The point about MMRs is that through modeling the actions of another person the child is able to form an internal representation of these actions that guides their reinstantiation on another occasion, making them available to practice on one's own without cueing or scaffolding by another. Donald (1991) argued that mimesis is a necessary foundation for human language. He held this to be true for two reasons: First, imitation of verbal productions is necessary to the acquisition of verbal forms, and second, mimetic gestures (verbal and nonverbal) can be used as signs in communication, establishing a symbolic form between people that can bridge between the egocentric experience of events and the mentalistic communication of true language. The fact that mimesis emerges in development coincidentally with the first language forms in late infancy underscores this point.

It should be noted that MERs and MMRs do not have the same form or function. MERs are based on the child's own action sequences, in conjunction with supporting cues from those of interactors; thus the child and others have complementary roles in an activity. The child knows and anticipates only his or her own role, similar to an amateur actor in a play who learns only his or her own part and the cues for his or her lines. MMRs are different; they convey a new way of acting through imitation of another. Thus, one can take on the knowledge of another in a situation and play his or her role as well as one's own. It is as though one has learned all the parts in the play and can play any part as required. MERs support joint coordinated action; MMRs support shared action knowledge. Through mimesis the child can engage in symbolic play sequences, playing out the father's role in food preparation, for example, or the mother's role in driving a car, and through mimesis the child can learn to produce words; thus, a shared set of word forms may be acquired and used among family members. Gradually the capacity for taking in longer and more complex representations of new knowledge through language and using language to articulate knowledge already acquired come into play, but the process is a slow one and depends on the acquisition of complex linguistic forms and practice.

This description of self developed during the second and into the third years may be compared with previous work by Kagan (1991), Lewis (1997; Lewis & Brooks-Gunn, 1979), and others that has implied a new level of self-consciousness toward the middle of the second year. It is possible that MMRs may lead to such a change, as an analysis of the structure of imitation reveals. One can envision different levels of mimesis in development, for example:

Level 1: Adult acts
        Child watches
        Child replicates adult's acts

This level appears at about 9 months according to many analyses, in common forms of imitation of babbling, peek-a-boo games, and so on. Meltzoff (1988) observed the reverse sequence, when the adult imitates the child's action, evoking new trial acts on the part of the child.

Level 2: Adult acts and achieves goal
      Child watches
      Child internally replicates other's actions
      Delay
      Child replicates other's actions in action

Meltzoff (1988) and others have demonstrated this level in infants as young as 9 months, and it is clearly evident by 1 year (e.g., Bauer et al., 1994). These studies stand in contrast to Piaget's (1962) claim that delayed imitation signals the onset of representation at the end of the sensorimotor period toward the middle or end of the second year. At this second level the child must have a differentiated view of the self in relation to another, in which the self is seen in terms of action possibilities as in the thought "I am like others—we can do the same things" but "I am different from others" in that the other acts in one context and the self acts at a later time in a different context. In this case self-awareness is not just self in relation to the experienced world but self in relation to specific others, an interpersonal self. As Meltzoff and Gopnik (1993) argued, a third level, in which the child internally represents the adult's intended goal, is observable and seems necessary. Toward the end of the second year the child will incorporate the goal into the activity, even when the adult's inferred goal has been frustrated and not achieved. Thus the child must have come to a point of interpreting another's intentions independent of the other's actions.

The achievement of the third level of self-awareness is coincident in time with the achievement of self-recognition in the mirror between the ages of 15 months and 2 years (Lewis & Brooks-Gunn, 1979). Here the child recognizes the view of the self from outside the self, that is, the other's view of the self, a kind of view of "me" as an object of others' perception and attention. As Lewis (1997) emphasized, self-recognition is accompanied by a new self-consciousness, together with the possibility of embarrassment and shame, which in turn suggests a new awareness of social rules of how things should be, which are different from the personal rules extracted from routines about how things are (and therefore should be) done. Personal event rules, when violated by others, give rise to frustration and anxiety on the part of the child. Violation of social rules, however, invokes displeasure on the part of other people, and awareness of the basis for this displeasure is evident in the child's newly self-conscious reactions.

The evidence, I believe, supports the view that the 2-year-old self is primarily still an Experiencing I. Although recognizing that self and other are the same kind, and that self and other engage in distinctive activities, the toddler's nascent sense of self is that of an actor among other actors. The child feels and expresses feelings, but events are represented cognitively as activities, as landscapes of action, not as landscapes of consciousness (Bruner, 1990). Thus the Experiencing I is an I in the midst of action and interaction, yet some enduring sense of the experiencing is maintained outside of the experience itself in terms of MERs. These representations are then available to support "knowledgeable" action when the activity recurs.

However, as many theorists have maintained (from Piaget, 1968, who distinguished between memory in the narrow sense and in the broad sense; to Karmiloff-Smith, 1992, who distinguished between implicit and explicit representations; to Tulving, 1983, who distinguished between semantic and episodic memory), these initial representations are generalizations from experience that are not open to self-reflection and deliberate recall. (The evidence on early MMRs is unclear in this regard.) Studies of infant memory (e.g., Rovee-Collier & Hayne, 1987) have shown that infants can retain object-action associations over several weeks, and studies of 1-year-old infants (e.g., Bauer et al., 1994; McDonough & Mandler, 1994) have demonstrated retention of an action sequence over 6 months or longer. It is controversial, however, as to whether these memories constitute a specific sense of a personal past or whether the memory is of a more general sort, analogous to Tulving's (1983) semantic memory (Nelson, 1994). It is only the self with a specific past that is endowed with the unique capacity to re-experience the past, unlike other creatures who can *use* past experience but not *re-experience* it, as Tulving (1983) claimed in comparing human memory with that of nonhumans. Episodic memory for Tulving involves what he calls *autonoesis*, the specific self-aware sense of "I was there when it happened to me."

Theorists approaching the issue of self-awareness in memory from different theoretical perspectives (Howe, Courage, & Bryant-Brown, 1993; Nelson & Fivush, 2000; Perner, 1991) agree that episodic memory in this specific self-aware sense is not evident before 2 years of age, although writers disagree about the age at which they do attribute this kind of memory. The memory issue is important to understanding emerging self-consciousness, as the designation *Continuing Me* implies. If there is no personal memory of episodes, then there is no basis for reflection on the "I" who was present at one time in comparison with the "I" who is now experiencing a similar or different event. This kind of reflection appears to be necessary to the establishment of a sense of continuity between the self who was and the self who now is.

The actor-experiencer self is aware of the "not present"—in the sense that present experience is surrounded by nonpresent previous experiences, possible future experiences, and pretense in the form of play and stories. These intimations of the nonpresent, however, do not have the specificity of actual episodes in the mind. I am arguing that all of these nonpresent realities are assimilated to the child's own experientially based internal working models of reality. This experiential child has a repertoire of knowledge about being in the world, a repertoire based on prior experience that guides action in the present, but does not have a self with a specific past and a specific imagined future. Put another way, for the young child the nonpresent exists but in a form that is not experiential. The Experiencing I knows that things have happened or might happen that are not present in the current ongoing situation, and it can call on specific episodes from the past, as well as familiar routines, to support action in the here and now. What the very young Experiencing I does not do is remember the self that was in the prior situation at some former specific time and place. Moreover, whereas adults, even when absorbed in the ongoing present, concentrating on a specific task, do not lose the continuing sense of who I am and can recapture it momentarily if the situation demands, very young children lack this sense of continuity. (Substantial evidence on this point comes from research on children's theory of mind; e.g., Astington, Harris, & Olson, 1988.) There appears to be no prior self or self-concept to be reconciled or integrated into the present. For the young child, "I am who I am right now," and that might be different (and in fact it is different) from who "I" was last month, or even a few minutes ago, or who "I" may be tomorrow.

THE CONTINUING ME

An important transition takes place between 2 and 5 years of age that supports the beginnings of a new sense of subjectivity and a continuing self. The basis for the transition, I claim, lies in the emerging function of language for talking about different experiences: the experiences of self and other at different times and places and the experiences of different others from different perspectives. The central point is that talk about past and future, self and other, provides the scaffold for constructing a continuing self.

In contrast to the restricted reality of the Experiencing I, the Continuing Me implies a broad awareness of the there and then—the not-present specifics of the past and future, the others of the world, and other places that have been experienced and might be experienced by the self or by others. The claim here is that this aspect of the extended self must be constructed in collaboration with others during the early childhood years. If it is not so constructed, the emergent self may be diminished or distorted.

The dimensions along which the extended self—the Continuing Me—must be constructed are threefold: spatial, temporal, and social. This construction is critical not only to the self-concept but also to understanding others as intentional persons and understanding a cultural world beyond the boundaries of direct experiential knowledge.

This extension and construction critically depends on experience in and with language: in conversational discourse with parents, siblings, and others; in narratives about self, others, and fictional beings; and in explanations about the world in which the child lives, whether natural scientific, historical, mythological, religious, or moral. These extensions of self obviously continue throughout life, but they begin crucially in the preschool years in everyday conversations with others. Just as the mirror presents a reflection of the perception of the self by others, so talk with others about experience reflects back to the child the self in the past and thus enables the representation of an objective conception of self through time and space.

The Self in Time: Talk of Then and There

Because an essential requirement of the self-concept—the Continuing Me—is an integration of self-perceptions over past, present, and future states, activities, motivations, and emotions, memory and imagination are critical to its construction. In recent years a great deal has been learned about the development of memory in the early years of life and the contribution of parental talk and narrative to its later development. By the age of 2 years children have the beginnings of memories for specific prior experience, that is, of episodic memories, although whether these include a sense of "me" ("I was there") is controversial, as previously noted (Nelson, 1994). Part of this controversy revolves around the issue of whether children begin to form autobiographical memories because they have established a "cognitive self," assumed to be in place by 2 years (Howe & Courage, 1993), or whether narratives of the self facilitate and are perhaps necessary to the beginnings of autobiographical memory (Tessler & Nelson, 1994). Here I take the position that it is not so much that autobiographical memory establishes the continuing self as that both are constituted through the same process. From autobiographical memory (the life story) emerges the sense not only of a Continuing Me but also of a temporally extended self that includes the self as baby and the adult self to come.

Parents begin talking with their young children about past events and about activities to come usually around 2 years of age, as children become able to engage in brief conversations and contribute some information to the account (see chaps. 3 and 4 in this volume, for discussion). These conversations lay the foundations for the child's dawning awareness of the continuity of the self in the past and present. Talk about the past and the projected future makes salient to the young child the reality that a younger self existed in activities and scenes that can be reinstated through talk and thus recognized as a same self in a different time and a self different from other actors in the scene. This temporal dimension of the developing self-concept has been overlooked in many theories that focus on characterizing its content and organization.

Of particular significance is the transformation of remembered scenes and incoherent images into narrative constructions that make sense of a whole experienced event. The narrative form that frames talk about the past is characterized by a goal orientation and by a sequence of events that are in general causally ordered toward an outcome with an evaluative component. Such narratives may be constructed in the course of an experience or in the reconstruction of what happened later (Nelson, 1993; Tessler & Nelson, 1994), scaffolded by an adult who shares or shared the experience and who is skillful in bringing out the meaningful connections that make up the whole and that highlight the perspective of the child in the experience, including a verbalization of the evaluation of the event from the child's point of view (e.g., "That was fun, wasn't it?"). Children who experience events in this way, and who are practiced in recounting with parents at this narrativizing level, both remember more of an experience and remember more of its personal meaning.

How narrativizing talk about the "there and then" facilitates the child's construction of a continuing sense of self involves two aspects of narrative: the landscape of action and the landscape of consciousness (Bruner, 1990). Narratives weave together an account of an event in terms of a sequence of actions that are temporally and causally related and that highlight a critical action, problem, or anomaly that makes this event different from the routine expectations of daily life. As I have noted, very young children focus on the routine in their event representations, the everyday way that things go, and should go. In these scripts of everyday life they are very good at keeping the order straight and anticipating what will happen next. These MERs are functional for supporting action in the present and predicting what will happen in the immediate future. They are not, however, accounts of specific experiences; rather, the unusual and novel details tend to get lost or to be remembered as disconnected bits not tied to specific times and places or orders. Recounting narratives of novel experiences imposes order on the action and makes clear the causal and temporal connections. This is the landscape of action in narrative; it serves an important function in crystallizing an experience into a whole that can be reconstructed on another occasion and reflected on or puzzled over.

Time, Narrative, Memory, and Self

Time is critically important in narrative, and it seems to hold the key to the intricate relation of self and time that has been puzzled over by many psychologists and philosophers (Freeman, 1998; Nelson, 1989, 1997;

Ricoeur, 1988). Sequence and duration are basic dimensions of the temporal mode on which a society builds a temporal structure that organizes the lives of individuals. Within the events and routines of the Experiencing I there is already a kind of temporal accounting, consisting of incipient understanding of both sequence and duration of the event, although the young child knows little about the society's transactional time conventions (McGrath & Kelly, 1986). For the infant, time is structured in terms of activities—whether engaging in solitary play in the crib, eating breakfast with the family, going for a walk in the park, or any other of a day's routines, the present here-and-now activity absorbs the child's consciousness. This sense of time does not extend beyond the boundaries of the event or activity within which the child is engaged; thus there is no self in the specific past or future, only a self in the present or in the "not now" (Nelson, 1989).

There are three aspects of time that are incorporated into talk about what happened and that eventually become organized as part of the person's autobiographical memory, that is, the ongoing account of the "story of my life," the "historical me" (Nelson, 1997). First is the immediate ordering of events and activities; to extend the dramaturgical metaphor, the sequence of actions, parts played in a scene. This is the sense of time that first emerges and that is present in incipient form in the child's event representations; young children are remarkably good at ordering actions in events (Nelson, 1986).

The second aspect is the locating of an event or a scene with respect to the present "now," whether as "yesterday," "tomorrow," or "last summer." This aspect appears to be remarkably difficult for young children, and it does not seem to be simply because of the difficulty of mastering conventional temporal terms, although the problem that children have with the deictic terms *yesterday* and *tomorrow* well into the late preschool years is surprising to most people (Nelson, 1991). Making the past real, stable, and recoverable by giving it a label involves an important transformation of the child's working model (based on experienced events), achieved through the joint work of memory and imagination.

The third sense of time involves ordering the events or scenes in relation to each other, and this sense apparently requires some scaffolding from tools, such as calendars, as well as parallel institutional realities that mark out experience, such as years in school, jobs, or births and marriages. Events do not just neatly arrange themselves in chronological order in our minds without some significant external help of this kind, and this kind of ordering is beyond the ability of the preschooler. Indeed, it ventures into the realm of the cultural and historical as well as the autobiographical. I have little more to say about it in this chapter, which is focused on the earlier period of childhood.

Time is intertwined with both place and people. The extended self must be aware of movement beyond the here into the there, and even into spaces as yet unknown, while maintaining self-identity. For the very young child, movement to a different spatial environment may not have the same meaning as it does for an adult. If the same people and comforting things are maintained, the larger space and movement may be ignored, but if these are absent, chaos may ensue for the child and for the family. Any parent who has inadvertently forgotten the child's favorite blanket or special stuffed animal on a visit to the grandparents knows the chaotic consequences only too well. Displacement of talk about places other than the present one is another aspect of the widening world that narratives open. Here the personal narratives of others—for example, parents' talk about their own childhood—as well as fictional stories, may provide the broader perspective that takes the child beyond the constraint of direct experience into a world not personally known.

The Self Among Others: Talk of You and Me

In the previous section I argued that talk about the past and the projected future makes salient to the young child the reality that a younger self existed in activities and scenes that can be reinstated through talk and that this self is recognized as a same self at a different time and a self different from other actors in the scene. Talk about others as well as the self in past events and in ongoing present experiences makes manifest as well different experiential perspectives and thus puts a new light on the self. Part of this is the realization that what was "me" (pre-enlightenment) is no longer "me" and cannot be reconstituted in the present. A parallel aspect of this enlightenment must be that others are different from the self in an important new way: They are not just different actors in an experienced event but are themselves *different experiencers*.

To tell another person an account of oneself is to represent oneself in an objective, differentiated framework. Similarly, to hear a story from someone else and to maintain it as a story about that person is to represent that person in an objective, differentiated sense. To tell or hear a story about both self and other in which each is represented as an objective, differentiated agent acting independently, each with different goals, knowledge, and beliefs, is a critical step toward the representation of self and other that goes beyond the recognition of different perspectives on the same shared ongoing experience. These developments begin and continue during the years 3 - 5 and later, as the child masters the representational function of language and is able to participate in the verbal construction of self and other in shared and nonshared activities.

The aspect of narrative that is concerned with the subjectivities of the actors within it is the *landscape of consciousness*. according to Bruner (1990). In the parental construction of a narrative about a child's experience this aspect appears in different guises, sometimes overtly as the evaluative component that Labov and Waletzky (1967) identified as critical to narrative (e.g., "That was fun," "You were angry"—see Fivush, 1994) but often in terms of setting, motivation, reactions, and problem solving within the narrative. Here the internal states of self and other are articulated as thoughts, feelings, wants and hopes, perceptions, efforts, disappointments, and so on. Narratives thus are ideal formats for learning both the language of internal states and the concepts that relate the child's own incipient understanding of self-consciousness to the actions and reactions of others. Fictional stories incorporate these aspects and often highlight them for children (Dyer, Shatz, & Wellman, 1999), but their articulation in terms of the child him- or herself in a past or present event, and in contrast with the feelings and thoughts of others, may have special impact on understanding the concepts involved. Moreover, their articulation in relation to self experience reifies an aspect of the self that may then become part of the emerging self-concept, for good or ill.

Between ages 3 and 5 years children begin to construct narratives of experience on their own and to report them to others in more or less coherent forms (Engel, 1995; Hudson, Gebelt, Haviland, & Bentivegna, 1992; Peterson & McCabe, 1983). At first these are shared and scaffolded with others, typically parents, but with time the "self stories" become the child's own. Beyond the individual narratives, the autobiographical project is one of constructing a "life story" composed of individual memorable event stories, involving episodes that somehow have significance to one's understanding of self over the course of developmental time. Of course, what is of significance to a 3-year-old may not be to a 30-year-old, yet often the 3-year-old's memories are retained as "the beginning" of the "real" story of one's life. The important idea here is that to become a part of the life story each episode must somehow be formulated as part of an ongoing overarching narrative that takes on significance in terms of life goals, achievements, failures, joys, and tragedies. Within it are contained representative or idiosyncratic episodes that in themselves are mininarratives about what happened one time. This "narrated self," individuated from all other selves, that emerges in the late preschool years for many, but not all, children, contains within it the essential temporal component of the Continuing Me as well as the self components reflected from others' views and is therefore a major source of the developing child's emerging personal self-concept.

The Self in the Future

To have a Continuing Me self is to have continuity with the future as well as the past, albeit the future is an imaginative construction built out of bits and pieces of tales and promises from other people. Unfortunately, we have little sense of children's growing conceptions of the future. We have just begun to recognize that parents talk with young children about the future at least as much as they talk about the past (Benson, 1994; Lucariello & Nelson, 1987; Nelson, 1989, 1993). Some studies of children's growing ability to plan have been the focus of recent research (see chaps. 4 and 7, this volume), but planning is a relatively complex cognitive activity involving the projection of self into the unknown and requires executive functions. The most significant talk about the future is usually talk about events that have never before been experienced, in contrast to the everyday routines that young children know and use to support anticipations of things to come. Parents often attempt to provide an anticipatory account that will set the stage for a new experience. Whether they are successful, and the degree to which children can visualize themselves in the projected plan, are questions to which there are no good answers at present.

When and to what degree children begin to take seriously the idea that ahead in time lies a lifetime composed of years of school and higher education, work, family, and so on, and their conceptions of the Continuing Me into these times, are very much up for grabs. To project oneself into the future requires a sense of a continuing cultural reality as well as a sense of a continuing personal and social reality. This aspect of time and the self calls out for examination.

The perspective of the future self implies the necessity of an effortful construction of self across time, space, and the social world. This is but the beginning, however, in that beyond the social world of childhood lies the cultural–historical world within which the self must be located once the familiar family space is left for the institutional world of school, with its formally defined social relationships, rules, and hierarchical progressions through age and grade.

The Self in Cultural-Historical Time: Talk of Other Times, Other Places, Other People

Thus far I have traced the beginnings of the human idea of self as extended in time, space, and social relationships in the early childhood years. Eventually, the extended self also incorporates a *historical self*, placed within an ongoing time that reaches beyond the personal and social to the cultural. This sense of self requires construction within an overall cultural scheme or mythology that determines the limits within which the construction takes place. The cultural scheme is constituted in terms of roles, myths, rules, and relationships that are at least in part conveyed through discourse and that have their beginnings in the early childhood years through parent-child and sibling-sibling conversations. The emerging self then is culturally constrained, a product of a specific social environment—the family—but individually constructed and maintained within these constraints and within the constraints of the Experiencing I, that is, the ongoing and developing person individually endowed with sensibilities and intelligences that begin as limited forms but grow in power over the childhood years. The child is then in the difficult position of constructing and maintaining a sense of ongoing self that is itself constantly changing in physical size, ability, experience, and consciousness.

These circumstances dictate that the construction of self is largely a project of the imaginative capacities of the individual child in collaboration with others who have some stake in how the project turns out. Indeed, one can imagine a kind of invisible voice emerging during the preschool years asking "who am I?" in varying circumstances, and trying on different answers, in play, in stories, and in real life. In some cultural environments the answer to this question is hard and fast: "You are the eldest son" (and therefore many specific things are expected of you), or "You are the youngest daughter of an impoverished farmer" (and therefore only crumbs are your due). But, in our complex and individualistic society the answers are likely to be diverse and ambiguous, and the quest is likely to be long lasting, as investigations such as those by Damon and Hart (1982) and Higgins (1991) have revealed.

BEYOND THE CONTINUING ME: MULTIPLE SELVES

The main thrust of this chapter has been to examine what it means to find a self in time, a Continuing Me in early childhood in North American middle-class society at the end of the 20th century. Part of that present reality has been the realization that modern life calls out, almost demands, multiple versions of the self (Gergen, 1991; Markus & Nurius, 1986; Neisser, 1988), each constructed for a different audience. The dilemma this reality presents is whether there is indeed a "real self" within each of the selves that different roles demand. The enterprises of autobiographical writing (Bruner, 1994) and psychoanalysis (Spence, 1982) propose that a coherent life narrative is the answer to this problem, wherein each alternative is integrated into a complex interwoven story.

A related way of viewing this problem comes from the levels view of human cognition, which has underlain the explanatory view of this chapter. From this perspective, the Experiencing I operates at one level:

the level of action and feeling, the basic level of experience. This level continues throughout life. Out of it emerges the reflective, self-awareness that is seen in the toddler who becomes aware of self as actor—like, but different from, other actors. When this level is reached it transforms the experiencer by making him or her aware of other participants' roles in the activity and, to some extent as well, their goals, perspectives, and feelings. A shared reality has emerged. Talk then becomes critical in extending this sense of shared reality, deepening it; making manifest what could not be seen in overt action, namely the thoughts, motives, and emotions of others, and the existence of other realities in other times and places. Narrative, as stressed here, is the effective vehicle of this talk and becomes a representational level differentiated from the basic experiential level.

But talk does not construct the self. Only the individual can undertake that project, through re-experiencing on a new reflective level the narratives about the self that have been the topic of talk. Out of these narratives continuity of self-conceptions (a "theory" of self) must be wrung. If these are conflicting or incoherent, an overarching life story narrative that consolidates the Continuing Me in an ever-changing social and cultural world will not be possible, and the possible selves will fly apart or disintegrate. Thus the construction and maintenance of the Continuing Me is a lifelong project whose foundation is laid in the preschool years but whose success is ultimately dependent on the reflective consciousness and organizing powers of the emergent person.

ACKNOWLEDGMENTS

This chapter extends the argument presented in "Finding Oneself in Time" (Nelson, 1997). Parts of the argument were incorporated in a paper coauthored with Sarah Henseler and Daniela Plesa presented at the 1997 Society for Research in Child Development symposium organized by Chris Moore on the Temporally Extended Self. Robin G. Fontaine contributed extensive commentary and bibliographic help on this version of the chapter. I am grateful to these doctoral students and to other members of our research group, in particular, Faye Fried Walkenfield, Sylvie Goldman, and Nechama Presler, for their contributions to the formulation of these ideas.

REFERENCES

Astington, J. W., Harris, P. L., & Olson, D. (1988). *Developing theories of mind.* Cambridge, England: Cambridge University Press.
Bauer, P. J., Hertsgaard, L. A., & Dow, G. A. (1994). After 8 months have passed: Long-term recall of events by 1- to 2- year-old children. *Memory, 2,* 353–382.

Benson, J. B. (1994). The origins of future-orientation in the everyday lives of 9- to 36-month-old infants. In M. M. Haith, J. B. Benson, R. J. Roberts, & B. Pennington (Eds.), *Development of future-oriented processes* (pp. 375–408). Chicago: University of Chicago Press.

Bowlby, J. (1982). *Attachment and loss: Vol. 1. Attachment*. (2nd ed.). New York: Basic Books.

Bruner, J. S. (1990). *Acts of meaning*. Cambridge MA: Harvard University Press.

Bruner, J. S. (1994). The "remembered" self. In U. Neisser & R. Fivush (Eds.), *The remembering self: Construction and accuracy in the self-narrative* (pp. 41–54). New York: Cambridge University Press.

Butterworth, G. (1990). Self-perception in infancy. In D. Cicchetti & M. Beeghly (Eds.), *The self in transition* (pp. 99–119). Chicago: University of Chicago Press.

Damon, W., & Hart, D. (1982). The development of self-understanding from infancy through adolescence. *Child Development, 53,* 831–857.

Donald, M. (1991). *Origins of the modern mind*. Cambridge, MA: Harvard University Press.

Dyer, J. R., Shatz, M. & Wellman, H. (1999, October). Children's books as a source of mental state information. Poster presented at the inaugural meeting of the Cognitive Development Society, Chapel Hill, NC.

Engel, S. (1995). *The stories children tell: making sense of the narratives of childhood*. San Francisco: Freeman.

Fivush, R. (1994). Constructing narrative, emotion, and self in parent–child conversations about the past. In U. Neisser & R. Fivush (Eds.), *The remembering self: Construction and accuracy in the self-narrative* (pp. 136–157). New York: Cambridge University Press.

Freeman, M. (1998). Mythical time, historical time, and the narrative fabric of the self. *Narrative Inquiry, 8,* 27–50.

Gergen, K. J. (1991). *The saturated self*. New York: Basic Books.

Higgins, E. T. (1991). Development of self-regulatory and self-evaluative processes: Costs, benefits, and tradeoffs. In M. R. Gunnar & L. A. Sroufe (Eds.), *Self processes and development: The Minnesota Symposia on Child Development Vol. 23* (pp. 125–165). Hillsdale, NJ: Lawrence Erlbaum Associates.

Howe, M. L., & Courage, M. L. (1993). On resolving the enigma of infantile amnesia. *Psychological Bulletin, 113,* 305–326.

Howe, M. L., Courage, M. L., & Bryant-Brown, L. (1993). Reinstating preschoolers' memories. *Developmental Psychology, 29,* 854–869.

Hudson, J. A., Gebelt, J., Haviland, J., & Bentivegna, C. (1992). Emotion and narrative structure in young children's personal accounts. *Journal of Narrative and Life History, 2,* 129–150.

James, W. (1950). *The Principles of Psychology*. New York: Dover. (Original work published 1890)

Kagan, J. (1991). The theoretical utility of constructs for self. *Developmental Review, 11,* 244–250.

Karmiloff-Smith, A. (1992). *Beyond modularity*. Cambridge, MA: MIT Press.

Labov, W., & Waletzky, J. (1967). Narrative analysis. In J. Helm (Ed.), *Essays on the verbal and visual arts* (pp. 12–44). Seattle: University of Washington Press.

Lewis, M. (1997). The self in self-conscious emotions. In J. G. Snodgrass & R. L. Thompson (Eds.), *The self across psychology: self-awareness, self-recognition, and*

the self-concept (pp. 119–142). New York: New York Academy of Sciences.
Lewis, M., & Brooks-Gunn, J. (1979). *Social cognition and the acquisition of self.* New York: Plenum.
Lucariello, J., & Nelson, K. (1987). Remembering and planning talk between mothers and children. *Discourse Processes, 10,* 219–235.
Markus, H., & Nurius, P. (1986). Possible selves. *American Psychologist, 41,* 954–969.
McDonough, L., & Mandler, J. M. (1994). Very long-term recall in infants: Infantile amnesia reconsidered. *Memory, 2,* 339–352.
McGrath, J. E., & Kelly, J. R. (1986). *Time and human interaction: Toward a social psychology of time.* New York: Guilford.
Meltzoff, A. N. (1988). Infant imitation and memory: Nine-month-olds in immediate and deferred tests. *Child Development, 59,* 217–225.
Meltzoff, A. N. (1990). Foundations for developing a concept of self. In D. Cicchetti & M. Beeghly (Eds.), *The self in transition* (pp. 139–164). Chicago: University of Chicago Press.
Meltzoff, A., & Gopnik, A. (1993). The role of imitation in understanding persons and developing theories of mind. In S. Baron-Cohen, H. Tager-Flusberg, & D. Cohen (Eds.), *Understanding other minds: Perspectives from autism* (pp. 335–366). New York: Oxford University Press.
Neisser, U. (1988). Five kinds of self-knowledge. *Philosophical Psychology, 1,* 35–59.
Neisser, U. (1997). The roots of self-knowledge: Perceiving self, it, and thou. In J. G. Snodgrass & R. L. Thompson (Eds.), *The self across psychology: Self-recognition, self-awareness, and the self-concept* (pp. 19–33). New York: New York Academy of Sciences.
Nelson, K. (1986). *Event knowledge: structure and function in development.* Hillsdale, NJ: Lawrence Erlbaum Associates.
Nelson, K. (Ed.). (1989). *Narratives from the crib.* Cambridge MA: Harvard University Press.
Nelson, K. (1991). The matter of time: Interdependencies between language and thought in development. In S. A. Gelman & J. P. Byrnes (Eds.), *Perspectives on language and cognition: Interrelations in development* (pp. 278–318). New York: Cambridge University Press.
Nelson, K. (1993). Events, narratives, memories: What develops? In C. Nelson (Ed.), *Memory and affect in development: Minnesota Symposium on Child Psychology* (Vol. 26, pp. 1–24). Hillsdale NJ: Lawrence Erlbaum Associates.
Nelson, K. (1994). Long-term retention of memory for preverbal experience: Evidence and implications. *Memory, 2,* 467–475.
Nelson, K. (1996). *Language in cognitive development: The emergence of the mediated.* New York: Cambridge University Press.
Nelson, K. (1997). Finding oneself in time. In J. G. Snodgrass & R. L. Thompson (Eds.), *The self across psychology: Self-recognition, self-awareness, and the self concept* (pp. 19–33). New York: New York Academy of Sciences.
Nelson, K., & Fivush, R. (2000). Socialization of memory. In E. Tulving & F. Craik (Eds.), *The Oxford handbook of memory* (pp. 283–295). New York: Oxford University Press.
Perner, J. (1991). *Understanding the representational mind.* Cambridge, MA: MIT Press.
Peterson, C., & McCabe, A. (1983). *Developmental psycholinguistics: Three ways of looking at a child's narrative.* New York: Plenum.

Piaget, J. (1962). *Play, dreams, and imitation.* New York: Norton.
Piaget, J. (1968). *On the development of memory and identity.* Barre, MA: Clarke University Press.
Ricoeur, P. (1988). *Time and narrative.* Chicago: Chicago University Press.
Rovee-Collier, C., & Hayne, H. (1987). Reactivation of infant memory: Implications for cognitive development. In H. W. Reese (Ed.), *Advances in child development and behavior* (Vol. 20, pp. 185–283). New York: Academic Press.
Schank, R. C., & Abelson, R. P. (1977). *Scripts, plans, goals, and understanding.* Hillsdale, NJ: Lawrence Erlbaum Associates.
Spence, D. P. (1982). *Narrative truth and historical truth.* New York: Norton.
Stern, D. N. (1985). *The interpersonal world of the infant: A view from psychoanalysis and developmental psychology.* New York: Basic Books.
Tessler, M., & Nelson, K. (1994). Making memories: The influence of joint encoding on later recall. *Consciousness and Cognition, 3,* 307–326.
Tulving, E. (1983). *Elements of episodic memory.* New York: Oxford University Press.

3

Owning Experience: Developing Subjective Perspective in Autobiographical Narratives

Robyn Fivush
Emory University

Our sense of self, of who we are, is intricately interwoven with our sense of who we have been and who we will be in the future. Certainly, as adults, we have a sense of continuous identity over time, and this identity is at least partly defined by the continuity of our autobiographical memories. As William James (1890/1950) commented, when we awake in the morning we are not confused about who we are, or whether the dream we recall was our dream or someone else's. Our dreams, our thoughts, and our memories are irrevocably ours. But how and when do young children come to understand this aspect of mental life? How and when do young children begin to understand that their inner thoughts and their memories are uniquely theirs? How and when do young children come to own their experience?

In this chapter I argue that one critical aspect of the development of a temporally extended self, a sense of self that is continuous in time, involves the construction of an autobiographical self, a self based on the specific experiences the individual recalls. I further argue that this construction relies on at least two developmental achievements: (a) understanding that memories are representations of what occurred in the past and (b) that, as such, memories are subjective. Even if we experience an event together, I may remember that event differently than you do, and understanding this unique subjective perspective is the heart of an autobiographical self. Before developing this argument in more detail, it is important to define autobiographical memories as distinct from episodic memories.

EPISODIC VERSUS AUTOBIOGRAPHICAL MEMORIES

All organisms must rely on memories of past experiences in order to survive. However, the form of these memories may vary widely both phylogenetically and ontogenetically (e.g., Donald, 1991; Nelson, 1996). Simple organisms may rely solely on the ability to remember past experiences in the form of conditioned responses, but more complex organisms develop the ability to remember specific past experiences as guides to future behavior. Nonhuman primates almost certainly have the ability to recall details of specific past events, at least when cued by the objects, places, or other animals present during that event. Although it is still not clear when human infants become able to recall specific past experiences (see, e.g., Mandler, 1990, vs. Rovee-Collier & Shyi, 1992), it is generally agreed that by the second half of the first year human infants are able to retain memories of specific experiences over a period of at least several weeks. Both the complexity of events recalled and the retention interval over which events can be recalled increases as children develop, and by the second year of life, we see unambiguous evidence of long-term explicit recall of specific details of events that were experienced only once (see Bauer, 1997, and Fivush, 1997, for reviews of this literature). At this point in development, however, these memories can be characterized as episodic but not yet autobiographical.

The distinction between episodic and autobiographical memories is one that is not often made in the memory development literature (but see Fivush, 1998b; Fivush, Haden, & Adam, 1995; and Nelson, 1996, for extended discussions), yet it is critical in understanding the developing relations between memory and self. An *episodic memory* represents a specific past experience as an event that has happened in the world; it is referenced to the external environment. An *autobiographical memory* represents a specific past experience as an event that happened to the individual; it is referenced to the internal self. Episodic memories are representations of what happened; autobiographical memories are representations of what happened *to me*.

To achieve this level of representational understanding, children must accomplish two developmental tasks. First, they must become aware that a memory is a *representation* of a past experience. In other words, they must develop a representational understanding of representation, or a metarepresentational understanding. Memories, although derived from external events, are internally generated and, as such, are subjective rather than veridical records. The second task, which is related to the first, is that children must come to understand that this memory may or may not be the same as memories of other people who have experienced ostensibly the same event. Two people who have experienced an event together may recall different aspects of the event, different details, and they certainly may have different affective and cognitive interpretations of that event. Once children achieve this level of representational awareness they are able to further understand that their memory of an event is unique to them, to their perspective. Understanding subjective perspective is the critical component of transforming episodic memories into autobiographical memories. Autobiographical memories begin when children understand that their experience is uniquely their own, that their experience is tied to their subjective perspective on their own experience. Moreover, this understanding heralds a new understanding of self, a self that is defined by one's subjective perspective on one's experiences. I am uniquely who I am because I have a unique perspective on the events of my life.

To flesh out this argument, I first outline research on the development of self-understanding, with a particular focus on distinguishing between the self as a concept and the self as an experiencer. I then turn to an examination of the development of subjectivity in children's autobiographical narratives: How and when do children begin to include information that marks their perspective on a past experience? Although these data inform us about the developmental course of subjectivity, they do not inform us as to the mechanism. Thus, I next present arguments and data indicating that children come to understand subjectivity through participating in joint reminiscing about the past with parents. I end the chapter by discussing the ways in which children come to own their experience as uniquely theirs and thus are able to form an autobiographical self that is at least partly defined by a subjective perspective on events experienced in the past.

DEVELOPMENT OF SELF-UNDERSTANDING

The problem of the self has been with us since well before psychology emerged as a discipline at the turn of the century, but James's (1890/1950) early explication of self-understanding set the stage for much of the psychological research on this issue. James distinguished between the categorical self, the "me"—that is known as an object with specific traits, characteristics, likes, dislikes, and so forth—and the "I," the subjective self that is reflected in the ongoing stream of consciousness, the central knower or experiencer. Modern psychologists have inherited this distinction, and the developmental work on self has focused almost exclusively on the development of the self-concept, the "me." Although there are many nuances to these research findings, in general, when asked to describe themselves, preschool children focus on physical traits and characteristics, such as gender, size, and hair color. During middle childhood children begin to use more psychological descriptions, such as being smart or funny, and with adolescence comes an understanding of a self in relation or comparison to other people (e.g., Damon & Hart, 1988; Harter, 1983; Lewis, 1992; but see Eder, 1990, for an alternative theoretical perspective). These tasks rely on children's ability to reflect on and verbalize their self-concept, and especially on children's understanding of self as a set of traits and characteristics. The question of the developing sense of self as the experiencer of events is not captured in these studies, neither has it been seriously addressed in the literature to date.

For James, the subjective sense of identity is dependent on a continuous stream of consciousness. Moreover, this stream of consciousness is not simply an awareness of thoughts but an awareness of "my" thoughts. In James's (1890/1950) words, "It seems as if the elementary psychic fact were not that *thought* or *this thought* or *that thought*, but *my thought*, every thought being *owned*" (Vol. 1, p. 226). So the first step in achieving a continuous identity through time is an understanding that one's thoughts exist over time and that, in addition, one's thoughts are one's own. For James, the self is a reflective process, "the result of our abandoning the outward looking point of view, and of having become able to think of subjectivity as such, to think of ourselves as thinkers" (Vol. 1, p. 296). Developmentally, then, a sense of continuous identity must rely on children's developing ability to reflect on their thought processes; that is, children must not only remember past experiences but, for a memory to be autobiographical in the sense that it is an integrated part of a personal history, children must also be able to reflect on their thoughts and feelings about their past experiences. In addition, to conceptualize oneself as a conscious thinker one must be able to provide a subjective perspective on the past.

DEVELOPING NARRATIVE SUBJECTIVITY

How might children's developing understanding of memories as subjective representations be manifest in their autobiographical narratives? In recounting a past experience one must tell what happened; one must provide what Labov (1982) labeled *referential information*. This is the bare bones of an account but if this is the only information included it is not really a narrative (e.g., Labov, 1982; Peterson & McCabe, 1982). For example, a child who lists the animals seen at the zoo is certainly recalling details of a past experience but cannot be credited with an understanding that this accounting represents a particular perspective on what occurred; there is no sense of story that relies on some kind of narrative tension. To create a true narrative, the narrator must go beyond recounting referential information to include orienting information, information that places the event in time and place, introduces the people involved, and provides information about how this event is related to other events, either temporally or thematically.

Most important, the narrator must provide some evaluation of the event, some way of expressing a personal perspective on what the event means. This kind of evaluative information is carried through a variety of linguistic devices, including intensifiers ("It was so hot"; "We saw really big turtles"), qualifiers ("It was a bad movie"; "He was mean") and internal responses referring to both emotion ("I was angry at my brother") and cognition ("I thought I was going to fall"; "I didn't want to go to the party"). By using evaluations, children are moving beyond simple descriptions of what occurred to mark how they felt about this event, to provide a sense of subjective perspective. Notice that evaluations mark two aspects of subjective perspective. Some kinds of linguistic evaluations refer to the objects, people, or activities in the external environment. Intensifiers and qualifiers almost always fall into this category. These kinds of evaluations provide subjective texture to the narrative in the sense that they implicitly mark the narrator's perspective, but it is internal responses that fully mark the subjective perspective. By bringing thoughts and feelings about an event into the narrative, the narrator is truly making the story his or her own. This is why the event was funny, or painful, or interesting, or important. This is what makes this event meaningful to me, and why it is worth recounting to you.

Fivush et al. (1995) examined children's developing narrative structure in a longitudinal study across the preschool years. They asked children to tell them about significant, novel experiences when they were 40 months old, 46 months, 58 months, and 70 months. Not surprisingly, children recounted more information as they grew older, and provided more detailed accounts of their past, increasing from a mean of about 10 propositions per narrative at 40 months to a mean of about 23 propositions at 70 months. Furthermore, children increased in their ability to place events in spatial–temporal context, providing more orienting information, and especially more information that linked the specific event being recounted to other similar events, providing a framework for placing this event in the context of other life events. Most important, children also increased their use of evaluative devices over time, marking their narratives with subjective perspective. For example, at 40 months of age, Patty recited her experience at a circus in the following way.

Child: We saw—we saw a clown riding on a—in a train.
Interviewer: You saw a clown riding on a train? Wow! What
        else?

Child: And there were lots of clowns that at the circus ... and
           lots of Indians at the circus.
Interviewer: What else happened?
Child: And there was lotsa of music going there too. And they
           squirt fire at the clowns.
Interviewer: Wow, that sounds like fun. What else happened at
           the circus?
Child: Um ... there was too much music and they play lots of
           music and when the circus is over we went to get
           some food at the food place.

Patty was clearly able to articulate specific details about her experiences,
but these details are presented as a series of descriptions about what
happened. She provided little orienting information to place this event in
context, and although she provided a good bit of evaluative information,
it is in the form of intensifying objective aspects of the event ("lots of
clowns," "lotsa music"). At the end, we get some hint of her personal
reaction to the event ("there was too much music") but this perspective
is not marked explicitly. In contrast, when asked about going to EPCOT
Center $2^1/_2$ years later, when she was 70 months of age, Patty responds:

Child: Well, when we went to EPCOT Center I saw, we saw
           the fireworks ... And we went to this Chinese
           restaurant ... At EPCOT, they had all these different
           country restaurants and we went to the Chinese ...
           but I got baby back ribs.
Interviewer: You got baby back ribs at the Chinese restaurant?
Child: Yeah, I didn't know they'd be in Chinese. I thought
           they'd be in English ... cause I like English ones. But
           instead they were in Chinese.

Patty went on to talk more about dinner and then moved on to reporting
the rides they went on in Disney World, but this excerpt already
demonstrates the change in her narrative perspective. She began by
orienting the listener to the specific event which she was narrating
("when we went to EPCOT Center") and provided background
explanation about their restaurant choice ("they had all these different
country restaurants"). She then went into great detail about what she
was thinking when she ordered her food, and why she wanted the ribs to
be in "English" ("cause I like English ones"). This narrative, in contrast
to her earlier one, clearly moves beyond reporting what happened by
referencing the events to her unique perspective, her thoughts and likes
and dislikes. Moreover, it is not just one's own perspective that children
report; they also report other people's perspective on the event. In

discussing a particular ride that she and her mother went on, Patty
recalled

Child: ...cause there's this little spinning wheel ... and it makes
          you go fast ... and slow. And my mom was, got sick
          on ummm .... When it went fast so, so, ummm, we,
          so when I drive with my mom, I had to turn it slow.
          Although I liked it fast.

Here we see Patty's ability to represent both her own perspective on the
event as well as her mother's and to comment explicitly on how they
differ.

It is intriguing that, although all children increased in both their
narrative length and their use of evaluations over time, girls'
autobiographical narratives were longer than those of boys. Moreover,
although girls and boys did not differ significantly in their use of
externally oriented evaluations (intensifiers, qualifiers), girls mentioned
significantly more internal states than did boys. One possible
explanation for this gender difference—and indeed, for the age
differences as well—may simply be that girls, and older children, are
more linguistically sophisticated than boys and younger children.
However, there were no gender differences on other measures of
language development, including mean length of utterance and
performance on the Peabody Picture Vocabulary Test. More specific to
narrative devices is that children's increasing use of evaluations over age
was also not related to other language measures. This is not to argue that
language skills play no role in developing narrative skills; clearly, they
must. Rather, the argument is that children's increasing narrative skills
cannot be *reduced* to increasing language skills. We must look to other
developmental explanations for how children come to include more
explicit information about their evaluative stance as they grow older and
why there are gender differences in autobiographical narratives.

There are at least two reasons why children may begin to include
their unique perspective when recounting their past experiences. First,
children learn that their internal reactions to events are interesting and
important to include when narrating the past. Second, children come to
understand that their reactions may be different than other people's
reactions. Explicitly providing one's own perspective is necessary once
one understands that this information is unique to the individual and
thus cannot be assumed to be shared knowledge. How might children
come to this understanding?

Certainly, specific cognitive advances are necessary for this level of
representational awareness. Perhaps most important are arguments put
forth by theorists exploring children's developing theory of mind
(Astington, 1993; Perner, 1990; Wellman, 1990). As children begin to

understand that others have internal states, beliefs, desires, and thoughts that may be different from their own they may also come to understand that others have representations of past experiences that may be different than their own. Perner (1990) argued that a sense of autobiography is dependent on the child's developing theory of mind. Children's developmental understanding of false belief, that individuals can hold conflicting mental representations, is the necessary cognitive prerequisite for constructing an autobiographical self. Recent research by Welch-Ross (1997) demonstrates an intriguing correlation between children's level of understanding of theory of mind and their level of contributions to memory conversations with their mothers. She argued, in line with Perner, that children's memory participation relies in part on their understanding that others may hold different mental representations. Thus, the individual's cognitive achievement of theory of mind leads to the ability to understand that others may hold different memory representations from the self.

I agree that certain cognitive milestones may need to be achieved for children to gain an appreciation that their representations of past events are uniquely their own, but I further argue that these cognitive achievements are embedded in a social context in which parents and children discuss past experiences together, and these joint reminiscings play a crucial role in facilitating children's dawning cognitive understanding. Following from Vygotsky's (1978) theory, I argue that cognitive skills develop in social contexts in which the forms and functions of behavior are highlighted. By engaging children in particular tasks, adults are teaching children that these are the important tasks to master to be a competent member of the culture (Rogoff, 1990; Wertsch, 1985). By scaffolding children's performance—essentially providing the structure to accomplish tasks children are not yet able to accomplish on their own—adults are modeling the forms of performance.

Moreover, language is a privileged means for the transmission of culturally appropriate skills (Schieffelin & Ochs, 1986). Language provides both the means of communication between the parent and child as well as the forms in which the task should be structured. For autobiographical narratives, which are by nature linguistic in form, the ways in which parents talk with their young children about past events provides both the context and the mechanism for children's developing narrative skills. It is in the context of jointly reminiscing about shared past experiences with adults, and in particular parents, that children learn how and why we share past experiences together.

Furthermore, it is during joint reminiscing that children come to realize that their representations of the past may differ from others' representations. This realization, in turn, leads to the understanding that memories are representations that may or may not be veridical and that may or may not be isomorphic with others who have experienced the same event. This is how children come to understand memories *as* representations, a critical step in the development of a subjective perspective.

EARLY PARENT-CHILD REMINISCING

Parents and children begin talking about the past together virtually as soon as children begin talking. However, at this early stage, beginning at about 18 - 20 months of age, parents provide virtually all of the content and structure, and children respond by confirming or repeating what the parent has said (Eisenberg, 1985; Sachs, 1983). For example, Sachs (1983, p. 152) gave the following illustration of a typical conversation about a past experience with her 22 month old daughter, Naomi.

Mother: Did you go on the slide?
Child: Go slide.
Mother: What did we do outside?
Child: Outside.

As can be seen in this example, although Naomi is quite willing to engage in this conversation by taking an appropriate conversational turn, she does not provide any new information about the event under discussion. Very quickly, however, children become much more participatory in these conversations, providing information about the previous experience when questioned, as the following example of a mother talking with her 29-month-old daughter (from Eisenberg's, 1985, p. 188 corpus) illustrates (translated by Eisenberg from Spanish).

Mother: Gabriela, did you fall out of bed last night?
Child: Yes.
Mother: Did you fall? How did you fall?
Child: (sits down on the ground) Like this.

In this example, Gabriela did more than simply confirm her mother's rendition of the past; she provided additional information (although partly nonverbal) about how this event transpired.

Still, it is obvious from these examples that in talking about the past, these very young children are relying heavily on the adult's scaffolding or structuring of these conversations for them. At these early stages of adult-child reminiscing children are learning to reflect on and report their past experiences. Within a few months, children begin participating more heavily in parent-guided reminiscing as well as introducing past events as topics in ongoing conversations. This transition into full participation in reminiscing marks an important developmental milestone in children's understanding of their own past. Through conversing with others about their previous experiences, children begin to reflect on their past experiences in a new way. They begin to understand that individuals who have shared an experience together can talk about that experience at a later time, sharing what they recall. Essentially, the memory of a past event becomes an object on which attention can be focused. In the act of joint reminiscing children become aware of memory representations as representations, as objects of shared attention and discussion.

Negotiating the Past

In the early stages of parent - child reminiscing there is no sense that children are aware that their memory representations may be any different from anyone else's. In confirming and repeating parental contributions to the conversations, and recalling information in response to a specific question, parents and children are coconstructing a past event in which both participants agree on what occurred. However, as children participate more fully in these conversations, as they begin to report more information and introduce past events as topics of conversations, the possibility for disagreement becomes more probable. Whereas in early reminiscing conversations children become aware of past events as objects of shared attention between people, with increasing participation in these conversations children become aware that memories of past experiences may be different even for people who have ostensibly experienced the same external event; that is, the object that is being jointly focused on, the past event, may be represented differently by the different people contributing to the shared construction of what occurred. It is at these critical conversational junctures that children are faced with constructing a subjective sense of one's own reality that may or may not coincide with those of others. It is through these kinds of interactions that children come to understand that they have a unique perspective on the world.

Some examples drawn from research my students and I have conducted over the last several years illustrate this phenomenon (Fivush & Fromhoff, 1988; Reese, Haden, & Fivush, 1993, 1996). The first excerpt is from a conversation between a mother with her 40-month-old daughter in which they discuss a day at Grandma and Grandpa's house.

Mother: What did Mommy find for you that you brought home?
Child: Rocks.
Mother: Yeah, we got some rocks, didn't we?
Child: And fire hats.

> Mother: And fire hats? Yeah that's right. Those little tiny fire
> hats. I forgot about those. Where did you get those?
> Child: Grandma and Grandpa.
> Mother: Grandma and Grandpa gave you those.

In this example, the mother asks a question to which she expects a specific answer: rocks. When the child supplies this information, the mother confirms, but the child then goes on to recall another object that she brought home from Grandma and Grandpa's house: little fire hats. This is information that the mother had forgotten; after acknowledging the veridicality of this response the mother explicitly tells her daughter that she herself had forgotten about the fire hats, thus informing her child that their memories of the event are different. They each recall different details about what occurred. The following is another example of a 40-month-old child's conversation with his mother, in which they discuss playing at a friend's house.

> Mother: What toy did you play with that you liked a real lot?
> Child: The sandbox.
> Mother: She didn't have a sandbox. Remember in that
> playroom, she had lots of toys. What was your
> favorite toy that you kept wanting to play with, do
> you remember?
> Child: The airplane.
> Mother: No, not the airplane. Do you remember?
> Child: What.

This is a very different example from the first. In this conversation the mother is explicitly asking her son what his favorite toy was, yet when he responds with what he recalls, the sandbox, she denies that this object even existed. Clearly, this must create a conflict for the child in trying to reconcile what he remembers with what his mother remembers. Both of these examples point to how actual objects are negotiated as to whether they were even part of the event as experienced. In the first example, although the mother had forgotten the fire hats, she acknowledges her daughter's recall of this object; in the second example, the mother simply denies that this object even existed. As it turns out from a later discussion with the father, there was, in fact, a sandbox at this friend's house, so the child is correct in his recall. In both examples the children are learning that different people recalling a shared past event may recall different objects associated with that event, but the first child is learning to trust her recollections, whereas the second child is not.

Moreover, in the second example, when the mother further questions the child about his favorite toy, and he responds with "airplane," the mother again denies this response. In this case, however, she is not explicitly denying that there was an airplane; she is denying that this was her son's favorite toy. Thus, past events are negotiated not only at the level of external reality but also at the level of internal reality. This child is denied his evaluations of the event, what his favorite toy was. This level of negotiation is even more apparent in the following example of a mother and her 35-month-old daughter discussing seeing bears at a carnival.

>Mother: They were big bears. Did they scare you?
>Child: Um-umm. (no)
>Mother: A little bit? Just a little bit?
>Child: Oh, I'm not scared of bears.
>Mother: You're not scared of bears. Well, that's good.

Here we see a very explicit negotiation between mother and child about the child's emotional reaction to an event. At first the child denies being scared, to which the mother responds by prompting the child that perhaps the child was just a bit scared. When the child still denies it, the mother accepts it, and the conversation moves on to other aspects of the carnival. Later in the conversation, the child returns to the topic of bears.

>Child: Bears scare me.
>Mother: They scare you. I thought they didn't scare you.
>Child: I'm scary (i.e., "I'm scared")

The child now claims that she is scared of bears. When the mother questions the child's previous report of not being scared, the child reaffirms that she was, indeed, scared. Whether the child was actually scared of the bears at the carnival is an open question; however, what is clear in this interchange is that the child is beginning to rethink her interpretation of the event, perhaps because of the mother's questioning. Thus, by the end of the conversation the child's subjective experience, the ways in which she interprets her internal reactions to and interpretations of what this event means, has been changed. She has developed a new subjective sense of this event and, by extension, of herself: She is someone who is scared of bears.

Learning to Evaluate the Past

Two components of parent–child reminiscing are highlighted in the previous examples. First, in the act of jointly re-creating a shared event in conversation there are critical conversational junctures at which children are confronted with the fact that what they recall may be different from what others recall. Furthermore, what differs may be recall of specific objects or details of the event itself or the subjective evaluation of the event. Both of these discrepancies are important fodder for children's developing understanding of memories as representations, but the latter is particularly interesting, because it is the subjective perspective on an event that makes it uniquely one's own experience. Earlier I presented evidence that as children develop they increasingly use subjective evaluation in reporting their past experiences. In this section I present evidence that children are explicitly learning how to include this kind of information during parent-guided reminiscing.

In an initial study exploring children's developing autobiographical narrative skills in social context, I compared the narrative devices mothers used in reminiscing with their 32-month-old children and children's independent autobiographical narratives with an unfamiliar interviewer just over a year later, when the children were 45 months old (Fivush, 1991). If children are learning how to evaluate their own past experiences through participating in scaffolded conversations with their mothers, then mothers who use more evaluative devices when reminiscing with their young children should have children who come to use more evaluative devices in their own narratives later in development. This is exactly what was found. Mothers used predominately two types of evaluative devices in these conversations, intensifiers and emotional language, as the following example illustrates.

Mother: What else did we see in Baltimore? Did we go to a big
         place that had fish in it? That wasn't one of your
         better days. Mommy carried you most of the way
         around the aquarium. The National Aquarium.
         What did you see there?
Child: Fish.
Mother: We saw fish. Big fish or little fish?

This mother both evaluates external objects (a big place, big fish or little fish) and also evaluates the child's internal state ("That wasn't one of your better days"). In contrast, children used almost exclusively intensifiers to evaluate their experience. Only 6% of their evaluative comments were emotional reactions or states. Thus, at this early stage of learning to evaluate one's experience, although mothers focus on both external and internal evaluation, children are focusing on external evaluation. The fact that mothers who evaluate a great deal have children who later evaluate a great deal in their independent narrations indicate that children are learning that evaluation is an important part of telling one's story. But that so little of this evaluation marks internal responses further suggests that, this early in development children have not yet achieved full autobiographical narratives. It is important to note again that this is not simply due to language limitations. Children of this age have quite extensive emotion vocabularies and are able to talk about their emotions and others' emotions in the ongoing context of emotional experiences (Bretherton, Fritz, Zahn-Waxler, & Ridgeway, 1986). The fact that they do not elect to discuss these aspects when reporting past experiences suggests that they have not yet learned to mark their experiences from a subjective perspective.

In order to examine the development of subjective perspective in more detail, Haden, Haine, and Fivush (1997) conducted a longitudinal study beginning with somewhat older children. They also wanted to extend their findings to other important adults in children's lives. Thus, they asked mothers and fathers, in separate home sessions, to discuss several special events with their 40-month-old children, and they repeated this procedure when the children were 70 months old. Mothers and fathers did not differ from each other in the types of narrative structures they used when conversing with daughters or sons, but both mothers and fathers increased in their use of evaluations over time. Children also showed an increase in overall use of evaluations over time, but girls showed a sharper increase than did boys. Moreover, in this study, children did use emotional language in evaluating their narratives at both ages, and this increased over time, especially for girls. These results suggest that as children grow older they begin to include more specific mention of their emotional reactions to events in their autobiographical narratives, with girls showing this to a greater extent than boys.

More important, regression analyses indicated that maternal use of evaluations when conversing with their 40-month-old children predicted children's use of evaluations when the children were 70 months old above and beyond what children's own use of evaluations at 40 months predicted or concurrent relations between maternal evaluations and child evaluations at 70 months (Haden et al., 1997). That is, mothers' use of narrative evaluations earlier in development predicted a significant proportion of unique variance in children's use of evaluations later in development. It is provocative that fathers' use of evaluations did not provide any predictive power. Overall, this line of research provides strong evidence that children are learning how to evaluate their past experiences through participation in parent-guided reminiscing. In particular, mothers who provide a great deal of evaluation when reminiscing with their preschoolers have children who use more evaluation when reporting their past than children whose mothers do not use as much evaluation.

Episodes, Autobiography, and Subjectivity

Over the course of the preschool years children not only begin to recall more detailed and elaborated information about their past, but they also begin to evaluate their past experiences when narrating them with and to others. Even the youngest children studied clearly recall the past; they are able to verbally recount bits of information and are willing to share this information with others in conversational reminiscing. However, the flavor of these conversations changes qualitatively from one of *describing* the past together to one of *sharing* the past together. Moreover, as I have demonstrated throughout this chapter, this developmental shift occurs as a function of joint reminiscing. In this context, children are learning the forms and functions for evaluating their past experiences and, critically, they are confronted with the fact that others may not view the past event in the same way as they do. By the time children are 5 to 6 years of age they demonstrate a clear understanding that memories are negotiated in joint reminiscing, as the following example of a conversation between a 70-month-old child and her father demonstrates.

Father: What was fun about the zoo?
Child: Uh ... I know what I liked.
Father: What did you like?
Child: I liked the g'rillas.
Father: The gorillas?
Child: Yeah.
Father: Yeah, we saw some neat gorillas, didn't we?
Child: What did you like?
Father: Well, gee, I may—you know that was one of my favorite things. You know, what was, what kind of gorilla did you like the best?
Child: Ummmm, the black ones.
Father: The black ones. And didn't they have some different size gorillas?
Child: I didn't....
Father: But didn't they have some little babies?
Child: Yeah!
Father: What, did they have little baby gorillas?
Child: Yes. I like those. I like those.

In this conversation the focus is almost exclusively on evaluating the event. Little work is done to establish external referents (there is some reminding about the baby gorillas), but there is a great deal of negotiated interaction about who liked what and whether they both liked the same parts. Notice that the implicit theme is that father and daughter may have very different evaluations of the event; the child asks her father quite seriously what his favorite part was, with the full understanding that it may be quite different than her own.

Through learning to evaluate one's past, one develops an understanding of one's unique perspective on past experiences. Obviously the development of autobiographical memory is a complex phenomenon, involving many cognitive and social skills, but the development of subjective perspective certainly plays a major role in the shift from episodic to autobiographical memory. Moreover, there are individual and gender differences in this process. Children whose mothers focus more on evaluation themselves come to include more of this kind of information in their own autobiographical narratives. Also, girls include more evaluation in their narratives across the preschool years than do boys (see Fivush, 1998a, for a full discussion of gender differences in autobiographical narratives). Children who enrich their memories of past experiences with evaluative texture may come to have a more subjective perspective on their past. These children may come to understand their current self as emerging from past experiences that shape them, and are shaped by them, in a continual dialectic between memory and self. If I am who I am because of the sum of my experiences, then my subjective perspective on those experiences is my subjective perspective on my self. Similarly, my subjective perspective on who I am will color the way in which I interpret my experiences. The richer the evaluative stance, the more complex and textured is my perspective and therefore my autobiographical self.

Following from these arguments, the individual and gender differences are particularly intriguing. Girls may be learning to develop a more nuanced and evaluative sense of their experiences and of themselves than are boys but, as the research on parental influences demonstrates, there are large differences within the gender groups as well. Children, and perhaps especially girls, who are learning to evaluate their past and to negotiate their memories in joint reminiscing in which their experiences and perspectives are valued, may come to own their experience in the sense that they trust what they recall and how they recall it. These are children who will come to have a sense of self grounded in their experience.

This is not to argue that one's memories are not influenced by the ways in which one jointly recalls them with others. In the process of sharing memories, the memories may change—mutate, not only in what details one may recall (yes, there were baby gorillas) but also in how one interprets those events (I am scared of bears). Rather, the argument is that in sharing one's experiences from one's own subjective perspective, as well as from understanding the other's perspective, one comes to own those experiences as part of one's past. As Barbara Wilson (1998) wrote in her memoirs of her childhood,

After the good times were over, as we grew older, we were to tell each other stories about the past, each adding his or her own fragments of pleasurable detail, until the joint memory became larger than each single memory, and yet became something that each of us possessed fully, as if it were solely our own. (p. 142)

Through joint reminiscing one learns to evaluate one's past, to interpret one's experiences, and at the same time to own them as part of oneself, indeed as the very heart of who one is. It is through joint reminiscing that one comes to have a personal past.

REFERENCES

Astington, J. (1993). *The child's discovery of mind*. Cambridge, MA: Harvard University Press.

Bauer, P. (1997). Development of memory in early childhood. In N. Cowan (Ed.), *The development of memory in childhood* (pp. 83-112). Sussex, England: Psychology Press.

Bretherton, I., Fritz, J., Zahn-Waxler, C., & Ridgeway, D. (1986). Learning to talk about emotions: A functionalist perspective. *Child Development, 57*, 529-548.

Damon, W., & Hart, D. (1988). *Self-understanding in childhood and adolescence*. New York: Cambridge University Press.

Donald, M. (1991). *Origins of the modern mind: Three stages in the evolution of culture and cognition*. Cambridge, MA: Harvard University Press.

Eder, R. A. (1990). Uncovering young children's psychological selves: Individual and developmental differences. *Child Development, 61*, 849-863.

Eisenberg, A. R. (1985). Learning to describe past experience in conversation. *Discourse Processes, 8*, 177-204.

Fivush, R. (1991). The social construction of personal narratives. *Merrill-Palmer Quarterly, 37*, 59-82.

Fivush, R. (1997). Event memory in childhood. In N. Cowan (Ed.), *The development of memory in childhood* (pp. 139-162). Sussex, England: Psychology Press.

Fivush, R. (1998a). Gendered narratives: Elaboration, structure and emotion in parent-child reminiscing across the preschool years. In C. P. Thompson, D. J. Herrmann, D. Bruce, J. D. Read, D. G. Payne, & M. P. Toglia (Eds.), *Autobiographical memory: Theoretical and applied perspectives* (pp. 79-104). Mahwah, NJ: Lawrence Erlbaum Associates.

Fivush, R. (1998b). The stories we tell: How language shapes autobiography. *Applied Cognitive Psychology, 12*, 483-487.

Fivush, R., & Fromhoff, F. (1988). Style and structure in mother-child conversations about the past. *Discourse Processes, 11*, 337-355.

Fivush, R., Haden, C., & Adam, S. (1995). Structure and coherence of preschoolers' personal narratives over time: Implications for childhood amnesia. *Journal of Experimental Child Psychology, 60*, 32-56.

Haden, C., Haine, R., & Fivush, R. (1997). Developing narrative structure in parent-child conversations about the past. *Developmental Psychology, 33,* 295-307.

Harter, S. (1983). The development of the self and the self-system. In E. M. Heatherington (Ed.), *Handbook of child psychology: Vol. 4. Socialization, personality, and social development* (4th ed., pp. 285-385). New York: Wiley.

James, W. (1950). *The Principles of Psychology.* New York: Dover. (Original work published 1890)

Labov, W. (1982). Speech actions and reaction in personal narrative. In D. Tannen (Ed.), *Analyzing discourse: Text and talk* (pp. 219-247). Washington, DC: Georgetown University Press.

Lewis, M. (1992). The role of the self in social behavior. In F. S. Kessel, P. M. Cole, & D. L. Johnson (Eds.), *Self and consciousness: Multiple perspectives* (pp. 19-44). Hillsdale, NJ: Lawrence Erlbaum Associates.

Mandler, J. M. (1990). Recall of events by preverbal children. In A. Diamond (Ed.), *The development and neural bases of higher cognitive functions* (pp. 485-516). New York: New York Academy of Sciences.

Nelson, K. (1996). *Language in cognitive development: Emergence of the mediated mind.* New York: Cambridge University Press.

Perner, J. (1990). Experiential awareness and children's episodic memory. In W. Schneider & F. E. Weinert (Eds.). *Interactions among aptitudes, strategies and knowledge in cognitive performance* (pp. 3-11). New York: Springer-Verlag.

Peterson, C., & McCabe, A. (1982). *Developmental psycholinguistics: Three ways of looking at a narrative.* New York: Plenum.

Reese, E., Haden, C. A., & Fivush, R. (1993). Mother-child conversations about the past: Relationships of style and memory over time. *Cognitive Development, 8,* 403-430.

Reese, E., Haden, C., & Fivush, R. (1996). Mothers, father, daughters, sons: Gender differences in reminiscing. *Research on Language and Social Interaction, 29,* 27-56.

Rogoff, B. (1990). *Apprenticeship in thinking.* New York: Oxford University Press.

Rovee-Collier, C., & Shyi, C. W. G. (1992). A functional and cognitive analysis of infant long-term memory retention. In M. L. Howe, C. J. Brainerd, & V. F. Reyna (Eds.), *Development of long-term retention* (pp. 3–55). New York: Springer-Verlag.

Sachs, J. (1983). Talking about the there and then: The emergence of displaced reference in parent–child discourse. In K. Nelson (Ed.), *Children's language* (Vol. 4, pp. 1–28). Hillsdale, NJ: Lawrence Erlbaum Associates.

Schieffelin, B. B., & Ochs, E. (1986). *Language socialization across cultures.* New York: Cambridge University Press.

Vygotsky, L. S. (1978). *Mind in society: The development of higher psychological processes.* Cambridge, MA: Harvard University Press.

Welch-Ross, M. K., (1997). Mother–child participation in conversations about the past: Relations to preschoolers' theory of mind. *Developmental Psychology, 33,* 618–629.

Wellman, H. M. (1990). *The child's theory of mind.* Cambridge, MA: MIT Press.

Wertsch, J. V. (1985). *Vygotsky and the social formation of mind.* Cambridge, MA: Harvard University Press.

Wilson, B. (1998). *Blue windows: A Christian Science childhood.* New York: Picador.

4

The Anticipated Self:
Mother–Child Talk About
Future Events

Judith A. Hudson
Rutgers University

Research on parent–child talk about the past has shown that the techniques that parents use to engage their children in verbal reminiscing may have long-term effects on children's autobiographical memory development (Fivush, 1991; Haden, Haine, & Fivush, 1997; McCabe & Peterson, 1991; Reese, Haden, & Fivush, 1993). By engaging their children in talk about the past, parents attach social significance to the sharing of memories and provide a verbal model of how to retrieve memories. Through participation in memory conversations, children learn to relate another person's representation of a past experience, expressed in language, to their internal memory of the experience. This insight depends on understanding how language is used as a representational medium, how individuals remember, and how one's own memory is related to others' (Fivush, 1991; Hudson, 1990; Nelson, 1993; Welch-Ross, 1995).

In everyday conversations, however, parents not only reminisce with their children about past events but also talk with them about future events. Comparatively little attention has been given to the role that talk about the future may play in children's conceptual development. Talk about the future is bound to future events in a different way than talk about the past represents memory of past experience. To participate in conversations about the future, children must understand the role of language in constructing hypothetical models and making plans that have not yet been experienced. When parents discuss future events with children, they are relating events along past to present to future. This temporal comparison may assist children in understanding temporal concepts. In addition, talk about the future may contribute to the development of planning skills as children are asked to anticipate and plan for upcoming events. Finally, talking about one's plans provides another perspective on the development of self-understanding. It can provide a model of a self that not only exists now and has existed in the past but that also will continue to exist and act into the future. Thus, a future perspective on the self is embedded in talk about future events.

DEVELOPMENT OF FUTURE UNDERSTANDING

There is ample evidence that during the first 2 years of life children are able to learn simple temporal sequences and anticipate "what happens next" (e.g., Bauer, 1995). They can also use anticipatory knowledge to adjust their behavior, for example, to alter their reach to obtain a toy so that they take into account the type of barrier they see ahead of them (Willatts, 1990). However, they do not provide evidence of understanding their own continued existence into future time. Evidence for this level of understanding comes from research on children's talk about future events.

Role of Language

Language provides the means for adults to establish reference to the future and becomes a means for children to express their expectations of future events. A large body of research on children's talk about time has focused on children's use of grammatical markers (tense, modality, and aspect) and lexical markers such as adverbs (*tomorrow*, *later*), prepositions (*on Monday*, *after*) and conjunctions (*and, then*), examining both spontaneous speech and speech used in experimental situations. There is general agreement that by the age of 2 years children can differentiate among past, present, and future reference using both tense and aspect (Harner, 1981; Nelson, 1991; Sachs, 1983). The question of when children have achieved an understanding of conventional time ("tomorrow," "next week") is more controversial (see Benson, 1997, for a review).

The controversy over children's understanding of "before" and "after" is representative of a conflict between two ways of thinking regarding the relation between children's talk about time and their understanding of temporal concepts. The Piagetian view maintains that language use merely reflects cognitive concepts that children have already mastered: The ability to use "before" and "after" correctly depends on the cognitive understanding of seriation and reversibility, which is achieved at about 6 years, during the concrete operational stage (Ferreiro & Sinclair, 1971; Trosborg, 1982).

In contrast, theorists who take a social–cultural perspective on cognitive development argue that social interactions between adults and children in everyday events provide a context in which new concepts are introduced to young children and within which children first understand time concepts (Nelson, 1986). In this view, the concept is itself a social construction, and it is conveyed to children through language: "The child alone cannot *discover* time, because (unlike concrete objects) it is not an entity that exists to be discovered. Rather, conceptions of process and change have led different societies to conceptualize time in different ways, and those ways are conveyed to children through language forms" (Nelson, 1986, p. 288). Children's temporal knowledge emerges from the use of temporal terms as applied to actual past, present, and future occurrences; time is not a concept that develops apart from or prior to correct use of temporal terms (French & Nelson, 1985; Nelson, 1996).

Coordinating Temporal Systems: Event Time and Speech Time

To engage in discussions about past and future events a speaker must master the various linguistic forms and must understand how past, present, and future are related in a hypothetical timeline. He or she must also coordinate systems of temporal reference and temporal relations in relation to a conversation that is also unfolding over time. Weist (1989) proposed that children progress through four stages in coordinating three systems: (a) *event time (ET)*, the time that the event under discussion actually occurred or will occur; (b) *speech time (ST)*, the time at which the speaker is talking; and (c) *reference time (RT)*, the time that is being referred to in speech. In the first stage, from 12 to 18 months, children talk about the "here and now" and do not use tense, modality, or aspect to differentiate ET from ST. In the second stage, from 18 to 30 months, children use tense and aspect to refer to separate ET from ST and to distinguish events that occurred in the past ("Mommy went bye-bye") from those occurring in the present ("I eating my lunch"). During this stage children express future desires, but there is also no delineation of the future into units of time. In the third stage, from 30 to 36 months, children are able to use adverbials to locate recent and distant past events, so that RT is separated from ST. Finally, at about 4 years, children use temporal adverbs that differentiate RT and use "before" and "after" clauses to coordinate RT with ET and ST.

Nelson (1996) pointed out that Weist's (1989) account may underestimate young children's understanding because it focuses on children's ability to coordinate temporal systems within single sentences, not connected discourse. Nelson's analysis of the bedtime monologues of a young child, Emily, from 22 to 23 months, indicates that Emily was capable of moving backward and forward in time in her references to past and future events within one evening's monologue. Looking at sequential mention of events across the entire narrative, it is apparent that Emily was able to effectively coordinate ET and RT as she referred to the past, the present, and the future.

Extended conversations with parents may assist young children in coordinating time systems by providing the extended narrative contact in which the relation between ET, RT and ST are understood. Before children are able to coordinate these systems in single sentences or even in independent narratives they may be able to provide appropriate event information as queried by parents in coconstructing narratives about past and future events. Because parent–child conversations are situated in the real-time unfolding of shared events, the relationship between events over time and how they are described is made explicit. To understand parents' temporal references, children can refer to the actual events as they unfold as well as their internal representations of familiar event sequences (general event representations). Conversations about both the past and the future would be most effective for children to acquire an understanding of how these systems are related in language and thought.

Parent–Child Talk About the Future

Although far less research has been conducted on how parents and children talk about the future than on how they talk about the past, some research indicates that talk about the future is quite frequent in everyday parent–child conversations. Lucariello and Nelson (1987) examined the extent to which mothers referred to the here and now (present), past events, or future action while talking with 2-year-old children in different event contexts. Across the 10 dyads studied there was a total of 38 episodes of past talk and 44 episodes of future talk. Both past and future talk were more frequent in the routine event contexts (e.g., bath time) than in play contexts, suggesting that shared event knowledge facilitated temporally displaced language use. However, the vast majority of future talk (95%) referred to actions that were anticipated to occur on the same days as the observation took place, whereas 63% of talk about the past referred to events that had occurred at least 1 day before. This finding suggests that the temporal frame of reference for past and future events may be different and mothers are more likely to refer to the immediate future. Lucariello and Nelson also found that children provided relatively few substantive contributions to either talk about the past or the future, providing no evidence of a superiority for either type of displaced time talk at this age.

Norton (1993) examined the relation between maternal time talk in naturalistic conversations and 3-year-olds' ability to temporally sequence events. Conversations were videotaped as part of a large, longitudinal investigation and took place as frequently as once every 6 weeks. Although talk about time represented less than 2% of the total language directed to children, there was a relation between maternal time talk and children's sequencing ability, measured by the seriation task of the McCarthy Scale. Children who scored in the top quartile had mothers who used more temporal references than mothers of children with lower scores. Norton's study provides some support to the notion that maternal talk about time affects the development of children's temporal concepts.

Benson, Talmi, and Haith (1999) recently examined parental time talk in 16 parent–child dyads over 16 months when the children were 14, 20, and 32 months. This study made use of data obtained from the Child Language Data Exchange System (MacWhinney, 1995). Approximately 47% of all utterances referred to events that could be dated as past, current, or future. Although the majority of adult utterances referred to current events (31%), there was significantly more reference to future events (14%) than to past events (2%). It is interesting that the percentage of parental talk about the past remained relatively constant over the 16-month interval, but the percentage of parental talk about the future increased from 36% at 14 months to 58% at 32 months.

The differences found in the rate of talk about past and future events across these studies are most likely due to variations in the contexts in which the conversation took place. Together these investigations (Benson et al., 1999; Lucariello & Nelson, 1987; Norton, 1993) provide evidence that parents do talk to very young children about future events at least as much as they talk about the past and perhaps even more often. However, these investigations provide scant information regarding how children interpret future talk and how they participate in conversations about the future. A complete understanding of the role of future talk in promoting children's concepts of the future and of their future selves depends on a more thorough investigation of children's participation in future talk and the long-term effects of participation.

Effects of Familiar Event Routines on the Development of Time Concepts

Friedman (1977, 1990; Friedman & Brudos, 1988) has conducted research on children's understanding of the temporal structure of real-world events by asking children to sequence photographs and construct temporal sequences spanning periods from hours to days to weeks. This line of research has found that by 4–5 years children are able to construct correctly ordered sequences for activities such as eating dinner, going to bed, waking up, and having lunch.

Using a variation of the picture-sequencing tasks, Benson, Grossman, and Hanebuth (1993) examined whether 4- and 5-year-olds could correctly sequence 12 daily activities from the past (yesterday), present (today), and future (tomorrow) along a timeline. Consistent with Friedman's (1977, 1990; Friedman & Brudos, 1988) research, children at both ages were able to correctly sequence these activities, but they were more accurate in sequencing activities from the past than from the future. These findings support the view that temporal understanding develops in the context of thinking about routine events but that thinking about a yet-undetermined future is more difficult than reasoning about an already-experienced past.

Planning for the Future

Although children under 5 years of age are generally unable to plan successfully in novel, spatial–planning tasks, such as planning routes through model towns (e.g., Rogoff, 1991), 3- to 5-year-old children are able to use general event knowledge to conduct and carry out plans for routine events. For example, when asked to construct event plans for going to the beach or grocery shopping, preschoolers can plan aloud for these events and consider alternative plans to correct mishaps that could occur (Hudson, Shapiro, & Sosa, 1995). There is also evidence that preschool children do not always know how to use event knowledge most effectively in planning. Three-year-olds provide more information when describing what happens in general in familiar events than when planning a future event, and 3- and 4-year-olds have difficulty coordinating multiple event goals. However, preschoolers' planning improves after planning with an adult partner (Hudson et al., 1995).

Thus, research indicates that parents do talk to their young children about future events; that temporal understanding may develop within a narrative discourse context; and that preschool children are able to plan for future, familiar events. Understanding how parents engage young children in talk about everyday, future events and how children participate in future–oriented conversations may provide insight into how children develop concepts of time and how to plan. The ability to think about and plan for the future may be important to the development of a concept of self that can be projected into the future.

A COMPARISON OF MOTHER–CHILD PAST AND FUTURE TALK

In this section I present data from a study of mother child talk about past and future events (Hudson & Sosa, 1995). The foremost goal was to examine the ways in which mothers engage young children in conversations about the future. Although there has been ample research on how mothers engage children in past talk, we were interested in whether mothers used similar techniques in eliciting children's future talk. A second goal was to determine whether stylistic differences in how mothers elicited their children's participation were consistent across contexts. On the one hand, mothers may use the same style across contacts, suggesting that these styles reflect general stylistic differences in how mothers interact verbally with their preschool children. On the other hand, parents' styles may vary across contacts, suggesting that these styles are task dependent and that parents use different styles depending on the goals of the interaction.

Also of interest was whether children would participate more or less in conversations about the future compared to conversations about the past. Greater difficulty in talking about the future would support the view that conceptualizing the future is cognitively more difficult than remembering an experienced, nonpresent past event. The final goal was to examine how general event knowledge contributed to the conversations. We predicted that general event knowledge would facilitate talk about the future more than talk about the past. When discussing past events, mothers would be more likely to focus on unique aspects of particular episodes to provide children with effective contrast; when talking about the future mothers could refer to general event knowledge to help create a verbal plan for what is likely to occur, and children could provide general event knowledge to contribute to that process.

Method

Fifty-six mothers and their children participated in this investigation. Twenty-eight children were approximately 2.5 years old (15 females, mean age = 30 months, age range = 28–31 months), and 28 children were approximately 4 years old (14 females, mean age = 47 months, age range

= 46–49 months). Participants were predominantly middle-income children with mothers of European descent.

An experimenter visited the dyads in their homes on two separate occasions separated by one week. During one visit past events were discussed, and during the other visit future events were discussed (order was counterbalanced). At the beginning of the first visit the experimenter discussed potential event topics with each mother, and eight topics were selected, four for each visit. During both visits, mothers discussed two novel events that had been experienced only once or had not yet been experienced, such as going to the circus and having chicken pox. They also discussed two routine events that had been experienced at least two times, such as going to the doctor and playing in the snow. Conversations were audiotaped. In most cases, the experimenter left the room while the mother and child conversed. Audiotapes were transcribed verbatim for coding.

Coding

Maternal speech. Each maternal utterance was first coded as one of eight conversational categories *(questions, contextual statements, evaluations, prompts, memory placeholders, metacognitive comments, placeholders, clarifications,* and *associative talk)* using a coding scheme adapted from Reese et al. (1993). The majority of maternal contributions consisted of questions (including general queries ["What happened when we went to Grandma's?"], requests for information ["Who's gonna be at the party?"], and yes–no questions ["Do you want to go to the playground tomorrow?"]) and contextual statements (statements that provided new information). Because these contributions represented mothers' substantive contributions and are generally considered the most revealing measures of material elicitation style (Reese et al., 1993) they were further coded as to whether they consisted of an *elaboration* or a *repetition*. *Elaborations* referred to new information about the event under discussion, whereas *repetitions* referred to information previously discussed. Finally, all questions and contextual statements were coded in terms of their temporal *point of reference: past episodes* ("What did you do the last time you went to the playground?"); *general event knowledge* ("What happens at preschool?"); *future actions* ("What are you going to do at the beach?"); and *future plans* which includes references to possible actions ("Maybe we'll see horses there"), predictions ("Do you think Amanda will be there?"), and elicitation of preferences ("Would you like to have a birthday party at McDonald's?")

Child contributions. All comments made by children were coded as 1 of 10 types of contributions, *elaborations, questions, yes–no responses, repetitions, placeholders, evaluations, metacognitive comments, associative talk, off-topic talk,* and *unintelligible utterances.* Children's substantive contributions to the conversations were largely in the form of elaborations, that is, statements that provided new information about the event under discussion. All elaborations produced by children were therefore coded for their temporal point of reference.

Stylistic Differences in Maternal Talk About the Future

Research on maternal styles in talking about the past has used an elaboration ratio score to examine stylistic differences in maternal elicitation style. The ratio is computed by dividing the number of elaborations produced by the number of repetitions produced. Two elaboration scores were computed for mothers using this formula: one for past conversations and one for future conversations. We compared mothers' elaboration ratio scores across types of conversations (past and future). Although mothers were more elaborative with 4-year-olds (M = 9.42) than with 2.5-year olds (M = 4.68), the elaboration ratios did not vary significantly by type of conversation. Thus, mothers as a group did not use a more or less elaborative style when talking about the future compared to how they talked with their children about the past.

To examine consistency in elaboration ratios, we computed correlations between mothers' elaboration scores for past and future conversation for mothers of younger children and of older children. The correlation for mothers of younger children was .21 (p = .27), and the correlation for mothers of older children was .41 (p < .05). These findings suggest that there was a small but significant correlation in maternal elaboration over past and future event conversations for mothers of 4-year-olds but not of 2.5-year-olds. Ratio scores were also used to divide mothers into separate categories of high and low elaborators. Mothers were categorized as high or low elaborators by dividing the sample into equal groups of 14 participants for each age group. The cutoff points were 5.00 for mothers of 2.5-year-olds in future conversations (M = 7.22, range = 0.96–16.25), 4.00 for mothers of 2.5-year-olds in past conversations (M = 4.97, range = 1.00–11.37), 6.00 for mothers of 4-year-olds in future conversations (M = 9.36, range = 2.41–49.00), and 6.00 for mothers of 4-year-olds in past conversations (M = 9.64, range = 1.08–442.00). In regard to categorization across conversations, 32 mothers (16 in each age group) were categorized the same way in both conversations, and 24 mothers (12 in each age group) were categorized differently across conversations. Thus, there was not a high degree of consistency in maternal elaboration across past and future conversations.

How Mothers Talk About the Future

Because there already are considerable data on how mothers talk about the past with preschool children, data on mothers' contributions to past conversations is not discussed here. To examine ways in which mothers talked about the future, analyses were conducted on the frequency of mothers' production of questions and contextual statements. As shown in Table 4.1, mothers rarely asked questions about past episodes, but they asked questions regarding general event knowledge as much as they asked questions regarding future actions and future plans. Mothers referred to general event knowledge significantly more often when discussing routine events than when discussing novel events, whereas future plans were mentioned significantly more often when discussing novel events than when discussing routine events. Mothers also mentioned fewer contextual statements about past episodes than any other type of contextual statement. They provided significantly more statements referring to future actions and future plans when discussing novel events than when discussing routine events.

Mothers' differential references to past events and their differential use of planning-related talk when talking about future novel and routine events suggests that they were using different methods to help their children think about the future depending on children's level of general event knowledge. When events were familiar, mothers tended to focus on what usually happens. In discussing future novel events of which children could not be expected to have prior knowledge, mothers were more likely to suggest possible actions and to elicit predictions and preferences. These differences are illustrated in the following examples. The first two excerpts are from conversations about routine events.

TABLE 4.1
Mean Frequencies of Maternal Questions and Contextual Statements by Point of Reference for Novel and Routine Events

Type of event	Past	General	Future	Future Plan
		Questions		
Novel events	2.84	12.80	10.93	14.68
Routine events	4.86	17.16	8.66	8.79
	Contextual statements			
Novel events	1.14	3.39	6.25	7.14
Routine events	1.39	4.54	3.84	4.39

Point of Reference

Example 1: 2.5-Year-Old, Visit to the Doctor (Routine)

Mother: You wanna go to the doctor's? Uh-huh? How come?
Child: I don't like doctor.
Mother: You don't like the doctor?
Child: No.
Mother: How come? Does he scare you?
Child: Yeah.
Mother: Yeah.
Child: Check my mouth.
Mother: He puts a tongue depressor in your mouth?
Child: A stick.
Mother: A stick in your mouth?
Child: Yeah.
Mother: Oh. And then what does he do? Does he look down your throat? Does he look down your throat when he puts a stick in your mouth? Does he check your heart, too? Does he have a stethoscope that goes like this and this? You don't mind that, do you?

Example 2: 4-Year-Old, Preschool (Routine)

Mother: Today's Wednesday, tomorrow is Thursday, what do we do on Tuesday and Thursdays? We do we do twice a week?
Child: Preschool.
Mother: Preschool. And tell me all about preschool. What's a day at preschool like? What do you do?
Child: Uhhmm.
Mother: Well first you get there and what do you do first?
Child: Uhhmm.
Mother: Well, do you say, first you shake the box?
Child: Yeah.
Mother: And you pick a name?
Child: Uh huh.
Mother: You shake the box and pull out a name and what does that person get to do?
Child: Hold the flag?
Mother: Who's your special friend?
Child: Jenna.
Mother: What did Jenna ask you on Tuesday? Jenna's mommy?
Child: She said that we could come over for lunch at her house.
Mother: Yeah, that would be nice.

Most of the conversation is conducted in the timeless present tense as the mothers ask, "What do you do...?" Note also how in the second example the mother shifts from talking about the general ("Who's your special friend?") to asking about what question was asked (in the past) regarding a future event. "What did Jenna ask you on Tuesday?" and "She said that we could come over for lunch at her house."

The following excerpts illustrate how mothers talked about future, novel events.

Example 3: 2.5-Year-Old, Going to the Fair (Novel)

Mother: Are you going to a fair on Saturday?
Child: Yeah.
Mother: Yeah? And what are you gonna do at the fair? What are you going to do at the fair?
Child: I don't know.
Mother: Are you gonna dance?
Child: Yeah.
Mother: Are you gonna get a balloon? Are you gonna have fun?
Child: Yeah.
Mother: Are you gonna go on a ride?
Child: Yeah.
Mother: Do you like horses? If it rains on Saturday, are we gonna go to the fair?
Child: Yep.
Mother: Yeah? Are you gonna get wet? Or do you think they should cancel it?
Child: Cancel.
Mother: Cancel it. And should they have it another day?
Child: Yeah.

Most of the conversation concerns what is "gonna" happen. A few questions at the end of the excerpt elicit the child's input into planning the event or expressing preferences: "Do you like horses? Or do you think they should cancel it?" The next excerpt, taken from a conversation with an older child, includes even more discussion of the child's views.

Example 4: 4.5-Year-Old, Party for Friends Who Are Moving (Novel)

Mother: On Sunday, we're going to cousin Annie, Aaron, and John's house and they're going to have a pizza party because Chris, Karen, Ken, and Deirdre are moving. Do you remember their house up the street?

Child: We're going or just the moms?

Mother: No, mommies and daddies and kids. Everybody's going to the party.

Child: And Stephanie and the babies, too?

Mother: And Stephanie and the babies, too. Do you remember what Aaron's basement looks like when you guys play downstairs? Remember how you guys play down there? What do you think we are gonna play when we go up to their house?

Child: Downstairs.

Mother: Downstairs. And where do you think the mommies and daddies are going to visit?

Child: Upstairs.

Mother: Upstairs. Do you think maybe we should bring a dessert when we go?

Child: No.

Mother: Should we make something?

Child: A present.

Mother: A present? Well, maybe when we go over and visit we'll maybe bring some cookies or something. Do you think that would be fun to go up with all of your friends with Taylor and her mom and dad and we'll go and have pizza and soda?

Child: Yep.

Mother: Yeah. What do you think you guys will play when you go downstairs in the basement?

Child: That thing, the cake is my favorite.

Mother: How many pieces of pizza do you think you might eat?

Child: I don't know. Eight or seven.

After referring to the children's general event knowledge about the house ("Remember how you guys play down there?"), the mother speculates with her child about what will happen ("and where do you think the mommies and daddies are going to visit?") and discusses plans for their participation ("do you think maybe we should bring a dessert?" and "maybe we'll bring some cookies or something").

These event differences indicate that mothers were sensitive to children's prior event knowledge and engaged their children in thinking about the future in different ways depending on whether the event under discussion was familiar or unknown to the child. When discussing routine events, children were encouraged to provide information about what they could expect to happen, whereas when discussing novel events mothers engaged their children in more hypothetical talk.

Lucariello and Nelson (1987) obtained similar findings in their investigation of temporally displaced talk with 2- to 2.5-year-olds in routine and play contexts. Mothers in that study used conditioned and hypothetical references almost exclusively while talking about future events.

Children's Talk About the Past and Future

Again, the focus of the analyses presented here is the ways in which children participated in conversations about the future. Data on children's participation in past conversations is presented only for comparison purposes. Unlike mothers' contributions, most of children's utterances could not be reliably coded for point of reference. Tense markers were either unclear because of articulation difficulties or could not be determined from the verb (e.g., "I put it down"). An indeterminate category (none) was therefore included. In addition, because children vary rarely used hypothetical or conditional references, all reference to future events were combined into a single future-point-of-reference code without distinguishing utterances with a future planning perspective.

As shown in Table 4.2, the majority of children's utterances could not be coded for point of reference. However, there was no difference across past and future conversations in the number of utterances with no identifiable time point of reference. In talking about the past, children referred to the past significantly more frequently than they used a general point of reference, and they used the general reference more frequently than a future reference. In conversations about future events, children used the general point of reference significantly more frequently than the past point of reference, but there was no significant difference between the frequencies of general and future time references. These

TABLE 4.2
Mean Frequencies of Children's Elaborations by Point of Reference and Age in
Past and Future Conversations

Age (Years)	Point of Reference			
	None	Past	General	Future
	Past conversations			
2.5	10.25	3.78	1.66	0.15
4.5	12.87	6.43	1.75	0.22
	Future conversations			
2.5	7.52	0.33	1.40	1.43
4.5	12.69	0.83	3.16	4.10

TABLE 4.3
Mean Frequencies of Children's Elaborations in Future Conversations by
Type of Event and Point of Reference

Type of event	Point of Reference			
	None	Past	General	Future
Novel events	10.22	0.70	1.26	2.91
Routine events	9.99	0.45	3.30	2.63

results indicate that children used tense markers to distinguish references to different points in time and appropriately used more past tense while discussing past events and more future tense while talking about future events. However, they referred to general event knowledge more frequently while talking about future events, suggesting that this type of event knowledge was more pertinent to the future discussions.

There were also significant age differences in point of reference. Older children contributed significantly more elaborations with no point of reference, general reference, and future reference compared to young children, but references to the past were infrequent for both ages.

While talking about the future, but not the past, children's use of point of reference varied by type of event (novel or routine) under discussion. As shown in Table 4.3, overall, children used general and future references more often than past references. When discussing novel events, however, children referred more to the future than to general event knowledge. General references were also significantly more frequent when discussing routine events than when discussing novel events.

IMPLICATIONS FOR CHILDREN'S UNDERSTANDING OF THE FUTURE

Children's Understanding of Future Time

There appear to be important differences in how parents and children talk about the past and future, which may affect how children learn to think about the past and the future. One striking characteristic of talk about the future is the variety of types of temporal reference that are used in these conversations. Mothers frequently talked about both future actions and general event knowledge and when talking about the future, used both future and hypothetical references. Even talk about the past, although less frequent than other temporal references, was nevertheless included on an average of four times per conversation. To illustrate how mothers moved from reference to past and future events and incorporated references to general event knowledge, consider the following example.

Example 5: 2.5-Year-Old, Easter (Novel)

Mother: Who comes at Easter?
Child: Easter Bunny.
Mother: That's right. And what does he bring?
Child: Candy.
Mother: And what else?
Child: Umm.
Mother: What does he bring that we're gonna color on Friday?
Child: Umm.
Mother: Eggs? Yeah, you're gonna help me color the eggs?
Child: Yeah.
Mother: Yeah, it's gonna be the first time you get to color the eggs, huh? Remember we bought the kit?
Child: Hmm?
Mother: You and me, and Drew, we bought the kit? And we're gonna make pretty colors on the eggs.
Child: Yeah.
Mother: And then on Easter Sunday we're going to Grandma's house.

The mother talks first about what typically happens at Easter (the Easter Bunny comes), then queries the child about what will happen at a time in the future (coloring eggs). She then refers to an event that has occurred in the past (buying the egg-coloring kit) and refers again to the future event of coloring the eggs. Finally, she refers to another future event that will occur after the egg coloring (going to Grandma's house on Easter Sunday). To follow along, the child must differentiate specific events in real time from general event knowledge and understand how these events are ordered along a timeline that starts before the present and extends into the future, with specific points marked along the future timeline. It is noteworthy that the child's substantive contributions consist of information about the events in general, not details of either the past or future events discussed by the mother. In the next example an older child is able to contribute more to the narrative that spans past, future, and general time:

Example 6: 4-Year-Old, Vacation (Routine)

Mother: Caroline, are we going on vacation this year?
Child: Yeah.
Mother: Where are we going?
Child: To Aruba.
Mother: No, we went to Aruba last year, but where are we
           going to down the shore? To whose house?
Child: Aunt Jean's.
Mother: Yeah, and what do we do at Aunt Jean's house? Did
           we go once before?
Child: Yeah.
Mother: Last year?
Child: Yeah.
Mother: And what did we do there?
Child: We find seashells.
Mother: Yeah, that's something you and Daddy did together.
Child: Yeah, we painted seashells.
Mother: So are we going to go again this year? What do you
           want to do this year when we go down there?
Child: I want to get more seashells and paint them.
Mother: You want to get more seashells and paint them. And
           then how about, what else would you like to do?
           Would you like to go to the amusement park?
Child: Yeah.
Mother: And what do you like to do there?
Child: Go down the slide.

How much of an understanding of the past, present, and future is necessary for children to participate in these conversations? To fully understand mothers' temporal references children must be able to distinguish general, semantic knowledge about familiar events from references to specific episodes, both past and anticipated, organized along a mental timeline. The data from children's contributions suggest that children are able to understand their mothers' questions and respond appropriately by providing information using reference to past events, future events, and general event knowledge. The finding that younger children provide fewer elaborations than older children in future conversations, but that there are no significant age differences for past conversations, suggests that participating in talk about the future is more difficult to understand. Although 4-year-olds may be able to participate in both types of conversations with equal ease, 2.5-year-olds may find the future conversations more challenging.

It may also be possible for children to provide appropriate information solely on the basis of their general knowledge about the events under discussion. They could provide this information using the tense of the question posed by their mothers without necessarily referring to past or future events. Nelson (1996) described this type of language production as "use before meaning" and hypothesized that it serves as a strategy for acquiring word meanings in specific discourse contexts. According to Nelson, children's understanding is not necessarily incomplete or inaccurate but rather is tightly constrained to a particular discourse and syntactic context so that children may not use the same forms appropriately outside of event conversations with parents. However, using the forms in the mother–directed conversations gives children experience that they can later generalize to different discourse contexts.

General Event Knowledge and Talk About the Future

Children's general event knowledge and memories of specific similar episodes may provide them with a type of cognitive support for understanding mothers' references to future events. As if to make this support more explicit, mothers frequently refer to both general knowledge ("Who comes at Easter?") and past episodes ("Did we go once before?") while talking about the future. Mothers appear to be creating a *zone of proximal development* for their children (Vygotsky, 1978). They are scaffolding discussions in such a way as to include their children's participation and guide them through a discussion of different time frames. This may be an important context in which children learn to juxtapose information about past and future events and understand the different ways that time references are used in language.

Mothers used different strategies to engage children in future conversations depending on the level of children's background knowledge about the events under discussion. When discussing routine events, mothers asked more questions about general event knowledge. When discussing future novel events, mothers engaged their children in more hypothetical talk. Thus, talking about the future novel and routine events provided children with different types of planning talk. It had been predicted that children would be able to participate more in discussion of future routine events because they could rely on their general event knowledge to consider what was likely to occur. However, mothers' strategy of asking hypothetical questions about what might happen and asking for preferences rather than simply asking their children what was going to happen may have facilitated children's participation in discussing novel events.

No Effects of Maternal Style?

In these data there were no effects of maternal elaboration on children's contributions to talk about the future. In contrast, several researchers have noted effects of maternal elaboration on children's contributions to talk about the past (Fivush, 1991; Haden et al., 1997; Hudson, 1990; McCabe & Peterson, 1991; Reese et al., 1993). Increased elaboration may be more critical for children's participation in talk about the past, because more elaborative mothers may provide more memory cues for children and facilitation of the retrieval of memory information. While talking about the future, however, mothers who provide more information about the event under discussion do not necessarily increase children's participation. Additional analyses can be performed to determine whether there are other maternal variables that influence children's participation in future conversations.

It is also important to keep in mind that effects of maternal elaboration on children's memory talk are more evident over time than concurrently (McCabe & Peterson, 1991; Reese et al., 1993). Maternal elaboration during future conversations may facilitate children's ability to talk about the future, but these effects may be evident only over time.

Children's Concepts of Self

Another question for further investigation is how conversations about the future contribute to children's emerging self-concepts. Just as talk about the past can provide children with a framework for thinking about themselves as continuing from the past into the present, talk about the future can extend that mental, self-referenced timeline. When parents engage their children in thinking and talking about the future they are coconstructing a representation of them engaged in future activities. The strategy of eliciting children's thoughts and desires in regard to the future, which mothers appear to do as frequently with 2.5-year-olds as with 4-year-olds, can promote thinking not only about what is going to happen but also "What do I want to happen?" and "How do I feel about what will happen?" This line of questioning engages children as individuals who can anticipate and reflect on the future and gives voice to children's particular wants, desires, and intentions.

By talking about the future in ways that engage their children as active agents, mothers may assist children in creating hypothetical models of themselves as individuals with the capacity of affecting the course and outcome of future events. Several theorists have proposed that talking about the past and, in particular, constructing coherent narratives about the past, is an essential component of the development of a concept of the self (Bruner, 1990; Fivush, 1991; Nelson, 1993). Bruner

(1990) proposed that the self is more than a constructor of autobiographical narratives; a second essential characteristic of the self is the capacity to "envision alternatives—to conceive of others ways of being, of acting, of striving" (p. 110). In talking about the future with children, parents may affect this component of the self, the ways in which children envision themselves acting or being in the future. One's future desires, plans, and intentions may be as important to one's concept of self as our past memories. Further research on parent–child talk about the future may provide a rich data source on variables affecting both the cognitive and evaluative components of self-concept in young children.

REFERENCES

Bauer, P. J. (1995). Recalling past events: From infancy to early childhood. *Annals of Child Development, 11*, 25–71.
Benson, J. B. (1997). The development of planning: It's about time. In S. L. Friedman & E. K. Scholnick (Eds.), *The developmental psychology of planning: Why, how and when do we plan?* (pp. 43–75). Mahwah, NJ: Lawrence Erlbaum Associates.
Benson, J. B., Grossman, S. E., & Hanebuth, E. (1993, March). *Young children's temporal representations: Past, present, and future daily activities.* Poster presented at the Society for Research in Child Development, New Orleans, LA.
Benson, J. B., Talmi, A., & Haith, M. M. (1999, April). *Adult speech about events in time: A replication.* Presented at the Society for Research in Child Development, Albuquerque, NM.
Bruner, J. (1990). *Acts of meaning.* Cambridge, MA: Harvard University Press.
Ferreiro, E. & Sinclair, H. (1971). Temporal relationships in language. *International Journal of Psychology, 6,* 39–47.
Fivush, R. (1991). The social construction of personal narratives. *Merrill–Palmer Quarterly, 37,* 59–81.
French, L. A. & Nelson, K. (1985). *Young children's knowledge of relational terms: some ifs, ors, and buts.* New York: Springer.
Friedman, W. J. (1977). The development of children's knowledge of cyclic aspects of time. *Child Development, 48,* 1593–1599.
Friedman, W. J. (1990). Children's representations of the pattern of daily activities. *Child Development, 61,* 1399–1412.
Friedman, W. J. & Brudos, S. L. (1988). On routines and routines: The early development of spatial and temporal representations. *Cognitive Development, 3,* 167–182.
Haden, C. A., Haine, R. A., & Fivush, R. (1997). Developing narrative structure in parent–child reminiscing across the preschool years. *Developmental Psychology, 33,* 295–307.
Harner, L. (1981). Children talk about time and aspect of actions. *Child Development, 52,* 498–506.

Hudson, J. A. (1990). The emergence of autobiographic memory in mother–child conversation. In R. Fivush & J. A. Hudson (Eds.), *Knowing and remembering in young children*, (pp. 166–196). New York: Cambridge University Press.

Hudson, J. A., Shapiro, L. R., & Sosa, B. B. (1995). Planning in the real world: Preschool children's scripts and plans for familiar events. *Child Development, 66*, 984–988.

Hudson, J. A., & Sosa, B. B. (1995, April). *Scripts and plans in mother–child talk about the future*. Poster presented at the biennial meeting of the Society for Research in Child Development, Indianapolis, IN.

Lucariello, J., & Nelson, K. (1987). Remembering and planning talk between mothers and children. *Discourse Processes, 10*, 219–235.

MacWhinney, B. (1995). *The CHILDES project: Tools for analyzing talk*. Hillsdale, NJ: Lawrence Erlbaum Associates.

McCabe, A., & Peterson, C. (1991). Getting the story: A longitudinal study of parental styles in eliciting narratives and developing narrative skill. In A. McCabe & C. Peterson (Eds.), *Developing narrative structure* (pp. 217–253). Hillsdale, NJ: Lawrence Erlbaum Associates.

Nelson, K. (1986). *Event knowledge: Structure and function in development*. Hillsdale, NJ: Lawrence Erlbaum Associates.

Nelson, K. (1991). The matter of time: Interdependencies between language and thought in development. In S. A. Gelman & J. P. Byrnes (Eds.), *Perspectives on language and cognition: Interrelations in development* (pp. 278-318). New York: Cambridge University Press.

Nelson, K. (1993). The psychological and social origins of autobiographic memory. *Psychological Science, 4*, 1–8.

Nelson, K. (1996). *Language in cognitive development: The emergence of the mediated mind*. New York: Cambridge University Press.

Norton, D. G. (1993). Diversity, early socialization, and temporal displacement: The dual perspective revisited. *Social Work, 38*, 82–90.

Reese, E., Haden, C. A., & Fivush, R. (1993). Mother–child conversations about the past: Relationships of style and memory over time. *Cognitive Development, 8*, 403–430.

Rogoff, B. (1991). Social interaction as apprenticeship in thinking: Guidance and participation in spatial planning. In L. B. Rescind & J. M. Leaven (Eds.), *Perspectives on socially shared cognition* (pp. 349–364). Washington, DC: American Psychological Association.

Sachs, J. (1983). Talking about the there and then: The emergence of displaced reference in parent–child discourse. In K. E. Nelson (Ed.), *Children's language* (Vol. 4, pp. 3–28). Hillsdale, NJ: Lawrence Erlbaum Associates.

Trosborg, A. (1982). Children's comprehension of before and after reinvestigated. *Journal of Child Language, 9*, 381–402.

Vygotsky, L. S. (1978). *Mind in society: The development of higher psychological processes*. Cambridge, MA; Harvard University Press.

Weist, R. M. (1989). Time concepts in language and thought: Filling the Piagetian void from 2 to 5 years. In I. Levin & D. Zakay (Eds.), *Time and human cognition: A life–span perspective* (pp. 63–118). Amsterdam: North-Holland.

Welch-Ross, M. K. (1995). An integrative model of the development of autobiographical memory. *Developmental Review, 15*, 338–365.

Willatts, P. (1990). Development of problem-solving strategies in infancy. In D. F. Bjorklund (Ed.), *Children's strategies* (pp. 23–66). Hillsdale, NJ: Lawrence Erlbaum Associates.

5

The Self: Elevated in Consciousness and Extended in Time

Daniel J. Povinelli
University of Louisiana at Lafayette

In his now-classic text, *Play, Dreams, and Imitation in Children*, Jean Piaget (1962) described two incidents involving the reactions of his daughter, Jacqueline, to her own image. The first occurred when she had just turned 23 months old. "On coming in from a walk, J. said that she was going to see: *"Daddy, Odette and Jacqueline in the glass"* as if "Jacqueline in the glass" was someone other than herself (although she could recognize herself very well in a mirror)" (p. 224). The second incident occurred when Jacqueline was 35 months of age. Piaget had just shown her a photograph of herself. Jacqueline looked at the photo and stated: "It's Jacqueline." Intrigued by the third-person nature of her reply, Piaget asked her: "Is it you or not?" Jacqueline answered: "Yes it's me, but what has the Jacqueline in the photo got on her head?" (p. 225).

Some scholars may interpret these anecdotes as nothing more than mere curiosities involving a young child's reactions to the cultural artefacts of mirrors and photographs. In contrast, in this chapter I reinterpret Jacqueline's comments in light of recent research that has explored the child's developing understanding of the self's place in time. In doing so I hope to show how Jacqueline's comments may be emblematic of the unique manner in which very young children conceive of the self—a manner that does not include the idea that the self extends in time. I show how mirrors, video images, and photographs can be used as tools to reveal transitions in the development of an adult-like understanding of the temporal breadth of the self. I propose that the development of an explicit and temporally extended self-concept can be understood as a developmentally complex process, tapping different conceptual and attentional structures at different ages.

THE SELF IN TIME

My original interests in the relation between time and the self-concept concerned chimpanzees, not human children. My curiosities about these matters were sparked many years ago after reading an article by Gordon G. Gallup, Jr. (1979), in which he had summarized his experiments showing that chimpanzees, but not most other primates, were capable of recognizing themselves in mirrors. To Gallup, this suggested that these apes might share with humans a kind of self-concept. He further speculated that if these animals had a concept of self, they might also be capable of projecting themselves into the past and future (see also Gallup, 1982). To me, the question seemed profound: Could chimpanzees conceive of their past and future, or was their notion of the self largely limited to the here and now?

However, as I mulled over the possible nature of the chimpanzee's self-concept, I began to appreciate the fact that we did not yet even understand at what age human infants and children develop the ability to conceive of the temporal dimensions of the self. One possibility, of course, was that young children's explicit awareness of their own past and future emerges in tandem with the very concept of self. Another possibility was that the temporal dimensions of the self are constructed gradually throughout late infancy and early childhood. However, there were no readily available experimental techniques that could address these questions.

Thus, I decided that before asking about another species' understanding of the temporal dimensions of the self it would be prudent to briefly shift my attention to our own species. However, what was intended as only a temporary methodological diversion has become a decade-long undertaking to explore how and when young children come to appreciate that they are more than just their own current set of experiences and sensations, that they are, in addition, historical beings—beings with a past, present, and future.

AN INITIAL IDEA—AND SOME INITIAL TESTS

My first thoughts on this matter were fairly naive: Perhaps the initial appearance of the self-concept was temporally restricted, perhaps extending for only a few minutes in time. From this starting point children might progressively come to understand how more remote moments in time are connected to the present, ultimately allowing them to arrive at the point where, following William James (1890/1950), they conclude, "*I am the same self that I was yesterday*" (p. 332).

What empirical method could be used for tracking the transition of the self from its initial state of temporal restriction to its later, temporally extended state? At the time, the standard procedure for diagnosing the emergence of the self-concept was to assess the capacity for self-recognition in mirrors. The standard procedure involved wiping the child's nose or cheek with rouge and then placing him or her in front of a mirror to see if he or she would wipe it off (e.g., Amsterdam, 1972; Lewis & Brooks-Gunn, 1979). On the basis of these techniques, it was widely accepted that by about 18–24 months of age most infants were capable of recognizing themselves in mirrors. Thus, if my initial idea were correct, 2-year-olds ought to be capable of understanding how very recent former instances of the self related to the present self—but how could one empirically explore this idea?

One way of asking children about their ability to relate past instances of the self to their present state was to confront them with previous visual instances of themselves. What was needed was a variation of the classic mark test of self-recognition. However, instead of confronting the children with a live image of themselves, one would need to have them observe a video recording of an event which, unbeknownst to them, had happened just several minutes earlier—an event that had direct implications for their present appearance (e.g., an experimenter secretly placing a large sticker on top of their heads). All things being equal, would the children be able to infer the connection between the previous event and their probable current appearance? My colleagues and I conducted a set of preliminary experiments to explore these ideas (see Povinelli, Landau, & Perilloux, 1996).

Reactions to Delayed Video Images of the Self

In a first experiment, we individually videotaped 2-, 3-, and 4-year-old children and a familiar adult as they played an unusual game that they had never played before. During the game, the experimenter praised the child several times by patting him or her on the head. The experimenter used the final pat as the opportunity to place a large, brightly colored sticker on the child's head. Three minutes later, the child was shown a video recording that clearly depicted the previous events of (a) the child playing the game, (b) the experimenter placing the sticker on his or her head, and (c) several ensuing minutes of the child with the sticker on his or her head.

We had expected that even the youngest children ought to be able to relate what had happened just minutes earlier to their present state, and so the actual results startled us. None of the 2-year-olds, and only 25% of the 3-year-olds, ever reached up to their own heads to search for the sticker. They paid attention to the video, especially as it depicted the experimenter placing the sticker on their heads. Indeed, a number of these children remarked about this event. So why did they not reach up? Did they not recognize the image as themselves? In one sense, they clearly did. In the informal questioning that followed the test (which we systematized in later experiments), we asked many of the children "Who is that?" while pointing to their image on the video. The children had no difficulty in labeling their images properly (either by stating "That's me!" or by using their proper name). When we pointed to the image of the sticker and asked them (in a number of different ways) if they could get the sticker, they were simply unable to do so. It was as if they recognized the features of the image but did not grasp what it had to do with them.

In contrast, 75% of the 4-year-olds removed the sticker within seconds of seeing the pivotal marking event on videotape. Unlike most of their younger counterparts, the 4-year-old children seemed to have an immediate and intuitive grasp of the connection between the delayed video images and their present state.

Reactions to Recent Photos of the Self

Because of the surprising responses of the younger children in the test just described, we decided to explore the generality of our finding by examining 3- and 4-year-olds' reactions to recent Polaroid photographs of themselves. We chose this approach for several reasons. First, it was possible that the ongoing motion of the video events, rather then helping the younger children, may have actually confused them—causing them to objectify the images more than they would otherwise. Second, perhaps like adults, seeing themselves engaging in various behaviors on videotape elevated the children's levels of embarrassment, thereby inhibiting their willingness to remove the sticker from their heads. Third, although there was ample evidence of mirror self-recognition in young children, we sought to include a control condition in which the children who did not reach up in response to witnessing delayed images of the self were allowed to see themselves in a mirror. Fourth, we sought to incorporate a stronger temporal marker into the procedure to assist the children in localizing when the events had actually occurred. Fifth, we felt that the static photos might help us focus the children's attention on the key aspects of the events (the sticker on the head, the experimenter in the act of placing it there, and a key temporal marker that we introduced into the routine). Finally, we felt that the photos might assist us in using a standardized (and somewhat leading) set of questions that might assist the younger children in making the connection between the image and themselves.

This study proceeded in much the same manner as the first one (playing an unusual game, secretly placing a large sticker on the child's head, etc.). However, instead of videotaping the children, we took two Polaroid snapshots of them at two critical junctures in the procedure. The first photo was taken just as the experimenter was praising the child and placing the sticker on his or her head. This procedure was carefully choreographed so that the photo clearly depicted the child's upper torso and head and the experimenter's hand putting the sticker in place. The second photo was taken at the end of the game. One of the experimenters introduced the child to a large stuffed gorilla that the child had never seen before and explained to the child that the other experimenter was going to take another picture—this time of the gorilla, the experimenter, and the child (with the sticker still on his or her head).

Approximately 2–3 minutes later, the main experimenter let the child look at the two photos, one at a time. For each photograph, the child was allowed to look at it and was then asked: "Who is that?", "What is that?" (as the sticker was pointed out), and then, "Where is that sticker right now?" In addition, for the first photograph, which depicted one of the experimenters in the act of placing the sticker on the child's head, the child was asked, "What's [the experimenter's name] doing right there?" Finally, the children who still did not reach up to their own heads were presented with a large mirror.

The results were consistent with those of our first experiment (see Fig. 5.1a). First, only 13% of the young 3-year-olds (35–42 months) reached up for the sticker (even after the verbal prompting). In contrast, 85% of the young 3-year-olds who did not reach up in response to the photos did reach up when they were allowed to see themselves in the mirror. Second, the results depicted in Fig. 5.1a show a clear developmental trend between 3 and 4 years in children's ability to use the delayed information to infer the location of the sticker of their heads.

Equally intriguing were the children's responses to our questions. First, even the group of young 3-year-olds had little difficulty when they were asked, "Who is that?": Eighty percent of them answered correctly by either saying, "me," their proper name, or pointing to themselves. The older children performed at even higher levels (see Fig. 5.1b). However, the 3-year-olds tended to use their proper name as much or more than the personal pronoun *me*, whereas the older children almost never used their proper names. Second, when asked "What is that?" (while the sticker in the photo was pointed out to them), the youngest children had little difficulty in identifying it correctly—again, 80% of them responded correctly (see Fig. 5.1c). In combination, these results revealed that, in

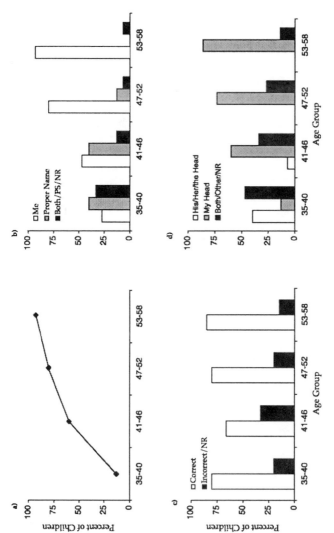

Fig. 5.1.   Children's reactions to photographs of the self that revealed that a sticker had been covertly placed on their heads. Panel a: percentage of children who searched for the sticker. Panel b: percentage of children who used 'me' vs. their proper name to label the photograph. Panel c: percentage of children who correctly identified the sticker. Panel d: percentage of children who used first vs. third-person descriptions of the image. Note: PS = point to self; NR = no response.

some sense at least, the 3-year-olds both recognized themselves in the photos and noticed the sticker on the head of the image in the picture. Apparently, there were some other reasons why the younger children did not seem to understand that there was a sticker on their heads at that very moment.

Finally, the children's answers to the final question were classified according to whether their answer used the expression "my head" (e.g., "He's putting the sticker on my head") or whether they used a phrase that dissociated themselves from the image such as "his/her/the head" (e.g., "He's putting the sticker on her head"). The results of this analysis are depicted in Fig. 5.1d. The youngest children preferred to use the dissociative phrases, the opposite pattern displayed by the older children. Indeed, there was a significant correlation between whether the children reached up for the sticker on their heads and the nature of the phrase they used. The group of children who did not reach up used both phrases equally often. In contrast, only a single child who reached up for the sticker used one of these dissociative phrases.

Although I have summarized the statistical evidence that the children who seemed unable to infer that they had a sticker on their head tended to provide verbal descriptions that distanced themselves from the images (e.g., using their proper name, or talking about the sticker as if it were on someone else's head), these statistical summaries do not completely capture how odd some of the younger children's answers seemed. For example, in response to our questions, one 3-year-old responded, "it's Jennifer" and "it's a sticker" and then added, "but why is she wearing my shirt?"

Reactions to Delayed Versus Live Video Images of the Self

The previous studies provide some surprising evidence that 2- and 3-year-old children may not understand the connection between recent past events and their current physical state. This suggested a dissociation between their reactions to live versus delayed visual feedback of the self. However, we had not yet conducted a test in which separate groups of children were tested under conditions in which the only parameter that differed was whether they saw themselves in live versus delayed video. So, in a third initial study we repeated the video test with two groups of 2- to 3-year-old children. After the sticker was covertly placed on their heads, one group was shown live video feedback, whereas the other group was shown delayed feedback from about 3 minutes earlier.

The results were in the direction predicted: Sixty-two percent of the children who saw themselves in live feedback reached up, whereas only 37% in the delayed group did so. Although this effect was only marginally significant, there was a significant difference in the timing of when the successful children in the two groups reached up. In the live group, 71% of the successful children reached up during the 2-minute presentation of their images, whereas the remainder reached up at some point during the prompting/questioning period. This pattern was reversed in the delayed group, in which only 22% of the successful children reached up during the video presentation.

These results suggest that the temporal dimension of the playback, by itself, may be a crucial factor in the developmental pattern obtained in the first two studies we conducted. For some reason, when the images are delayed, young children seem less able to grasp the connection between the images and themselves. We realized that we needed a more formal framework in which we could think about this difference, as well as the developmental pattern we had obtained.

A MODEL OF YOUNG CHILDREN'S UNDERSTANDING OF THE TEMPORAL DIMENSIONS OF THE SELF

The purpose of our model was threefold (see Povinelli, 1995). First, we sought to develop an account of a possible transition from the representation of the self as an on-line, experiencing agent, to a representation that explicitly includes the connection among the present, past, and future states of the self. Second, we sought a more integrated account of the psychological processes that initially allow 18- to 24-month-old human infants (and chimpanzees) to recognize themselves in mirrors. Finally, we sought an explanation for why it is not until about 4 years of age that children pass the analogous test using delayed feedback.

The Present Self

The model begins with an assumption that at around 18 to 24 months of age most infants develop an explicit self-concept—an ability for various dimensions of the self to be held in consciousness as objects of thought. This development is seen as a more or less direct consequence of other, domain-general cognitive developments that emerge during this same period. Furthermore, these domain-general abilities are seen as allowing infants to form explicit relations between objects and events in the world, on the one hand, and their representation of various aspects of the self, on the other. A number of specific proposals for cognitive development during this time period are compatible with this view (e.g., Case, 1992; Olson & Campbell, 1993; Perner, 1991). Our model (Povinelli, 1995) posits that these changes allow certain kinds of information about the self that were previously implicitly available, to become consolidated into a conceptual structure. In this way the self can become an explicit object of thought and thus related to events out in the world (see Povinelli, 1995).

Which specific aspects of the self become explicitly represented at this age? The model supposes that, in human infants, the initial self-concept includes the infant's representation of both his or her current kinesthetic and mental states. For reasons to which I briefly allude later, the model supposes that the kinesthetic information is the most salient and omnipresent for the infants. Of course, because of the rapidly changing nature of the infant's postural states and actions, this kinesthetic representation is likely to be constantly updated and hence largely restricted to the present sensory input. Following James (1890/1950), I have referred to this representation as the *present self*.

What about information about previous states of the self—is this information included as part of the 2- to 3-year-olds' self-concept? On the one hand, one might be tempted to say yes, given that the model allows that children of this age store information about past events, including past states of the self. However, the model also stipulates that these memories are not conceptualized as experiences that a former instance of the present self underwent. Indeed, somewhat radically, the model stipulates that even memories of quite recent events—events that the 2- to 3-year-old child can verbally recall—are not explicitly represented as temporal trailings of their present self. The reason is because our model supposes that the general difficulty that 2- to 3-year-olds have in understanding how one object or event can have multiple natures (e.g., Flavell, 1988), applies with equal force to their understanding of the self. And, as I explain later, this may have some fairly striking implications for the temporal breadth of the 2- to 3-year-old's present self.

By focusing on the kinesthetic dimension of the self, the model provides a fairly specific account of the process by which 18- to 24-month-olds come to react to the mark test by reaching up to their own faces. In doing so, the model shares certain features with previous accounts of mirror self-recognition (see Gallup, 1970; Mitchell, 1993). However, it begins with a novel and seemingly counterintuitive idea: namely, that the ability to pass the mark test has nothing to do with understanding what mirrors do (i.e., understanding that mirrors provide an accurate and contingent image of things that are in front of them).

But if infants do not understand that mirrors provide a reflection of themselves, how is self-recognition possible? I propose that the first step in answering this question is to set aside the term *self-recognition* altogether and to instead speak of various *equivalence relations* that infants may or may not form between their representations of themselves and the images of the self that they confront in mirrors. The necessity of invoking the idea of equivalence relations stems from the realization that the term *self-recognition* is not fine grained enough to develop a proper theory of the multiple dimensions along which infants may explicitly map the relation between their physical and mental states and their images in mirrors.

The model posits that infants detect an equivalence between their explicit representation of their bodies (their kinesthetic states) and the actions of the images in the live feedback before them. If the infant possessed the domain-general ability just described (the ability to form a relation between a concept held in mind and external objects and events), then the infant could form the following sort of relation between its kinesthetic state and the image in the mirror: "Everything that is true of this (my body here) is also true of that (the image), and vice versa." Presumably, the formation of this relation may occur quite rapidly, as infants in preindustrialized cultures with little or no access to mirrors may pass the mark test with as little as 5 minutes of experience with a mirror (see Priel & de Schonen, 1986).

In summary, the causal account of the factors that lead 18- to 24-month-old infants to reach up and touch marks on their faces is that they conclude that there is an equivalence between the bodily self (held in mind) and the stimuli they confront out there (the image in the mirror), not that they realize that the image is a representation of themselves.

One of the most important aspects of this account of self-recognition is that it explicitly models the impact of the separate dimensions along which infants may detect an equivalence relation between their representations of the self and the images they confront. Two of these dimensions are seen to be especially important in making sense of the patterns of the children's responses: (a) the infants' detection of the equivalence between their representation of their physical features and the physical features portrayed in the images and (b) the infants' detection of the equivalence between their representation of their kinesthetic states and the movements of the images.

For several reasons, I suspect that the most important and earliest emerging dimension is the kinesthetic one. First, unlike the features of one's face (and the rest of the body), one's kinesthetic state can be constantly experienced and does not depend on looking at the body, let alone confronting oneself in a mirror. In addition, the evolutionary emergence of the first nonhuman primate with an explicit self-representation may have been associated with the evolution of the common ancestor of the great apes and humans and may have been driven by the need to represent and integrate the self's kinesthetic states (see Povinelli & Cant, 1995). This evolutionary model argues that an unprecedented increase in body size for an arboreal mammal that occurred in the common ancestor of the great apes and humans, created a specific set of ecological problems, the solution to which involved integrating various low-level streams of proprioceptive and kinesthetic information into an explicit representation of the self's bodily position and movements. I suspect that this evolutionarily primitive self-concept—a kinesthetic self-concept—remains the most salient dimension of the self early in human development.

Returning to the developmental emergence of the ability to pass the mark test, this model holds that once the equivalence relation between one's own actions and the actions of the image are formed, other equivalences may soon be explicitly represented as well—for example, between the appearance of aspects of the body that are directly visible and the image of the body in the mirror and, ultimately, the otherwise-invisible aspects of the body, such as the face (see Povinelli, 1995, for a detailed account of this process).[1]

Although the question of self-recognition in mirrors has often been cast as a problem of how the infant comes to know that the face he or she sees in the mirror is his or her own face (e.g., Mitchell, 1993), this model would view this as a false issue. Once the infant has formed an explicit representation of the self that includes its kinesthetic states and those featural aspects of the body that are directly observable, updating the representation while confronting a mirror becomes straightforward. After all, once the infant concludes that there is an equivalence between their kinesthetic and partial featural self-representation on the one hand, and the image on the other, then the mirror simply allows him or her to update the (incomplete) featural self-representation.

Do Children "Recognize" Themselves in Delayed Videos and Photos?

Assuming that this model is roughly correct, let us move on and consider what must occur when 2- or 3-year-olds confront their images in delayed versus live visual feedback. If, as I have speculated, the kinesthetic dimension of the self is the most salient aspect of the self that is explicitly represented, then when these children confront themselves in live feedback they will detect a perfect match between their kinesthetic self-representation and the movements in the mirror. The child therefore concludes, "That is equivalent to me." In contrast, when the image is

---

[1]This account raises the question of whether infants reach up for the mark because it violates a schema they have of their face, or simply because the mark is of some intrinsic interest. Our model suggests different answers at different points in development. If one were to take a 24-month-old infant who had not yet mapped out his or her facial features through experience with mirrors, mark his or her face, and then confront him or her with a mirror, we suspect that the infant's intrinsic interest in the mark would drive the reaching response. On the other hand, an additional factor is likely to be involved in the reaching response of the 24-month-old who already possesses a default scheme of what his or her face looks like—for this infant, the mark "shouldn't be there."

delayed, this equivalence is not present, and the infant concludes, "That is not equivalent to me." In the former case, the mark is noted by the child, and his or her relation to his or her own body understood; in the latter case, however, although the mark may be noted it bears no explicit relation to the child's body.

A further complication arises, however, because, depending on his or her prior history with mirrors, the 2-year-old child may have already formed a self-representation that includes information about his or her facial features (through the process described earlier). Thus, if the very young child focuses his or her attention on the facial and general bodily features of the image, an equivalence relation may be formed in either live or delayed situations. After all, the featural appearance of the self is, for all practical purposes, invariant across fairly long temporal intervals. Thus, depending on how any given 2- or 3-year-old child partitions his or her attention to the various aspects of the self, he or she may confront seemingly contradictory, or rapidly alternating, information concerning whether the image is equivalent to him- or herself: the kinesthetic information says 'no," but the featural information says "yes."

Indeed, this would seem to be exactly the kind of dual interpretation of their images that 2- and 3-year-olds seem to express as they observe their delayed images. On the one hand, they seem to understand the name of the image, but on the other hand they seem to distance themselves from the image. Furthermore, because the kinesthetic information is the most salient aspect of the current self-representation, most children of this age conclude that the image is not equivalent to themselves. However, a smaller percentage of the children may background the kinesthetic information, allowing them to focus on the featural information for long enough to conclude (at least temporarily) that there is an equivalence. In the former case, they would not reach for the sticker; in the latter case, they would.

These considerations led us to speculate (e.g., Povinelli, 1995), that the temporal dimension of 2- to 3-year-olds' representations of the present self might be very narrow indeed—perhaps on the order of 1–2 seconds. Some authors have found this idea inherently suspect, arguing that our model implies that 3-year-olds cannot conceive of themselves beyond several seconds in the past or future (e.g., Zelazo & Sommerville, chap. 12, this volume). However, what the model actually stipulates is 2- to 3-year-olds' inability to integrate successive present selves along a purported temporal–causal dimension, not their inability to store or imagine past or future states of the self (Povinelli, 1995, p. 167). Thus, the possible temporal restriction of 2- to 3-year-olds' current self-representations in no way necessitates the absence of a memory of past self states or the inability to imagine future ones. They have simply not yet adopted an ontology in which those states can be placed within a temporal–causal continuum. By implication, they have no way to relate their current self to such future or past states (for a discussion of the possible ways in which 3-year-olds may conceive of the past, present, and future, see Povinelli, Landry, Theall, Clark, & Castille, 1999). Indeed, on our account, certain future-oriented behaviors (especially those that are highly routinized, script-like, or are based on procedural rules) should prove quite simple for 2- to 3-year-olds, whereas other behaviors, which require an explicit understanding of the relation between the child's present self and some imagined future state, ought to prove far more difficult (see Atance & O'Neill, chap. 7, this volume).

The Proper (or Temporally Extended) Self

What about older children? When and how do they develop a representation of self that extends in time? This model highlights the importance of a second domain-general cognitive transition that may occur at around 4–5 years of age—a transition that may have the consequence of allowing the child to hold in mind multiple representations of the self (past, present, and future states) as all referring to the same entity: the self. I have labeled this the *proper self* after the proper names that we typically use to embrace all the present, past, and future states of the self. Thus, with the emergence of the proper self the present self becomes simply the most salient of the multiple instances of the self that extend forward and backward in time. Some theorists who have argued for a strong domain-general developmental transition in conceptual abilities at around 18–24 months have also argued for another domain-general transition at around 4–5 years of age (see Case, 1992; Olson & Campbell, 1993; Perner, 1991). In these and certain other theories, the child is seen as becoming capable of sustaining multiple, and contradictory representations of the same object or event. This model posits that this general ability applies to the child's self-representation as well. Thus, this domain-general ability paves the way for the child to sustain not simply one current representation of the self but also to organize previous, current, and future representations under a temporally extended, metaconcept of "me."

RECENT DIRECTIONS

With this framework in place, my colleagues and I have sought to probe additional aspects of the child's developing awareness of the self's place in time. In what follows I briefly mention several of these recent studies.

Extending the Self in Time: Brief Versus Extreme Delay

Earlier in this chapter, I argued that younger preschoolers experience a dual interpretation of their delayed images. On the one hand, the featural information leads them to detect an equivalence between themselves and the image; on the other hand, the kinesthetic information suggests a nonequivalence. Thus, a certain percentage of young preschoolers reach up for the sticker on their head, but for different reasons than the majority of the older preschoolers. This raises a sticky problem. We are suggesting that the exact same behavioral response (reaching up to the head to remove the sticker) may have different psychological causes at different ages. Is there any way to demonstrate this empirically? In other words, is there any way to show that 3-year-olds who pass the test do so on the basis of featural cues, whereas older children pass the test on the basis of inferences derived from a representation of the self that is temporally extended?

It occurred to us that if our general model were correct, then older preschoolers ought to appreciate that, other things being equal, very recent events have more causal bearing on the present than do more distant events. Younger children, in contrast, should fail to appreciate such a distinction, either because they do not conceive of previous events as "previous" at all or simply because to them time is not seen as a causal arrow.

Our first test of this idea was reported by Povinelli and Simon (1998), who invited 88 young 3-, 4-, and 5-year-olds (32 children in each age group) to two visits to our laboratory. Each visit was separated by 7 days. On the first visit the children played a distinctive game in a particular room. As usual, we secretly marked them with a large sticker while a video camera recorded the events and the game. However, just as the children were finishing, rather then showing them the video, we secretly removed the sticker from their heads. Thus, although they left the center none the wiser, we had obtained a video of them playing a distinctive game and being marked on their head with a sticker.

A week later, the children were invited to play a different game in a different room at the center, and we again covertly placed a sticker on their heads. Now, however, we allowed the children to witness themselves on videotape. The critical manipulation was that in each age group, half of the children (N = 16) observed the recording from 5 minutes earlier, whereas the other half observed the recording from the week before.

The results for the presentation period of this study are depicted in Fig. 5.2. As predicted, the older children understood the distinction between the two tapes. Very few of the 4- and 5-year-olds who were

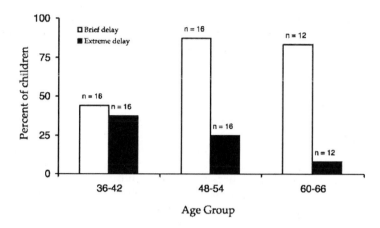

FIG. 5.2. Percentage of children who reached up to search for a sticker on their head in response to briefly versus extremely delayed images of themselves.

confronted with images of themselves from the previous week reached up to search for the sticker—exactly as if they appreciated that the events that they were seeing had no direct relevance to their current appearance. In contrast, the majority of the 4- and 5-year-olds who observed the events from just a few minutes earlier reached up for the sticker. This logic of the experimental design allows us to conclude that the factor responsible for this difference is *when* the images were recorded. One more particular interpretation is that the older children appreciated the causal structure of time and their current place within this structure.

The 3-year-olds showed a very different pattern of results—again, consistent with the predictions of the model. Almost the same percentage of children reached up in both the briefly and extremely delayed groups (see Fig. 5.2), and this percentage was roughly comparable to the levels obtained in previous studies in this age group. In other words, although some of the 3-year-olds did reach up for the sticker, there was no evidence that they did so because they appreciated the temporal–causal significance of the events that they were observing. Rather, this result provided support for the idea that the same measure (reaching up to the head for the sticker) is triggered by different psychological processes in young versus older preschoolers. Most 3-years-olds conclude from the kinesthetic information that the images are not equivalent to themselves, although a certain percentage may reach up because they detect the featural equivalence between the image and their representation of their appearance. However, because this featural information is more or less constant across the time intervals examined, they do not understand the crucial difference between the briefly versus extremely delayed video. Although older preschoolers also conclude that the delayed video is not equivalent to their current self, their metarepresentation of self allows them to assess the differential significance of the two tapes with respect to their current appearance.

Developing a General Understanding of the Self in Time

In our most recent work we have explored the development of preschoolers more general understanding of how the past and present interrelate—an understanding that goes beyond temporal transitions in the self's physical appearance. Indeed, our model of the development of the child's understanding of the temporally extended self suggests that older, but not younger, preschoolers ought to understand how events in the world in which they have participated causally connect to the present state of the world—even when these events do not directly involve alterations of the self. In a series of six studies, we recently explored the ability of young children to understand how the very recent past is causally bound to the present (see Povinelli et al., 1999). In particular, we sought to determine if we could detect a parallel between children's understanding of alterations of the self through time and alterations of the external world through time.

We initially tested this idea by introducing 3- and 4-year-old children to two empty boxes along a wall. After the children saw that both were empty, one experimenter sat down between the boxes. The other experimenter seated the children at a table so that their backs were to the boxes (and the other experimenter) and then proceeded to play a game with the children. About halfway through the game, the experimenter who was seated between the boxes silently took out a familiar puppet, held it up, and placed it inside one of the two boxes. Although the children were unaware that this event had happened, a video camera clearly captured them playing the game, the experimenter behind them, and her actions as she hid the puppet.

Approximately 2 minutes later the children were turned around to face the boxes and were invited to watch themselves on a video monitor that was placed between the two boxes (thus preserving the veridical left–right position of the boxes on the video). Two brief videotapes were then played for the children (in counterbalanced order). The *self* tape depicted the child playing the game 2 minutes earlier and the experimenter hiding the puppet in one of the boxes; the *other–child* tape was a virtually identical, but prerecorded, image of another child (of the same gender and approximate age) playing the game and the

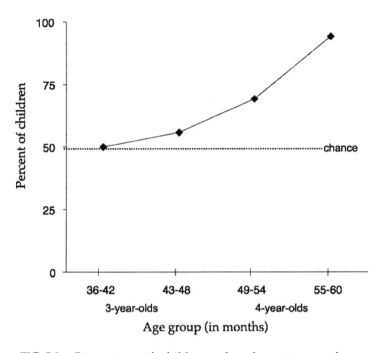

FIG. 5.3   Percentage of children who chose to use the
information provided in a videotape of the self (as opposed to
a video of another child) to locate a puppet that had been
secretly hidden as the child played an unrelated game.

experimenter placing the puppet in the opposite box. The children were
then asked to go and get the puppet. In effect, these procedures asked
the children whether they grasped that the information in the self tape
was relevant to the puppet's current location, whereas information in the
other–child tape was not.

   As predicted, the children's answer to this question depended on
their age (see Fig. 5.3). The 3-year-olds performed at chance levels—they
were just as likely to look in either box—suggesting that they did not see
any special significance in the information provided in self tape. Also, as
in previous studies, this was not because the 3-year-olds failed to
recognize their images in the videos: Ninety-four percent of the 3-year-
olds correctly identified themselves when they were asked about their
image. In contrast, the 4-year-olds, especially the older group, clearly
grasped the differing significance of the information about the puppet's
location depicted in the self versus other-child tapes. Indeed, a clear

developmental trend was apparent across the four age groups tested (see Fig. 5.3). These results provided some initial support for the idea that the development of young children's temporally extended selves may involve a more general (or parallel) understanding of the causal structure of time.

Several follow-up studies helped to constrain our interpretation of these findings. First, we addressed a critique of our work by Suddendorf (1999), who questioned whether our previous results (and, by implication, these results as well) were simply artefacts of some general difficulty that 3-year-olds might have in understanding how video corresponds to reality. Although several aspects of our previous results cast direct doubt on this critique, we decided to test the issue empirically. For example, in one study, 3-year-olds were shown a single video that depicted a puppet being hidden in one of two boxes. Every child (N = 24) searched in that box when asked to find the puppet (see Study 2 of Povinelli et al., 1999). Obviously, they had no difficulty in understanding the general correspondence between the video images and the objects in the world. This result stands in direct contrast to the results reported by Suddendorf (1999), but are consistent with related findings reported by Troseth (1997).[2] Furthermore, in another study, we conducted a verbal analogue of the puppet task. In it, we provided the information about the hiding incidents through two verbal scripts (without video). One script referred to events that had just happened while they were playing the game, and the other referred to events that had happened "a long time ago," to a different child. Not only did this simple verbal script not help the 3-year-olds, but also it was actually harder for the 4-year-olds! These studies strongly suggest that the results of our tests with 3-year-olds are not due to some general inability to understand the correspondence between video and reality; rather, the difficulty may lie in their inability to understand the extension of the self in time or, perhaps more broadly, the causal arrow of time.

Finally, several additional studies tested even more directly the idea that the older preschoolers (i.e., 4- and 5-year-olds) are explicitly able to understand the causal structure of the extension of the self in time. These studies revealed that when older preschoolers were shown two recent events in which they had participated they understood that the

---

[2]These discrepancies may be attributable to some specific aspects of the procedure used by Suddendorf (1999). In particular, when the children in his study were shown the video playback of an object being hidden under one of several cups, the image was apparently left–right reversed from the real location of the cups on the table in front of the child. Thus, the children's difficulty in decoding the video information might easily have been the result of this spatial reversal. Note that in our studies (as well as that of Troseth, 1997) this confound was not present.

information from the most recent event was crucial with respect to the current location of the puppet (see Povinelli et al., 1999, Studies 5 and 6).

"JACQUELINE IN THE GLASS": SUMMARY AND FUTURE DIRECTIONS

I opened this chapter by recounting Piaget's (1962) observations of the curious attitude that his daughter, Jacqueline, seemed to adopt toward her image in photos and mirrors, and in particular the dual interpretation she seemed to possess. On the one hand, she clearly understood something about her image and its relation to herself, but on the other hand she seemed to distance herself from the image—as if it were not her at all, but some other Jacqueline. The work reported in this chapter suggests that Jacqueline's reactions are not simply curious anecdotes but rather are manifestations of the various dimensions along which the self is, and is not, explicitly represented at different ages. Indeed, studies of children's reactions to their own images, if properly structured, can reveal striking transitions in how the temporal dimension of the self comes to be grasped by young children.

Clearly, our work is but one thread in an ongoing effort to understand how and when infants and children come to understand the historical and future aspects of the self. Our results highlight the multiple dimensions along which the self may be represented—both in the here and now and in the past. As always, however, numerous fascinating questions remain waiting to be explored. For example, are there other transitions in the child's ontology of time not captured by our simplistic model? For example, do 3-year-olds possess an explicit notion of the past, present, and future but simply not grasp the causal relations that bind successive states of the world together? Perhaps even more interesting, do the transitions I have documented in this chapter have implications for the child's imagistic representation of past events? For example, as children gain an increasingly sophisticated ability to think about the self in time, does this allow them to imagine specific representations of their own bodies in these previous events—allowing them to imagine the self in previous events from a third-person point of view (a view they never actually had)?

Finally, these studies highlight the importance of the still unanswered question that motivated me to conduct these studies in the first place: whether chimpanzees, who share with human infants the ability to recognize themselves in mirrors, also develop an understanding that they are unique and unduplicated selves, caught ever–changing in the irreversible dimension of time.

ACKNOWLEDGMENTS

The research reported in this chapter was supported by National Science Foundation Young Investigator Award SBR-8458111 and a grant from the University of Louisiana Lafayette Foundation. The writing was supported by a Centennial Fellowship from the James S. McDonnell Foundation.

REFERENCES

Amsterdam, B. (1972). Mirror self-image reactions before age two. *Developmental Psychobiology, 5,* 297–305.

Case, R. (Ed.). (1992). *The mind's staircase: Exploring the conceptual underpinnings of children's thought and knowledge.* Hillsdale, NJ: Lawrence Erlbaum Associates.

Flavell, J. H. (1988). From cognitive connections to mental representations. In J.W. Astington, P. L. Harris, & D. R. Olson, (Eds.), *Developing theories of mind.* (pp226–243). Cambridge: CUP.

Gallup, G. G., Jr. (1970, Jan). Chimpanzees: Self-recognition. *Science, 167,* 86–87.

Gallup, G. G., Jr. (1979). Self-awareness in primates. *American Scientist, 67,* 417–421.

Gallup, G. G., Jr. (1982). Self-awareness and the emergence of mind in primates. *American Journal of Primatology, 2,* 237–248.

James, W. (1950). *The principles of psychology.* New York: Dover. (Original work published 1890)

Lewis, M., & Brooks-Gunn, J. (1979). *Social cognition and the acquisition of self.* New York: Plenum.

Mitchell, R. W. (1993). Mental models of mirror–self-recognition: Two theories. *New Ideas in Psychology, 11,* 295–325.

Olson, D. R., & Campbell, R. (1993). Constructing representations. In C. Pratt & A. F. Garton (Eds.), *Systems of representation in children: Development and use* (pp. 11–26). New York: Wiley.

Perner, J. (1991). *Understanding the representational mind.* Cambridge, MA: MIT Press.

Piaget, J. (1962). *Play, dreams, and imitation in childhood.* New York: Norton.

Povinelli, D. J. (1995). The unduplicated self. In P. Rochat (Ed.), *The self in early infancy* (pp. 161–192). Amsterdam: Elsevier.

Povinelli, D. J., & Cant, J. G. H. (1995). Arboreal clambering and the evolution of self-conception. *Quarterly Review of Biology, 70,* 393–421.

Povinelli, D. J., Landau, K. R., & Perilloux, H. K. (1996). Self-recognition in young children using delayed versus live feedback: Evidence of a developmental asynchrony. *Child Development, 67,* 1540–1554.

Povinelli, D. J., Landry, A. M., Theall, L. A., Clark, B. R., & Castille, C. M. (1999). Development of young children's understanding that the recent past is causally bound to the present. *Developmental Psychology, 35,* 1426–1439.

Povinelli, D. J., & Simon, B. B. (1998). Young children's understanding of briefly versus extremely delayed visual images of the self: Emergence of the autobiographical stance. *Developmental Psychology, 34,* 118–194.

Priel, B., & de Schonen, S. (1986). Self-recognition: A study of a population without mirrors. *Journal of Experimental Child Psychology, 41,* 237–250.

Suddendorf, T. (1999). Children's understanding of the relation between delayed video representation and current reality: A test for self-awareness? *Journal of Experimental Psychology, 72,* 157–176.

Troseth, G. L. (1997). *The medium can obscure the message: young children's understanding of video.* Unpublished master's thesis, University of Illinois at Urbana-Champaign.

6

Personalizing the Temporally Extended Self: Evaluative Self-Awareness and the Development of Autobiographical Memory

Melissa Welch-Ross
National Institute on Early Childhood Development and Education
Office of Educational Research and Improvement
U.S. Department of Education

Thinking about a self as existing through time depends on making personal sense of everyday experiences and integrating these into a coherent story of the self. Thus, a temporally extended self is fundamentally and necessarily an autobiographical self that includes an awareness of self-continuity and enduring, personally meaningful memories. Developing this temporally extended and autobiographical self-concept occurs in the context of children's everyday lives as they learn to evaluate and interpret events with significant others and to make connections between events using relevant cognitive tools available to them at the moment. Therefore, in this chapter I outline a model that situates the development of an autobiographical self in social contexts and cognitive achievements of early childhood. First, representational abilities involved in social metacognition are discussed that may help children become active participants in conversations through which they learn how to organize representations of experience and remember the past. I then emphasize the importance of developing a personal and evaluative subjective perspective for interpreting experience and constructing an autobiographical self. Last, I compare the proposed model with other current views on the emergence of the temporally extended self and its relation to autobiographical memory.

THE CONCEPTUAL FRAMEWORK

Overview

According to this model, particular social and cognitive factors converge in early childhood to provide a context that supports an understanding of self-continuity and the long-term recall of personal experience. These factors include (a) the content and structure of talk about past events; (b) the development of an evaluative, subjective perspective; (c) the ability to engage in causal spatial–temporal reasoning; and (d) particular social metacognitive skills (see Fig. 6.1). Specifically, parent-child conversations about events provide a social context for learning a narrative structure and constructing an evaluative, subjective perspective that children use to interpret, organize, represent, and recount personal experience. In addition, children need specific cognitive tools, such as social metacognitive skills, in order to learn in conversation how to organize event representations into narrative forms and how to evaluate everyday events. The emotional content of parent-child conversations is one type of evaluative framing likely to play a critical role in the development of this subjective orientation toward events that imparts meaning to experience. The ability of children to represent their evaluative mental

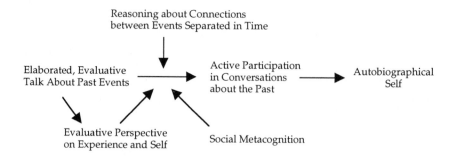

FIG. 6.1. Proposed social and cognitive influences on the development of an autobiographical self.

attitude toward personal experiences provides a basis for establishing meaningful connections among temporally disconnected episodes and thus motivates an awareness of psychological self-continuity. The general cognitive ability to infer causal, spatial–temporal connections between events is necessary to this process. The child's emerging ability to explicitly represent personal subjective evaluations, or mental attitudes, in memory may initiate a self-referential frame for organizing experience that earlier event memories lacked. This qualitative change in event representation may allow children to construct memories that have the potential to become personally meaningful, enduring, and autobiographical.

Social Metacognitive Skill

Conversing with children about past experiences appears to be a cultural means through which children learn to structure their verbal reports of past events and, therefore, perhaps their internal representations of the past, into detailed narrative forms (Fivush, 1991; Hudson, 1990; Reese, Haden, & Fivush, 1993). During the preschool years children develop increasingly structured and coherent narratives about past events (Fivush, Haden, & Adam, 1995). Parents who use an elaborated and evaluative narrative structure when talking with children about past events have children who structure their independent recall of past experiences into elaborated and evaluative narrative forms (Haden, Haine, & Fivush, 1997). Moreover, children whose mothers talk about the past in elaborated detail recall more information about past events than do children whose mothers are less elaborative (Reese et al., 1993). Together these results suggest that, through talking with children about past events, parents help children organize event representations into narrative forms that facilitate the long-term recall of personal memories. What skills must young children develop to benefit from the elaborative scaffolding that parents provide for representing and recounting past experience?

According to this framework (see also Welch-Ross, 1995), the development of specific representational skills involved in social metacognition may provide children with the cognitive tools needed for learning how to remember past events in conversation (see also Nelson, 1993; for a related discussion on cultural learning see Tomasello, Kruger, & Ratner, 1993). Two types of representational capabilities that appear to emerge between ages 3 and 4 may be most critical for engaging in this particular form of collaborative learning: (a) an understanding of the concept of knowledge, particularly the understanding that knowing requires an informative experience, and (b) an understanding that the self and others experience mental representations of past experience that the child can coordinate in conversations about past events.

An awareness of the relation between experiencing an event and knowing about it may enable children to represent their event knowledge as connected to an experience in their personal past. With this understanding, children can begin to link events discussed in conversation with their experiential history (Welch-Ross, 1995, 1997). The ability to recognize that one's memory of an episode is associated with an originating experience is characteristic of the personal memories of normally functioning adults who not only know the content of their representations of past events but also recognize that this knowledge originated with a previous informative experience (Gardiner, 1988; Tulving, 1985, 1993). This explicit understanding that knowledge is rooted in a previous experience is probably not sufficient, however, for fostering the development of autobiographical memory or an awareness of self-continuity (for an alternative view see Perner, chap. 10, this volume). Social and emotional factors probably interact with a variety of developing representational skills to construct temporally coherent and personally meaningful self-representations. An understanding of knowledge, together with the ability to coordinate multiple mental representations of past experience, for example, may enable preschoolers to engage in an act of intersubjective, joint attention during conversations about past events. Children can become enculturated more fully into the social activity of remembering because they can recognize that the "object," or referent, of conversation is an event memory that they represent as linked to their pasts. As a result, children can establish with others a shared representation of past events that provides a common ground for constructing shared evaluative meaning and a shared narrative organizational form for representing experience. Certainly, talking with children about past events would be expected to play a role in developing these aspects of mental-state understanding in the first place. Once these concepts are acquired, however, they in turn should foster a new understanding of the process of talking about past events that benefits children's recall and changes the organization of their personal memories and self-representations.

According to this view, children who have developed particular social metacognitive skills should recall more details in conversations about past events than children who have not. Correlational data obtained from the conversations of 40 mother–child dyads support the hypothesis that two types of mental-state reasoning—coordinating multiple mental representations and understanding the relation between knowing and experiencing—moderate the amount children recall in conversations with mothers about shared past events (Welch-Ross, 1997). In this research, mother–child dyads discussed three past events. Maternal narrative style was examined using a coding scheme adapted from Reese et al. (1993). The results presented here focus on the type of questions mothers asked about past events and the type of responses children provided to these questions. Mothers' questions were coded as either elaborative or repetitive. *Elaborative questions* provided additional information about the event, asked the child to recall a piece of information that the dyad had not yet discussed, or both. *Repetitive questions* consisted of repeating the exact wording or gist of a previous question or simply prompting children to remember more details without providing additional information. Children completed two sets of tasks taken from the literature on children's developing understanding of mind. One set of tasks consisted of false-belief and representational change tasks (e.g., Gopnik & Astington, 1988; Wimmer & Perner 1983) that require children to reason about conflicting mental representations of a situation. The ability to reason specifically about mental representations that *conflict* was not of primary interest. Instead, the rationale for including tasks that involved reasoning about conflicting mental representations was to provide the strongest test of whether children understood that the processes of the mind are representational and, as a result, that the mind does not create a single and true representation of the world (for further discussion on this point, see Flavell, 1988, and Perner, 1991). A second set of tasks indexed an understanding of knowledge (e.g., O'Neill & Gopnik, 1991; Pillow, 1989; Taylor, 1988). For example, one task required children to determine that a person who looks inside a container will know its contents, but a person who does not look will not know (see also Pratt & Bryant, 1990; Ruffman & Olson, 1989; Wimmer, Hogrefe, & Perner, 1988).

Semipartial correlations showed that performance on these tasks correlated positively with the amount of new information children provided in conversation after controlling for age and linguistic skill (mean length of utterance [MLU]). In addition, analyses performed on conditional probabilities showed that children who performed at above-chance levels on conflicting mental representation tasks and understanding of knowing tasks were more likely than children who did not perform above chance levels to provide new information whenever their mother asked an elaborative question (Welch-Ross, 1997). These patterns remained significant after controlling for age and MLU. Performance on conflicting mental representation tasks and understanding of knowing tasks was unrelated to the frequency with which mothers asked elaborated questions in the first place. Longitudinal data are needed that include measures of children's independent memory reports to determine if children must first develop these social metacognitive skills in order to engage in and benefit from the narrative scaffolding that has been shown to affect the amount and quality of children's recall of personal memories.

EVALUATIVE, SUBJECTIVE PERSPECTIVE

In addition to developing narrative skills for representing and recounting past experience, parent–child conversations about the past provide evaluative information and a subjective framing through which children learn how to interpret and make sense of their pasts (Fivush, 1993; Miller, 1994; Miller, Mintz, Hoogstra, Fung, & Potts, 1992; Miller, Potts, Fung, Hoogstra, & Mintz, 1990). Thus, a second claim of this model is that parent–child conversation about past events plays a critical role in the development of a personal, subjective perspective, which is defined as an evaluative representation of how the self is connected with the social and physical world. Consider that isolated events in themselves are neutral. The value that individuals in the child's immediate environment, and broader culture, attribute to events and the causal–temporal structure of language provides the child with a basis for connecting events across time in personally meaningful ways (for related discussions see Gergen, 1994; Nelson, 1996). That is, talking with others about events involves selecting particular episodes that are important to remember and placing these episodes in meaningful relation to other temporally displaced episodes. Clearly, one would expect variability among families and among cultures in the types of events selected and in the particular evaluations emphasized. Yet, in many cultures, individuals use evaluative, affective, causal–temporal language when talking with children about personal experiences. One would expect that children learn how to impart personal meaning to experience during this sense-making activity of collaborative remembering. Moreover, much of this personal meaning may emerge in discussions that focus explicitly on how children and others feel or should feel about particular past experiences.

Through participating regularly in such conversations over time, a child would be expected to develop a shared subjective perspective for interpreting experience and for organizing representations of past events with respect to their personal meaning. Also, over time, this subjective perspective should become increasingly consistent as children begin to interpret and represent connections among new experiences. This gradual process of developing a personal, subjective focus, or evaluative orientation, toward representing the self in relation to the world should be evident in the organization of the child's psychological self-view, or self-concept. A psychological *self-concept* is defined as a recognition of one's particular preferences, typical patterns of emotional expression, and typical ways of appraising people and situations (Damon & Hart, 1988; Eder, 1989, 1990). This correspondence between the development of a subjective perspective and an organized self-view would be expected because the psychological self-concept includes the child's personal view of how he or she is connected to, reacts to, and feels about his or her social and physical environment. A subjective perspective enables children to represent events not only as experienced but also as experienced with particular mental attitudes or personal evaluations.

One possibility is that the gradual and continuous process of developing and representing an evaluative perspective and establishing personally meaningful, causal connections between events provides a sense of psychological continuity that motivates a transition from a static representation of the physical self to a temporally extended representation of the psychological self. This understanding of psychological continuity requires an ability to represent one's personal concerns, evaluations, and mental attitudes and thus one's psychological connectedness to social and physical contexts. With the ability to represent a subjective perspective, the child can construct personally meaningful connections among temporally disconnected episodes. Thus, the personal meaning that a child is able to impart to experience and represent in memory is what situates a particular event in causal relation to the child's other experiences. Incorporating this subjective, psychological continuity into one's representations of events may contribute to a qualitative change in event representation that enables children to weave together meaningful life stories and thus establish enduring personal memories.

To represent events in causally connected, evaluative frameworks, children must be able to reason about causal connections between events across time. Early in development children are sensitive to the meaningfulness of causal connections, and this capability enhances memory. For example, toddlers remember acts that are causally related better than acts that are only temporally contiguous and not causally ordered (see Bauer, 1997). Later, by age 4, children appear to reason about the causal connections between events across delays (e.g., Povinelli, Landau &, Perilloux, 1996). A general cognitive ability to reason about causal relations between temporally disconnected episodes would enable children to engage in and benefit from the narrative structure and evaluative perspective that parents use when they talk with children about past events. Such causal reasoning skills do not provide evaluative meaning and thus would not be sufficient for supporting a temporally extended self-representation or the long-term recall of personal memories, according to this model. Because the development of a personal, evaluative perspective is expected to provide children with a basis for connecting events across time, children who demonstrate a consistent evaluative, subjective perspective should connect events that are talked about in mother–child conversation with their own personal pasts. Therefore, these children should engage in and benefit from the narrative and evaluative structures that mothers provide in conversation more than children who do not show this evaluative subjectivity. Moreover, children who organize representations of events into personally meaningful connections would be expected to recall past events without parental support.

EMPIRICAL EVIDENCE

Clearly, a challenge of conducting research relating to this conceptual framework lies in operationalizing abstract constructs, such as the development of a personal and evaluative subjective perspective. In the first data set discussed next, the child's subjective perspective was measured with an index of the consistency of the child's psychological self-view. The first claim of the model is that mother–child talk about past emotional experiences contributes to the development of a subjective perspective that is evident in the consistency of the child's psychological self-view. Thus, one expectation is that individual differences in the amount that mothers and children talk about the emotional aspects of past events should relate to individual differences in the consistency of children's psychological self-concept. The second claim is that maternal talk about emotion fosters a personal, evaluative perspective on events that children use to organize events for long-term recall. Therefore, a second expectation is that the amount that mothers talk about emotion should correlate positively with the amount that children talk about emotion. Furthermore, the amount that mothers talk about emotion should predict the amount that children recall about the aspects of events that are not emotion related. A third claim is that the development of a subjective perspective helps children connect events that are talked about in mother–child conversation with their own personal pasts and thus to engage in and benefit from the narrative and evaluative structures that mothers provide in conversation. Thus, a third prediction is that a consistent, psychological self-view moderates the relation between maternal style and the amount of new information children contribute to mother–child conversations about the past.

Welch-Ross, Fasig, and Farrar (1999) recorded conversations about four past events between thirty-two 4-year-olds and their mothers. Conversations were coded for mother and child reference to emotion, including initial references to emotion and subsequent emotion elaborations that (a) provided an explanation for the emotion, (b) requested an explanation for the emotion, (c) provided a resolution for the emotion, (d) described how others responded to the emotion, (e) confirmed or denied the emotion, or (f) other. In addition, conversations were coded for mother and child references to mental states to determine the unique relation between emotion-related conversation after controlling for other evaluative references, such as thinking, knowing, wanting, and believing. For example, one child stated, "I *thought* they were gonna tear up my bed." In another instance, a mother asked, "What did you *think* about the haunted house?" and later said, "You didn't *want* Mommy to leave you there."

At a second session, children completed the 62-item Children's Self-View Questionnaire (CSVQ; Eder, 1990), which measures children's self-views with respect to 10 dispositional constructs, such as aggression, achievement, and harm avoidance. The questionnaire is presented as a puppet show in which two puppets state pairs of opposing statements that correspond to each of the 10 constructs. The pairs of statements describe a variety of behaviors, preferences, and emotional reactions to people and situations (e.g., "I like to tease people" and " I don't like to tease people"). Children choose which statement best describes them. In previous research using the CSVQ, factor analyses were conducted on the responses of 3-, 5-, and 7-year-olds. The results showed that all groups endorsed statements in an organized manner rather than choosing items randomly (Eder, 1990). For example, a factor labeled *Self-Control* emerged for 3- and 5-year-olds in that research. Children who chose an item indicative of low aggression, such as "I don't like to tease people," were also likely to choose other items indicative of low aggression, such as "I don't ever try to push in front of people in line," and to choose items indicative of high harm avoidance, such as "I don't climb up on things that are high." On the basis of this previous work, Welch-Ross et al. defined an organized self-view as a consistent representation of the psychological qualities of the self that enables children to determine consistently across several items of a factor whether the statements described them. Thus, both the child who endorsed many statements that were indicative of a factor, such as Self-Control, and the child who endorsed few statements that were indicative of the factor would be credited with a consistent self-view. A child who endorsed, for example, half of the items would not. A continuous score from the CSVQ was obtained for each child that indexed the consistency of responding, independent of the particular view children described (i.e., regardless of whether the child's self-view indicated high self-control or low self-control). In addition to the factor of Self-Control, children's responses were measured on the Self-Acceptance Via Affiliation factor and the Self-Acceptance Via Achievement factor. Scores across the three factors were combined to obtain a single, total score that indexed the overall consistency of the child's self-view (see Welch-Ross et al., 1999, for additional details).

The results of this study showed that the proportion of mother–child turns that related to emotion (i.e., the ratio of emotion references to total conversation turns) predicted the consistency of children's self-views after controlling for both MLU and mother–child references to mental states. References to emotion accounted for 10.7% of the variance ($p < .055$) in consistency of self-view scores. Moreover, the data for emotion references were consistent with a socialization interpretation in that mothers in this sample initiated talk about emotions more than children did. Maternal initiations accounted for 75% of the total initiations of talk about emotion. Twenty-six of the 32 mothers initiated talk about emotion more frequently than their children did. Moreover, mother initiations and child initiations of talk about emotion were positively correlated ($r = .458$, $p < .008$). Clearly, correlational data obtained from a single time point only suggest that mother–child talk about emotion may influence the development of a consistent self-view and that mothers initiate and guide this process. However, the pattern of findings is at least consistent with the hypothesis that mothers initiate talk about emotion that in turn supports the development of a consistent self-view. Longitudinal data are needed to address this issue.

A second hypothesis was that, if the development of a subjective perspective supports the recall of past events, then children who choose items consistently on the CSVQ should recall more information about past events than children who choose items inconsistently (Welch-Ross et al., 1999). To test this hypothesis, conversations were coded with the narrative style scheme discussed earlier adapted from Reese et al. (1993). An index of the degree of elaboration evident in mothers' narrative styles was obtained by summing the number of elaborations and dividing this sum by the number of repetitions and prompts. A child recall ratio was calculated by adding memory responses and dividing this sum by the number of placeholders (turns that did not provide new information). In this sample, the consistency of self-view scores did not predict child recall after controlling for maternal style. Rather, consistency scores tended to moderate the relation between maternal style and children's recall. The correlation between maternal style and child recall was significant for children who chose consistently on more than one third of the items ($r = .41$), but this correlation was nonsignificant for children who chose consistently on less than two thirds of the items ($r = .13$). Given the modest sample size, these correlations do not differ significantly, and therefore any interpretations must be tentative. Additional research is needed to confirm whether a consistent self-view moderates the relation between maternal style and child recall. Moreover, longitudinal research is needed to explore how this moderating effect may change in direction and magnitude across the preschool years. Finally, whether or not the consistency of the child's self-view predicts recall in independent interviews with an experimenter must be determined.

The next set of analyses addressed the third claim that talk about emotion is important for constructing a personal perspective that, in turn, supports child recall (Welch-Ross et al., 1999). In this case, maternal talk about emotion would be expected to predict the amount children recall, even if the details children recall are not emotion related. The results of a regression analysis showed that the proportion of maternal references to emotion predicted child recall (a ratio of memory responses to placeholders), after controlling for MLU, child references to emotion, and maternal style ($pr = .37$, $p < .05$). Thus, the results support the hypothesis that the amount that mothers talk with children about emotions may play a general role in the ability of children to recall events from their pasts. According to the current view, the development of a personal subjective perspective that is constructed in part through maternal reference to emotion mediates this relation between maternal emotion references and child recall through providing a meaningful structure for organizing memory. These findings should be interpreted with caution, because the sample size was smaller than some recommend for regression analyses involving four predictor variables. However, preliminary results from a second study (Welch-Ross, 2001) provide converging evidence that a developing evaluative subjective perspective is related to children's recall of past events.

In this second sample, the degree to which children emphasized in their everyday behaviors an evaluative perspective on the self and others was the measure of children's evaluative, subjective perspective. Fifty 36-month-olds and their primary-caretaker mothers participated as part of a larger longitudinal study. Mothers and children talked about three past events. Indices of maternal narrative style (ratio of elaborations to repetitions and prompts) and child recall (ratio of memory responses to placeholders) were obtained from the conversations. Mothers completed the Self-Development Questionnaire (SDQ; Stipek, Gralinski, & Kopp, 1990). This 25-item scale consists of four factors that correspond to different aspects of self-knowing: Self-Description and Evaluation, Self-Recognition, Emotional Response to Wrongdoing and Self-Regulation, and Autonomy. Of particular interest was the 12-item Self-Description and Evaluation factor, which was used to index the frequency with which children demonstrated an evaluative, subjective perspective. As Stipek et al. (1990) emphasized, six items on this factor focus on neutral–objective self-description (e.g., "Child uses the word 'me,'" "Child knows whether she or he is a girl or boy."), and six items focus on children's evaluative perspectives. Mothers report, for example, if their child uses general evaluative terms about himself or herself (e.g., "I'm a good girl," or "I'm nice"), uses general evaluative terms when talking about someone else (e.g., "bad dog," or "Johnny's mean"), uses descriptive terms that contain some evaluation (e.g., "sticky hands," or points to a toy and says, "dirty"), and describes the self using physical characteristics. An additional item, "Child communicates likes and dislikes verbally" also correlated strongly in the current sample with the other evaluative items. Thus, a 7-item Evaluative Perspective index was obtained from the SDQ and was expected to predict the amount children recalled about past events.

The other three SDQ factors were not expected to predict recall, thereby showing the specificity of the relation between the Evaluative Perspective index and memory. For the 4-item Self-Recognition factor, mothers report if their child recognizes the self in pictures, mirrors, or calls attention to something that the child has done by saying, for example, "Look what I did." For the 3-item Autonomy factor, mothers indicate, for example, if their child ever resists help by pushing the mother's hand away or by saying "no," asserts his or her own will for the sake of being contrary, and resists physical intervention during activities such as dressing. Mothers responded "definitely not" (1 point), "has just begun to do this, but not consistently" (2 points), and "definitely" (3 points) to these questions. For the Emotional Response to Wrongdoing and Self-Regulation Factor, mothers responded "yes" or "no" to questions such as "Does your child ever seem upset, ashamed, or remorseful when found doing something wrong?" and "Does your child ever try to hide evidence of wrongdoing?"

In addition, children completed a delayed video self-recognition task (Povinelli et al. 1996, Experiment 1) in order to index their ability to reason about causal connections between events across time. In this task, the researcher videotapes the surreptitious placement of a sticker on the heads of children who are allowed to view the videotape 3 minutes later. The researcher records whether or not children reach to remove the sticker while watching the video. According to Povinelli et al. (1996), performance on this task should predict directly the amount children recall about past events, because reaching indicates the child's awareness of temporal self-continuity, which is necessary for establishing autobiographical memory (see also Povinelli, chap. 5, this volume). However, the expectation based on the current model was that reaching to remove the sticker indicates causal, spatial–temporal reasoning that is in itself insufficient for predicting autobiographical memory. Instead, the ability to make causal inferences across temporally disconnected episodes would enable children to benefit from the elaborative and evaluative narrative support that mothers provide in conversation. Therefore, children who reach to remove the sticker in the delayed video task should recall more about past events in conversation, particularly if they also have highly elaborative mothers. Finally, children completed the Peabody Picture Vocabulary Test (PPVT; Dunn & Dunn, 1997), a measure of receptive vocabulary known to correlate with standard IQ scores.

A regression was conducted in which the predictors were PPVT scores, the Evaluative Perspective index, and scores for the remaining three SDQ factors. The Evaluative Perspective index was the only significant predictor of child recall in conversation after controlling for PPVT scores ($pr = .41, p < .006$). Partial correlations between the remaining three factors and child recall were .08, .07, and -.067. A second regression showed that, after controlling for PPVT scores and maternal narrative style, both Evaluative Perspective scores and performance on the delayed self-recognition task predicted child recall (prs = .42, and .33, respectively). Thus, these findings suggest that both an evaluative subjective perspective and the ability to infer causal connections between events are unique predictors of the amount children recall about personally experienced events in conversation.

Additional analyses were performed to determine if Evaluative Perspective scores and performance on the delayed self-recognition task interacted with maternal style to moderate the amount children recalled. For the first analysis, children were divided into three levels (low, medium, and high) according to whether their scores on the Evaluative Perspective index were (a) below the median, (b) at the median or within 1 SD above the median, or (c) more than 1SD above the median. An analysis of covariance (ANCOVA), controlling for PPVT scores, showed that the interaction term was nonsignificant. However, planned comparisons showed that the ratio scores between children of high-elaborative and children of low-elaborative mothers differed significantly only for those children who had Evaluative Perspective scores that fell more than 1SD above the median (Table 6.1). Moreover, among children with highly elaborative mothers, children who had the highest Evaluative Perspective scores had recall ratio scores that were greater than children whose Evaluative Perspective scores fell in the two lowest levels. In contrast, among children with low-elaborative mothers, ratio scores did not differ as a function of Evaluative Perspective. Finally, note that memory scores exceeded placeholders only for the group of children who had both highly elaborative mothers and the highest Evaluative Perspective Scores.

A second ANCOVA of maternal style (high elaborative vs. low elaborative) by delayed self-recognition (reach vs. not) was performed on children's ratio scores. A significant main effect showed that children of high-elaborative mothers had a higher ratio of memory responses to placeholders than did children of low-elaborative mothers. In addition,

TABLE 6.1
Recall as a Function of Evaluative Self-Awareness and
Maternal Elaborative Style

| *Maternal Elaborative Style* | *Level of Evaluative Self-Awareness* | | |
	Low (n = 19)	*Medium* (n = 15)	*High* (n = 16)
Low elaborative	0.57	0.71	0.61
High elaborative	0.61	0.90	2.47

Note. Percentages indicate the mean ratio of child memory responses to placeholders.

TABLE 6.2
Recall as a Function of Reaching and Maternal Elaborative Style

Maternal Elaborative Style	Not Reach (n = 34)	Reach (n = 16)
Low elaborative	0.61	0.64
High elaborative	0.75	2.83

Note. Scores indicate the mean ratio of child memory responses to placeholders.

children who reached on the delayed self-recognition task had higher ratio scores than children who did not reach. However, a significant interaction qualified these main effects and showed a pattern of results that was similar to the ones involving the Evaluative Perspective index. First, ratio scores between children with high-elaborative mothers and children of low-elaborative mothers differed significantly only for those children who reached on the delayed video self-recognition task (see Table 6.2). Moreover, among children with high-elaborative mothers, children who reached had a higher ratio of memory responses to placeholders than children who did not reach. In contrast, among children with low-elaborative mothers ratio scores did not differ as a function of whether children reached. Finally, the group of children who reached and who also had highly elaborative mothers was the only group for whom memory responses exceeded placeholders. It is important that Evaluative Perspective scores did not differ between children who reached ($M = 7.18$) and children who did not reach ($M = 7.56$) on the delayed video self-recognition task ($p < .51$), indicating that these measures index different constructs, although the pattern of results involving these measures was similar.

Together, the findings suggest that maternal narrative style interacts with both the child's evaluative subjective perspective and the ability to reason about causal connections between events to play an important role in children's participation in mother–child reminiscing. One interpretation of these results is that maternal elaboration, the development of an evaluative subjective perspective, and the ability to engage in temporal–causal reasoning converge to provide children with the social scaffolding and cognitive support needed for contributing new information to conversations about past events. Moreover, according to the present model, children's social metacognitive skills would be expected to moderate further the amount of new information children provide in conversation.

In sum, the findings presented here are consistent with the hypotheses that (a) individual differences in the amount that mothers and children talk about the emotional aspects of past events predicts individual differences in the consistency of children's psychological self-views, (b) maternal talk about emotion predicts the amount children recall about past events, and (c) an evaluative subjective perspective moderates the relation between maternal style and the amount of new information that children contribute to mother–child conversations about the past. The results suggest that emotional evaluation in conversation about past events contributes to the development of a subjective perspective, which in turn helps children connect events talked about in elaborated mother–child conversation with their own personal pasts and thus produce new information about past events. Ultimately, studies may show that some children develop an evaluative perspective and self-view earlier than others and that it is this perspective that allows them to interpret and represent events in relation to the self earlier in development. As they grow older, these children may recall events from earlier in childhood. However, much additional research is needed to test the claims of this model, and alternative explanations for the findings presented here must be explored. Clearly, longitudinal research that examines both children's participation in conversations about past events and independent personal narratives will be critical for determining precisely how social metacognitive skills, references to emotion, and causal spatial–temporal reasoning might interact with an elaborated maternal narrative style over time to affect the development of the child's subjective perspective, awareness of psychological self-continuity, and long-term personal memories.

COMPARING THE FRAMEWORK WITH OTHER PROPOSALS

Defining the Role of Metacognition

Recently, several researchers have offered proposals concerning interrelations among self-representation, metacognition, and the development of autobiographical recall. For example, Povinelli (1995) proposed that representing conflicting mental representations enables children to infer that representations of the past have causal implications for the current, and different, state of the self. This causal spatial–temporal integration of events results in an awareness of temporal self-continuity necessary for the emergence of autobiographical memory. Povinelli et al. (1996) showed that 25% of 3-year-olds who watched a delayed video recording of a researcher marking their heads with a sticker reached to remove the sticker, whereas 75% of 4-year-olds reached. Povinelli (1995, chap. 5, this volume) credits children who reach with an understanding of temporal self-continuity necessary for integrating events into the temporally extended representations of personal memories that may become autobiographical.

Consider that this proposal does not attribute a special status to the self in that self-representation is not distinguished from object representation. The child's awareness of temporal self-continuity emerges because he or she integrates temporally disconnected and causally related event representations, which happen to involve the self. Thus, reaching behavior in this task may actually demonstrate an ability to use inferential reasoning to conclude that past states of the world, including actions on physical objects, are related causally to the current state of the world. Therefore, the most cautious conclusion relating to evidence for *self*-awareness is that reaching for the sticker shows an ability to represent the temporal continuity of the physical self. As a result, a precarious leap is needed to infer from a child's abstract reasoning about changes in the physical appearance of the body the development of a quality of self-knowing and remembering that involves representing personally meaningful and enduring life stories. In short, this version of autobiographical memory development is curiously void of subjective lives.

The current proposal emphasizes a process of self-development that involves the ability of children to engage in contextualized, subjective reflection on their psychological continuity rather than emphasizing abstracted, objective reflection on physical, causal–temporal continuity. Children strive to make sense of the world, and conversations with others about past experiences are rich opportunities for learning within one's immediate social world which experiences are meaningful and why. In these conversations, others link the child to the past and future using causal, affective, and other evaluative language that situates the child in relation to activities, objects, and people and conveys how to interpret events with respect to the self. According to the present framework, understanding that the self and others are experiencers and thus knowers of the past (which an understanding of mental states affords) and representing evaluations or mental attitudes toward experience (which conversation with others affords) result in representing one's psychological self-continuity and constructing personally meaningful representations of events that could become part of autobiographical memory.

The understanding of causal, spatial–temporal relations children probably need to reach for the sticker on the delayed self-recognition task is important to an understanding of self-continuity and to the development of personal event memory in the present model, although it is considered (a) insufficient for initiating autobiographical recall and (b) unlikely to occur as a function of an ability to reason about conflicting mental representations of events. Focusing first on the issue of insufficiency, the data presented earlier indicated that whether or not children reached to remove the sticker on the delayed self-recognition task moderated children's recall, but only when children also had highly elaborative mothers. These data are consistent with the interpretation that causal, spatial–temporal reasoning interacts with elaborated conversation about past events to support children's recall rather than affecting children's recall only directly. A likely possibility is that causal, spatial–temporal reasoning emerges, in part, through exposure to linguistic markers of causal–temporal relations, and this reasoning in turn supports the ability of children to engage further in elaborated conversations about events through which children acquire narrative forms and evaluative perspectives for organizing personal memories.

Regarding the relation between the temporally extended self and the ability to reason about conflicting mental representations, children in the second sample who completed a delayed self-recognition task completed three appearance–reality tasks (see Flavell, Green, & Flavell, 1986) and three representational change tasks (see Gopnik & Astington, 1988) adapted from the literature on theory of mind. These tasks were intended to index an ability to coordinate conflicting representations of a situation. A t test showed that the mean percentage of items correct for the representational change task did not differ significantly between children who reached to remove the sticker ($M = .18$) and children who did not ($M = .21$; $p < 77$). Of the 16 children who reached, 5 did not answer any of the representational change questions correctly, and 5 provided a correct answer to only one of the questions. In addition, children who did not reach to remove the sticker performed better on appearance–reality tasks than children who reached ($Ms = .38$ and $.19$, respectively; $p < .03$), although this difference was not significant after controlling for PPVT scores. Of the 16 children who reached, 8 did not answer any of the appearance–reality questions correctly. These data indicate that an understanding of conflicting mental representations may not be a prerequisite for reaching to remove the sticker. Therefore, the results call into question the assumption that this representational ability motivates reasoning about temporal self-continuity, causal spatial–temporal connections between events, or both. Additional data clearly are needed to address this issue.

Perner (Perner, 1990, 1991, chap. 10, this volume; Perner & Ruffman, 1995) also has proposed that metacognition, especially an understanding of knowledge, may cause fundamental changes in event representation that initiate autobiographical memory and, as a result, an awareness of the temporally extended self. The specific claim is that an understanding of knowing provides children with the metacognitive skill needed for incorporating a conscious phenomenal experience of remembering into one's representations of past events. This conscious remembering of past experience makes possible an awareness of self that is extended across time (chap. 10, this volume). According to Perner and Ruffman (1995), parents' contributions to memory conversations serve a simple cueing function that triggers children's memory for the event.

In contrast to Perner's (Perner, 1990, 1991, chap. 10, this volume; Perner & Ruffman, 1995) view, an understanding of knowing is insufficient for establishing an awareness of self-continuity, according to the present model. Rather, a variety of mental-state concepts may operate in conjunction with social and emotional processes to support autobiographical self-representations. For example, both an understanding of knowing and effective reasoning about multiple representations of events may be necessary for children to engage in and benefit from the process of collaborative remembering through which autobiographical memory is constructed (for a more detailed discussion see Welch-Ross, 1995). Developing these concepts may be critical for reaching a qualitatively different understanding of talk about past events and thus a new level of participation in these conversations. An understanding of mental states helps children establish a history of "common ground" with their conversation partner that consists of shared evaluations of experience and to represent events in memory consistently using these shared evaluative frameworks. Thus, in order to recognize their self-continuity and develop autobiographical memories, children must begin to represent events routinely as more than merely experienced and thus known, as in Perner's model, but as experienced and known with a particular evaluative and personally meaningful perspective.

Developing a Personal, Subjective Perspective

In chapter 3 of this volume Fivush proposes that talking with others about past events enables children to encounter perspectives that conflict with their own. Such sociolinguistic evidence of conflicting perspectives may encourage children to become explicitly aware that their memories of events are unique, subjective interpretations. In this case, the term *subjective* refers to the fact that different individuals may interpret the "objective" facts of events differently, leading to unique perspectives of the same event. With this understanding, a child can begin to organize episodes into his or her own personal history, distinguish this subjective history from the subjective histories of others, and thereby construct a representation of a temporally extended self.

Indeed, theory-of-mind research indicates that people acquire increasingly sophisticated understandings of individual subjectivity throughout childhood and adolescence. Studying these relations between understanding individual subjectivity and constructing an autobiographical self might reveal how different processes contribute to self-representation and remembering at different points in development. Toddlers seem to learn during early social interactions—for example, in play with siblings and peers—that their own goals, wants, and needs can conflict with those of others (Dunn, 1988), an understanding that 2- and 3-year-olds can demonstrate more explicitly on a variety of structured tasks (e.g., Wellman, 1990). Preschoolers' understanding of subjectivity is more advanced and involves an explicit recognition that individual representations of events can conflict as a result of having different experiences, as passing false-belief tasks apparently shows. Later on, sometime between ages 5 and 8, children begin to understand that individuals may interpret and represent even shared experiences differently as a function of having different histories of experience (e.g., Pillow, 1991; Ruffman, Olson, & Astington, 1991). A truly constructivist and interpretative understanding of subjectivity may not develop until late childhood or adolescence (e.g., Carpendale & Chandler, 1996; Chandler, 1988). Adults probably continue to fine-tune their understanding of subjectivity as they encounter diverse perspectives. Thus, developmental transitions in understanding aspects of individual subjectivity may indeed contribute to an increasingly rich, differentiated, and private representation of the self that foregrounds the distinctiveness of one's self-history and autobiography, as Fivush suggests.

Instead of emphasizing how conflict between unique representations of experience may influence representations of self-continuity, however, the present model emphasizes the importance of establishing an empathic, representational connection with a more knowledgeable other. The present model predicts that very young children experience detailed representations of events but do not represent explicitly that they think or feel one way or another about them. Through talking with others about the evaluative aspects of experience, children learn to represent these evaluations explicitly. The assumption is that children develop an evaluative framework and narrative organization for representing events through using social metacognitive skills to establish a common ground, or shared representation of experience, with a more knowledgeable conversation partner. This evaluative perspective connects episodes to one another in ways that are personal and subjective in the sense that the child represents his or her mental attitude toward those events. However, children may not explicitly recognize these interpretations as subjective in the sense that they are potentially unique to the self; though these attitudes effectively organize memories of events. In fact, children may initially ignore discrepancies between their own perspective and that of their conversation partner, and perhaps even revise their perspective, in an attempt to make sense of experience through their partner's representations of those events.

The distinction between these two treatments of subjectivity is important in that it emphasizes the particular role that an understanding of mental representation plays in the present model. The social process that is proposed here for learning to construct self-continuity is analogous to one Bruner (1985) described in his conceptualization of Vygotsky's (1978) concept of the zone of proximal development. Bruner explained that a more knowledgeable other serves as the child's "vicarious consciousness" as he or she helps the child move from incompetence to competence in performing a task. The more knowledgeable other mentally represents the goals of the task; reasonable alternatives for reaching those goals; and, for each alternative, an organized sequence of steps for achieving them. The representations of the more knowledgeable other organize the child's behavior until the child shares these representations of the task and thus becomes "conscious" of how to perform the task on his or her own. The ability of the child to enter into this shared representation is critical to learning the task. In the present context autobiographical memory and an awareness of self-continuity may emerge initially because children begin to organize events according to personal and emotional evaluations that are shared with others. Children may interpret events using this evaluative mental attitude toward experience and begin developing an explicit self-history even if they do not yet recognize their perspective on events as potentially unique.

The current model differs also from other, more traditional views that explain the development of self and autobiographical memory as a process of becoming aware of how one is distinct, separate from others, and unique. One recent model (Howe & Courage, 1993) describes a purely cognitive process of abstract self-reflection through which children begin to differentiate self from other and organize events according to their individual, unique characteristics and perspectives. Adults in many cultures may indeed, in retrospect, conceptualize their earliest memories and sense of self in terms of internal, private, and unique reflections on personal experience. However, the process through which toddlers first begin to represent the existence of self and through which preschoolers begin to represent their temporal self-continuity may not be characterized best this way. The self-history we now construe in adulthood as necessarily private and unique to us may actually begin and develop primarily through forms of shared awareness with another. Thus, the current proposal focuses on how self-continuity and autobiographical memory develop in a social process of establishing psychological connectedness and a mutual, empathic understanding with others concerning how the self is situated to events and people in the world.

CONCLUSION

In this chapter I have presented a sociocultural view of the development of the temporally extended self and autobiographical memory in which the child applies particular social metacognitive tools to the task of making sense of experience through conversations with others about the evaluative meaning of past events. This contextualized and personalized approach to studying the development of self and memory may help us to understand how children construct an understanding of self-continuity and memories that are long lasting. In this effort, the framework offered here emphasizes the critical importance of sociolinguistic mechanisms to the development of self and autobiographical memory rather than organismic ones. Moreover, the development of a temporally extended self is viewed as more than an act of pure cognition in that the development of thought about the self is considered inseparable from the emotional and evaluative content of the self that is thought about. Thus, it will be important to examine in future research how children become able to think about and evaluate their experiences in terms of self-representations that include the kinds of people they are, and have been, in particular contexts with significant others (see Tessler & Nelson, 1994, for a related discussion). We may find that, as children begin to interpret the meaning of events with respect to a new dimension of experience—namely, personal relevance—this evaluative perspective facilitates an awareness of psychological continuity and enduring memories.

REFERENCES

Bauer, P. J. (1997). Development of memory in early childhood. In N. Cowan (Ed.), *The development of memory in childhood* (pp. 83–112). Hove, East Sussex, England: Psychology Press.

Bruner, J. (1985). Vygotsky: A historical and conceptual perspective. In J. V. Wertsch (Ed.), *Culture, communication, and cognition* (pp. 21–34). Cambridge, MA: Harvard University Press.

Carpendale, J. I., & Chandler, M. J. (1996). On the distinction between false belief understanding and subscribing to an interpretative theory of mind. *Child Development, 67,* 1686–1706.

Chandler, M. (1988). Doubt and developing theories of mind. In J. W. Astington, P. L. Harris, & D. R. Olson (Eds.), *Developing theories of mind* (pp. 387–413). New York: Cambridge University Press.

Dunn, J. (1988). *The beginnings of social understanding.* Cambridge, MA: Harvard University Press.

Damon, W., & Hart, D. (1988). *Self-understanding in childhood and adolescence.* New York: Cambridge University Press.

Dunn, L. M. & Dunn, L. M. (1997). *Peabody Picture Vocabulary Test–III.* Circle Pines, MN: American Guidance Service.

Eder, R. A. (1989). The emergent personologist: The structure and content of $3^1/_2$-$5^1/_2$-, and $7^1/_2$-year-olds' concepts of themselves and other persons. *Child Development, 60,* 1218–1228.

Eder, R. A. (1990). Uncovering young children's psychological selves: Individual and developmental differences. *Child Development, 61,* 849–863.

Fivush, R. (1991). The social construction of personal narratives. *Merrill–Palmer Quarterly, 37,* 59–82.

Fivush, R. (1993). Emotional content of parent–child conversations about the past. In C. A. Nelson (Ed.), *The Minnesota Symposia on Child Psychology, Vol. 26: Memory and affect in development* (pp. 39–78). Hillsdale, NJ: Lawrence Erlbaum Associates.

Fivush, R., Haden, C., & Adam, S. (1995). Structure and coherence of preschoolers' personal narratives over time: Implications for childhood amnesia. *Journal of Experimental Child Psychology, 60,* 32–56.

Flavell, J. H. (1988). The development of children's knowledge about the mind: From cognitive connections to mental representations. In J. W. Astington, P. L. Harris, & D. R. Olson (Eds.), *Developing theories of mind* (pp. 244–270). New York: Cambridge University Press.

Flavell, J. H., Green, F. L., & Flavell, E. R. (1986). Development of knowledge about the appearance–reality distinction. *Monograph of the Society for Research in Child Development, 60,* 201–213.

Gardiner, J. (1988). Functional aspects of recollective experience. *Memory and Cognition, 16,* 309–313.

Gergen, K. J. (1994). Mind, self, and society: Self-memory in social context. In U. Neisser & R. Fivush (Eds.), *The remembering self: Construction and accuracy in the self-narrative* (pp. 78–104). New York: Cambridge University Press.

Gopnik, A., & Astington, J. W. (1988). Children's understanding of representational change and its relation to the understanding of false belief and the appearance–reality distinction. *Child Development, 59,* 26–37.

Haden, C. A, Haine, R. A., & Fivush, R. (1997). Developing narrative structure in parent–child reminiscing across the preschool years. *Developmental Psychology, 33,* 295–307.

Howe, M. L., & Courage M. L. (1993). On resolving the enigma of infantile amnesia. *Psychological Bulletin, 13,* 305–326.

Hudson, J. A. (1990). The emergence of autobiographical memory in mother–child conversation. In R. Fivush & J. A. Hudson (Eds.), *Knowing and remembering in young children* (pp. 166–196). New York: Cambridge University Press.

Miller, P. J. (1994). Narrative practices: Their role in socialization and self-construction. In U. Neisser & R. Fivush (Eds.), *The remembering self: Construction and accuracy in the life narrative* (pp. 158–179). New York: Cambridge University Press.

Miller, P. J., Mintz, J., Hoogstra, L., Fung, H., & Potts, R. (1992). The narrated self: Young children's construction of self in relation to others in conversational stories of personal experience. *Merrill–Palmer Quarterly, 38,* 45–67.

Miller, P. J., Potts, R., Fung, H., Hoogstra, L., & Mintz, J. (1990). Narrative practices and the social construction of self in childhood. *American Ethnologist, 17,* 292–311.

Nelson, K. (1993). The psychological and social origins of autobiographical memory. *Psychological Science, 4,* 7–14.

Nelson, K. (1996). *Language in cognitive development: The emergence of the mediated mind.* New York: Cambridge University Press.

O'Neill, D. K., & Gopnik, A. (1991). Young children's ability to identify the sources of their beliefs. *Developmental Psychology, 27,* 390–397.

Perner, J. (1990). Experiential awareness and children's episodic memory. In W. Schneider & F. E. Weinert (Eds.), *Interactions among aptitudes, strategies, and knowledge, in cognitive performance* (pp. 3–11). New York: Springer-Verlag.

Perner, J. (1991). *Understanding the representational mind.* Cambridge, MA: MIT Press.

Perner, J., & Ruffman, T. (1995). Episodic memory and autonoetic consciousness: Developmental evidence and a theory of childhood amnesia. *Journal of Experimental Child Psychology, 59,* 516–548.

Pillow, B. H. (1989). Early understanding of perception as a source of knowledge. *Journal of Experimental Child Psychology, 47,* 116–129.

Pillow, B. H. (1991). Children's understanding of biased social cognition. *Developmental Psychology, 27,* 539–551.

Povinelli, D. J. (1995). The unduplicated self. In P. Rochat (Ed.), *The self in early infancy* (pp. 161–192). Amsterdam: Elsevier.

Povinelli, D. J., Landau, K. R., & Perilloux, H. K. (1996). Self-recognition in young children using delayed versus life feedback: Evidence of a developmental asynchrony. *Child Development, 67,* 1540–1554.

Pratt, C., & Bryant, P. (1990). Young children understand that looking leads to knowing (so long as they are looking in a single barrel). *Child Development, 61,* 973–982.

Reese, E., Haden, C. A., & Fivush, R. (1993). Mother–child conversations about the past: Relationships of style and memory over time. *Cognitive Development, 8,* 403–430.

Ruffman, T., & Olson, D. R. (1989). Children's ascriptions of knowledge to others. *Developmental Psychology, 25,* 601–606.

Ruffman, T., Olson, D. R., & Astington, J. W. (1991). Children's understanding of visual ambiguity. *British Journal of Developmental Psychology, 9,* 89–103.

Stipek, D., Gralinski, J. H., & Kopp, C. B. (1990). Self-concept development in the toddler years. *Developmental Psychology, 26,* 972–977.

Taylor, M. (1988). The development of children's understanding of the seeing–knowing distinction. In J. W. Astington, P. L. Harris, & D. R. Olson (Eds.), *Developing theories of mind* (pp. 207–225). New York: Cambridge University Press.

Tessler, M., & Nelson, K. (1994). Making memories: The influence of joint encoding on later recall by young children. *Consciousness & Cognition, 3,* 307–326.

Tomasello, M., Kruger, A. C., & Ratner, H. H. (1993). Cultural learning. *Behavioral and Brain Sciences, 16,* 495–552.

Tulving, E. (1985). How many memory systems are there? *American Psychologist, 40,* 385–398.

Tulving, E. (1993). What is episodic memory? *Current Directions in Psychological Sciences, 2,* 67–70.

Vygotsky, L. S. (1978). *Mind in society.* Cambridge, MA: Harvard University Press.

Welch-Ross, M. K. (1995). An integrative model of the development of autobiographical memory. *Developmental Review, 15,* 338–365.

Welch-Ross, M. K. (1997). Mother–child participation in conversation about the past: Relationships to preschoolers' theory of mind. *Developmental Psychology, 33,* 618–629.

Welch-Ross, M. K. (2001). *Self-development, causal–temporal reasoning, and maternal reminiscing style: Relations to preschoolers' narrative memories for personally experienced events.* Manuscript in preparation.

Welch-Ross, M. K., Fasig, L. G., & Farrar, M. J. (1999). Predictors of preschoolers' self-knowledge: References to emotion and mental states in mother–child conversation about past events. *Cognitive Development, 14,* 401–422.

Wellman, H. M. (1990). The child's theory of mind. Cambridge, MA: MIT Press.

Wimmer, H., Hogrefe, A., & Perner, J. (1988). Children's understanding of informational access as a source of knowledge. *Child Development, 59,* 386–396.

Wimmer, H., & Perner, J. (1983). Beliefs about beliefs: Representation and constraining function of wrong beliefs in young children's understanding of deception. *Cognition, 13,* 103–128.

7

Planning in 3-Year-Olds: A Reflection of the Future Self?

Cristina M. Atance
Daniela K. O'Neill
University of Waterloo

The ability to project oneself into the future in order to plan effectively, and to contemplate possible courses of action, is fundamental to one's existence. Yet few studies have had as their focus the development of children's ability to engage in this process. What we mean when we speak of children's ability to project themselves into the future is, specifically, how children begin to anticipate future events in which the self is mentally transported. This ability has been characterized as part of what comprises a *temporally extended self* (Moore, 1997, but see also Tulving, 1985; Tulving, Schacter, McLachlan, & Moscovitch, 1988; and Povinelli, 1995) and, specifically, with respect to the domain of the future, a *temporally extended future self* (hereafter referred to as the *future self*). We could contrast the notion of a future self with having knowledge of the future that may not be explicitly linked to the self. This latter type of knowledge may be more of a function of recognizing the pattern of past events and applying this knowledge to the future. For example, suppose you ask a 3-year-old child what she'll be doing for her birthday, and she replies, "I'm gonna eat cake." Is this reply reflective of her ability to place herself in this future event of "eating cake," or is she simply reciting this event as part of an impersonal script that describes what typically happens at birthday parties? Although, in theory, one can think about these two alternative notions of thought concerning the future, to our knowledge this distinction has rarely, if ever, been drawn. However, this same sort of distinction has been made with respect to past events.

For example, some authors (see Tulving, 1985; Tulving et al., 1988; Perner & Ruffman, 1995) have referred to this distinction as the difference between *knowing* versus *remembering* past events. The former is part of what Tulving (1985) characterized as semantic memory, whereas the latter is a function of the episodic memory system. For instance, a person can *know* that he or she used to drive a blue truck, without necessarily *remembering* any specific instances in which he or she did so (Tulving et al., 1988). Thus, if this distinction exists with respect to past events, it is not implausible to hypothesize that a similar distinction also exists with respect to future events. To determine whether this may be the case, we begin this chapter with a review of the literature that is related to children's understanding of the future.

Only a few studies exist that have had as their focus children's understanding of the future. These studies have used widely varying methodologies, which makes it difficult to directly compare the findings of each. At one end of the spectrum are naturalistic studies in which the focus has been children's talk about the future; at the other end are experimental studies that have looked at children's performance in delay-of-gratification and sequencing paradigms. Furthermore, not all of these studies have specifically tapped an understanding of the self with respect to the future. Despite this, we begin by looking first at the experimental work in this area and then at work that is more naturalistic.

As stated, experimental work has tended to examine children's understanding of the future in sequencing and delay of gratification tasks. There are many studies that have examined the development of sequencing abilities (e.g., Bauer & Thal, 1990, Friedman, 1990; O'Connell & Gerard, 1985); but only a few have explored children's ability to sequence future events. More typically, in infants, for example, researchers have looked specifically at their performance in elicited imitation paradigms, in which sequences of events are modeled with props by an experimenter, in front of the infant, and then infants are given the props and encouraged to imitate these events. Although the sequencing of past events is likely relevant to the ability to sequence possible future ones, such studies tell us little about children's ability to think into the future.

Friedman (1990), however, examined forward-sequencing abilities in preschool children. Specifically, he looked at how preschoolers begin to sequence events that are part of their daily routine. For example, Friedman gave children a forward-ordering task in which they had to place four cards that depicted "waking up," "eating lunch," "eating dinner," and "going to bed," in the order in which they occur in the day. Three-year-old children were below chance level in their ability to complete the task correctly; only by 4 years of age were children's performances beginning to exceed chance. However, it is not clear whether the difficulty that the 3-year-olds experienced was due to an inability to project themselves into the future or whether other factors, such as a limited knowledge of the pattern of daily events, may have contributed to their difficulty.

Alternatively, Thompson, Barresi, and Moore (1997) examined how children between 3 and 5 years of age begin to deal with future situations in a delay-of-gratification paradigm. So, for example, in one of their experimental conditions, labeled "delay of self-gratification," children were given the option of obtaining one sticker immediately or two stickers in the future. Only by 4 and 5 years of age did children begin to prefer the larger delayed reward rather than the smaller immediate one. Thompson et al. suggested that the 3-year-olds were impeded in part "by the introduction of a situation in which they were required to imagine future desires which conflicted with their current desires" (p. 207). Yet it is unclear whether the 3-year-old children in this study were truly incapable of placing themselves in the future, or whether this ability may have been confounded with the ability to delay gratification. For example, obtaining one sticker immediately may simply have been more desirable for children than waiting to obtain two.

If we now shift our focus to naturalistic data, we find that children as young as 2 years of age begin to talk about both the past and the future (Anglin, Ward, & White, 1999; Eisenberg, 1985; Nelson, 1989; Sachs, 1983). Sachs (1983) looked at the development of displaced reference in her firstborn child, Naomi, when Naomi was 17–36 months of age. Between 26 and 31 months of age Naomi began to talk both about events that had happened earlier in the day and about those that would happen later in the day. Sachs noted that Naomi seemed to be particularly concerned with the sequencing of these future events. For example, at approximately 29 months of age Naomi produced the following utterances (Sachs, 1983, p. 15).

Mommy's away. Coming back again.
(at bedtime) We'll have breakfast together.
Gotta put a bandaid on a little later.
I gotta feel better in the morning, when we have dinner in the morning.
We gotta drive pretty soon.
My mom will get up pretty soon.

These utterances suggest that, even at this young age, Naomi seemed to be aware not only of the future but also of future events that would involve the self. Between 32 and 36 months of age Naomi began to make more spontaneous references to the past and the future, which included events that had occurred, or would occur, at some time beyond the scope of the present day.

Katherine Nelson (1989) also documented the use of temporally displaced speech by a 2-year-old child, Emily, and similarly found that Emily's monologues included talk about both the past and the future. For example, the following narrative was constructed by Emily when she was 28 months of age.

> We are gonna...
> at the ocean.
> Ocean is a little far away.
> baw, baw, buh (etc.)
> far away...
> I think it's...
> couple blocks ... away.
> Maybe it's down, downtown,
> and across the ocean,
> and down the river,
> and maybe it's in,
> the hot dogs will be in a fridge,
> and the fridge (would) be in the water over by a shore,
> and then we could go in,
> and get a hot dog and bring it out to the river,
> and then sharks go in the river and bite me,
> in the ocean... (Nelson, 1989, p. 66)

In the previous narrative, Emily incorporated details told to her by her father but also included her own speculations about the particulars that might occur. For example, in talking about this event to Emily, her father had mentioned hot dogs but had not included information about refrigerators. Furthermore, Emily's mother reported that Emily had had no previous experience with the beach, or with eating hot dogs prior to her construction of this narrative. It is clear from her account that Emily has begun to develop a true concern for how an event that has not yet occurred will unfold.

More recently, Anglin et al. (1999) also documented, among a larger sample of 60 children, that temporally displaced speech about both the proximal and distal future shows a significant increase between the ages of 1.5 and 4.5 years. Naturalistic evidence thus suggests that by 2 and 3 years of age children engage in a substantial amount of talk about the future.

Finally, there is one area of previous research that comes closest to capturing not just an understanding of the future but the origins of the future self. Haith and Benson (1992) developed a parent-report questionnaire, the Development of Future-Oriented Processes Questionnaire, which was described by Benson (1994), to specifically examine the origins of future orientation in children between the ages of

9 and 36 months. They developed this questionnaire on the basis of preliminary interviews with mothers of 9- to 36-month-old children who were asked to provide examples of their child's behavior that seemed to suggest a nascent understanding of the future. For example, the mother of a 24-month-old boy reported the following: "One day I said to him, 'Tomorrow we are going to the zoo.' All of a sudden he ran to his room, laid down on his bed and closed his eyes—it seemed like he was thinking it would be tomorrow and we could go to the zoo when he opened his eyes" (Benson, 1994, p. 386).

The Development of Future-Oriented Processes Questionnaire provides more systematic data about the development of these types of behaviors. This questionnaire is filled out by the child's parent and contains two parts: one that focuses on the contextual factors in the family that may contribute to an understanding of the future and one that focuses on the child's behavior across various domains conceptualized as involving an understanding of the future. Questions in the family-context section seek to address parental beliefs about what the child understands about the future and parental theories of how the child will acquire knowledge about the future. Because we are more interested in the behavior of the child, we focus our discussion on the second part of this questionnaire. This section of the questionnaire assesses six domains of future understanding: Order, Routines, Planning, Expectation, Time, and Problem Solving. Parents are asked to rate the items in each of these domains on a 4-point scale that ranges from *very true* to *not at all true*. The Order domain assesses children's understanding of sequences; a sample question from this domain is, "My child understands that some things must happen before other things." The Routines domain includes items such as "My child goes through the same routine every night before bed." The Planning domain measures children's ability to prepare for the future, as captured in the item "My child does things that show preparation for the future (e.g., my child gets a toy to take to Grandma's)." The Expectation domain assesses the different types of expectations that children form from their daily experiences, for example, the item "My child knows what will happen later from the things that happen earlier." The Time domain assesses children's understanding of different aspects of time, such as the item "My child knows what later means (e.g., You can have a cookie later means not right now)." Finally, the Problem Solving domain looks at children's flexibility, goal orientation, and use of social agents in their problem solving, as captured in the following item: "My child will try to get a toy she or he wants even if it is way across the room."

In an initial study (Benson, 1994), this questionnaire was given to 68 sets of parents whose children were within 2 weeks of one of the following six ages: 9, 12, 18, 24, 30, and 36 months. The parent who spent the most time with the child was asked to complete the questionnaire; in most cases this was the child's mother. Results from the second part of the questionnaire (i.e., child's behavior) indicated that it had successfully captured changes in behavior between 12 and 36 months of age that seemed to reflect an understanding of the future. Parents reported high levels of child behavior at 36 months of age in the domains of Expectation, Routine, Problem Solving, and Order, but only moderate levels of planning behavior and behavior reflecting an understanding of time. The authors argued that children's poorer performance in these last two domains was not surprising, because the items in the Planning domain assess children's ability to prepare for the longer term future (i.e., later in the day) and, similarly, items in the Time domain assess whether children understand events occurring up to 1 week in the future. Nevertheless, there is a substantial increase between the ages of 12 and 36 months in both of these domains, which seems to corroborate the findings from naturalistic data showing that between 2 and 3 years of age children begin to talk about the more remote future.

Our literature review suggests that in some experimental settings, 3-year-olds experience difficulty with tasks that can be framed as requiring some understanding of the future (e.g., delay of gratification). However, it is not clear whether extraneous factors may have hindered the performance of these 3-year-olds or, even more important, the extent to which each task actually tapped an understanding of the future. To date, there is not nearly enough evidence to make a firm conclusion about 3-year-old children's understanding of the future in experimental settings. Turning to more naturalistic data, the picture that emerges is that 2- and 3-year-olds, in their talk and in their behavior, are clearly beginning to display, at the very least, a rudimentary understanding of the future. Thus, we believe that it is not unreasonable to search for the roots of an understanding of the future, and of the future self, in 3-year-old children.

Before we move on to an account of our own empirical work in this area it is worthwhile to discuss a taxonomy of "future thinking" that Haith (1997) proposed. Haith pointed out that one difficulty in studying the future lies in the fact that there exists no taxonomy for talking about it. This contrasts with the domain of past thinking, or memory, in which various subcategories have been developed, including iconic memory, short-term memory, and long-term memory. Haith conceptualized future thought as involving the following four categories: (a) the continuation of a repeating past (e.g., the ability to form an expectation of what will happen next in a set of repeating events), (b) the projection of past trends (e.g., scientific models that are based on the past, but project to an unprecedented future circumstance), (c) induction from observation (e.g., forming expectations about events on the basis of the experience of others), and (d) imagination and invention (e.g., the ability to imagine events that have never occurred before). Conceptualizing the future as based on projections or inductions from past events has also been noted by other researchers. For example, it has been argued that one of the ways in which children begin to anticipate future events is by drawing on their knowledge of scripts (Hudson, Fivush, & Kuebli, 1992; Nelson, 1991). In fact, Nelson (1991) stated that "Accounts of future events are often remarkably similar to accounts of past events, save for the temporal markers. Indeed, our expectations of future events are usually based to a large extent on our generalizations from the past" (p. 113).

Within these categorizations of future thought there is no distinction drawn between processes that involve the self to a lesser or greater extent, or even not at all. Yet we argue that this distinction is an important one to draw, and we hypothesize that thinking about the future may rely on different processes depending on whether the self is explicitly involved. Of course, we do not simply mean whether the event that is being talked about involves the self, but rather, along the lines of the distinction between "knowing" and "remembering" past events, which we discussed earlier, whether the self is projected into these events.

We draw support for this hypothesis from neuropsychological research. In particular, Tulving (1985) made some striking observations of an amnesic patient, N.N., that are relevant to the distinction concerning the involvement of the self. First, at a general level, Tulving has found that N.N. has an excellent knowledge of chronological time, so, for example, he can accurately represent the units of time and their relation to one another. It is striking, however, that his knowledge of subjective time is highly impaired, which is evidenced by his complete inability to recount what he did "yesterday" or what he will do "tomorrow." When asked questions of this nature, N.N. cannot go beyond answering them with a simple "I don't know." However, what is more interesting for the sake of our argument is the following: If N.N. is asked to recount a script—for example, a "restaurant" script—he is able to do so with ease. Yet, at the same time, he cannot recount one single past event of having gone to a restaurant! N.N. is not only unable to recall past events, but he is similarly unable to predict any future ones. When questioned about what he plans to do after leaving the laboratory, or what he will do the next day, he is unable to respond and characterizes his resultant state as "blankness." For N.N. it is impossible to conceptualize personal events, both past and future. Tulving characterized this inability as reflecting a lack of *autonoetic consciousness*, which he defined as "the kind of consciousness that mediates an individual's awareness of his or her existence and identity in subjective time extending from the personal past through the present to the personal future" (p. 1). It is clear from Tulving's characterization of N.N. that N.N.'s ability to recount a script is in a very important way *independent* from the process required to recount a personal event or to project a self-relevant future one. Similarly, we could conceptualize N.N. as having the ability to delineate events in time (as reflected by his ability to recount a script) but impaired in his ability to subjectively place himself in these events, either in the past or in the future.

If we focus specifically on N.N.'s difficulties with the future, what becomes apparent is his inability to engage in any sort of future planning. In fact, Tulving (1985) himself stated that "episodic memory and autonoetic consciousness lead to more decisive action in the present and more effective planning for the future" (p. 10), so indeed, it is not surprising that N.N. is unable to plan. In fact, Haith (1997) recently put forth the following thought piece: "Imagine an individual who has no comprehension of the future, and you have imagined a person who is unable to plan" (p. 28). However, given the findings with N.N., this statement may be too general; more precisely, it may be that a notion of the future *self* is what is necessary to be a successful planner.

If planning may in fact require one to project *oneself* into the future, then young children's planning could potentially reflect this ability and, as such, provide a good forum in which to investigate the development of the future self. It would intuitively seem that this would be the case, yet Haith (1997) made the surprising observation that, in the existing literature, the future is rarely discussed with respect to planning. This is in spite of the fact that young children's ability to think about the future may limit the level at which they can plan (Haith, 1997), thus making it a crucial variable to consider in any study involving planning in young children.

The literature that exists with respect to children's planning has included such diverse methodologies as the Tower of Hanoi (i.e., Klahr & Robinson, 1981), mazes (i.e., Gardner & Rogoff, 1990), searching behavior (i.e., Wellman, Fabricius, & Sophian, 1985), and navigating through a pretend grocery store (Gauvain & Rogoff, 1989). This research has typically not been carried out with children younger than 4 years of age and, as noted, has not been linked to children's understanding of the future. There are, however, some exceptions. For example, Wellman et al. (1985) stressed that engaging in a goal-directed sequence may be a necessary component of planning but does not on its own constitute planning. Rather, they argued, what is necessary evidence of planned action is the ability to "look ahead," a concept on which we touch later. What we can garner from Wellman et al.'s account is that planning involves thinking into the future in order to create a goal-directed action sequence. Thus, it would seem crucial in any evaluation of young children's planning to obtain evidence that they are in fact thinking into the future or, in other words, looking ahead.

What is also surprising in much of the planning research is that the tasks that children are given rarely require planning in a manner that stresses the involvement of the self. For example, in tasks such as the

Tower of Hanoi, it is unclear whether children view these as explicitly involving the self. Even in real-world planning tasks given to children younger than 4 years (i.e., Hudson & Fivush, 1991; Hudson, Shapiro, & Sosa, 1995) it is unclear whether the self is being tapped. For example, Hudson et al. (1995) assessed how 3-, 4-, and 5-year-old children planned for two types of events: "going to the store" and "going to the beach." These researchers were specifically interested in whether children's general event representations could support their planning and thus chose to assess children's planning in familiar situations. In addition to obtaining children's plans for going to the store and going to the beach, Hudson et al. were interested in obtaining the children's scripts of these two events. Thus, each child was assigned to either a script condition or a planning condition. More interesting for our purposes is the planning condition. In this condition, children were first provided with a model plan for going to the zoo and, after hearing this, were required to provide their own plans for going to the beach and for going grocery shopping. Results indicated that the 3-year-olds provided fewer information units (e.g., "you go there," "you swim," etc.) in their plans than did the older children, and in general their plans were found to rely heavily on scripted knowledge.

   Although this task was set in a "real-world" context, there is at least one reason why the actual involvement of the self is unclear. The model plan for going to the zoo that Hudson et al. (1995) presented to children was quite similar to a script. For example, the pronoun *you* was used throughout (e.g., "You have to get up early. And you have to bring your lunch and camera. And you have to buy tickets to go in..." p. 996). The use of the pronoun *you* may have contributed to the fact that the children's plans that are provided in the Appendix of the article also predominantly included the pronoun *you*. In fact, the use of *you* in the model plan may have led children to adopt a more impersonal mode in their planning. Relating this back to the distinction with N.N., if children were in fact structuring their plans similarly to how they would structure a script, then it is unclear whether the self was truly involved. It is interesting that there is at least one example given in which a child used *I* in a plan, but because children were assigned to either a planning condition or a script condition, and not both, it would be impossible to determine whether planning and script reports differed within children in terms of pronoun use (which could potentially be taken as evidence for differing levels of self-involvement when formulating a plan). Once again, it is difficult to determine how much of children's planning in this study was a genuine reflection of their ability to place themselves in these plans and how much was a reflection of their reliance on purely script-based information.

   What seems key then, in beginning to assess the development of the future self, is to design planning tasks that minimize script-based demands as much as possible while at the same time that maximize the involvement of the self. This was precisely the goal in our first study reported here of the emergence of a future self among 3-year-old children. Thus, in designing our planning tasks we first ensured that children's performance would not simply reflect their ability to conjure up a script for an event and then use this as the basis for a plan. In other words, we did not want to give children a planning task that would rely heavily on a script, as then it becomes unclear whether children are going beyond thinking about the future as a recurrence of the past. Our second concern was that children plan in a manner that would force them to form a representation of the self as being involved in this future event. Two final concerns related to the difficulty and verbal requirements of the task. Because there exist virtually no established paradigms in which 2- to 4-year-old children's planning abilities are assessed (Benson, 1997), we needed to develop tasks that would place both age-appropriate problem-solving and verbal demands on 3-year-old children. Although it is well established in the literature that by the second year of life children are able to order events in time, it is a much harder feat for them to actually generate a sequence of events that will lead to a goal (Benson, 1997). In fact, there is evidence from children's abilities in other domains, such as the Tower of Hanoi, that even 4-year-olds are not able to form plans that involve more than two moves (Klahr & Robinson, 1981). Indeed, in our pilot work it quickly became apparent that delineating multistep future sequences was not within the capability of 3-year-old children. As a result, we limited our planning tasks to one-step actions instead of overwhelming children with multistep ones that they would most likely have difficulty executing (and for which they would thus be very unlikely to provide a plan). Finally, we designed these tasks in a manner that would not require children to provide elaborate verbal plans. In many instances, one-word plans were sufficient.

Thirty-six 3-year-old children participated in this study: eighteen younger 3-year-olds (range 3;3 to 3;7; $M = 3;5$) and 18 older 3-year-olds (range 3;8 to 4;0; $M = 3;10$). Children were given 8 one-step planning tasks, as well as two other tasks that are not discussed here (see Atance & O'Neill, 2001). Each one-step planning task required children to execute one action to achieve the goal. Thus, children were not required to provide a plan involving a series of actions but rather of one possible action that would achieve the goal. At the beginning of the session, an Elmo puppet was introduced to children under the pretext that he needed instruction in "playing these games." Children were told they would first need to tell Elmo how to play the game and only after to show him how. Thus, for each task, Elmo first asked children "Can you tell me how you're gonna...?" Immediately after children had provided an answer, Elmo provided the following reply: "That's a good idea; can you show me?" By asking children to tell Elmo beforehand we hoped to establish whether children were in fact looking ahead, which is one of Wellman et al.'s (1985) planning criteria. The eight tasks that we discuss in this chapter were broken down into the following four categories:

Category 1: Body Action

Bell: Children were shown a bell that could be rung by pressing a knob on top. The experimenter demonstrated this action by using her hand. The children were then told that, in this game, they too should make the bell ring but that they could not use their hands. Elmo then asked children how they were going to do this (possible answer: "I'm gonna use my head"). In each task this question was repeated twice if necessary, before children were given the option of showing Elmo a solution.

Bucket: Children were shown a bucket and a Nerf ball, which were both placed on the floor by their feet. The experimenter demonstrated how the ball could be placed in the bucket by using her hand. The children were then told that in this game they should get the ball into the bucket but that they could not use their hands. Elmo then asked children how they were going to do this (possible answer: "I'm gonna use my feet").

Category 2: Action With Tool

Bunny: Children were shown a small plush bunny, and a bunny house, which were both placed on the table in front of them. The experimenter showed children how the bunny could be moved into the house by using her hand. The children were then told that they should get the bunny into the house without using their hands. At this point, children were provided with two tools: one that was more useful, a stick, and one that was less useful, a piece of string, and were told that they could use them if they wanted. Elmo then asked children how they were going to get the bunny into the house (possible answer: "I'm gonna use the stick").

Frog: Children were shown a plastic frog, which was placed at the edge of the table, and a bucket, which was placed on the floor underneath the frog. The experimenter showed the children how the frog could be pushed into the bucket, using her hand. The children were then told that they should get the frog into the bucket without using their hands. At this point, children were provided with two tools, one that was more useful, a ball, and one that was less useful, an elastic band, and children were told that they could use them if they wanted. Elmo then asked children how they were going to get the frog in the bucket (possible answer: "I'm gonna use the ball").

Category 3: Gaining Object

Box: Three boxes—red, blue, and yellow—were placed on the table in front of children. The experimenter told children that she was going to hide a sticker in the red box and then turned away from the child to do so. The experimenter turned back around and then placed the boxes back on the table in front of children. Elmo then asked children how they were going to retrieve the sticker (possible answer: "I'm gonna open it up").

Tube: A long, narrow, tube closed on one end and open on the other was shown to children, and then placed upright on the table in front of them. While the child was watching, the experimenter proceeded to drop a sticker into the upright tube. Elmo then asked children how they were going to retrieve the sticker (possible answer: "I'm gonna dump it out").

Category 4: Gaining Information

Water: Children were shown a bowl of water, and then Elmo asked them how they were going to find out if the water was cold or warm (possible answer: "I'm gonna put my finger in").

Ball: Children were shown a small rubber ball, and then Elmo asked them how they were going to find out if the ball was squishy or hard (possible answer: "I'm gonna squish it").

Thus, in all of these tasks children were asked to provide a verbal description of a future action that involved the self. Script-based demands were reduced in these tasks, as it was presumed that these were situations that children would have rarely, if ever, encountered. At the very end of the test session, children were administered the Test of Early Language Development–2 (TELD–2; Hresko, Reid, & Hammill, 1991) to obtain a measure of their language ability.

Children's performance on the eight planning tasks was coded along a *planning* dimension and along a *success* dimension. For the planning dimension, children received a score of 1 if they stated a means to the goal, before engaging in any goal-directed action. In addition, children's utterances had to include information about *how* to achieve the goal (see examples provided in task descriptions) as opposed to a simple intention *to* achieve the goal (e.g., "I'm gonna get it"). However, we did not require that children's plans be linguistically complex. So for example, in the bucket task, children were awarded a score of 1 if their plan simply contained the word *feet*. Examples of children's plans are provided in

TABLE 7.1
Sample Plans

Task	Plan
Bell	"Use my head" (4;0)
Bucket	"By using my feet" (3;7)
Box	"I'm gonna open up the box" (3;7)
Tube	"Dump it out" (3;10)
Water	"I'm just going to touch the water and see if it's cold or hot" (3;5)
Ball	"By squeezing it" (3;8)

Note. Numbers in parentheses are children's ages.

Table 7.1. Finally, plans that were only provided simultaneously as the child was carrying out a goal-directed action did not qualify as plans but instead were considered a verbal account of "on-line" action and were given a score of 0. If children did not state how they would achieve the goal, or provided a statement that did not meet the criteria presented above, then a score of 0 was also given.

Children's ability to execute a successful action (i.e., an action that was successful in achieving the goal) for each task was considered separately from their ability to provide a plan. For the success dimension children were given a score of 1 if they were able to achieve the goal (e.g., place the ball into the bucket without using their hands, retrieve the sticker from the tube, etc.). If children were not able to achieve the goal, then they received a score of 0. Thus, it was possible to obtain a score of 1 on either of these two dimensions without necessarily obtaining a score of 1 on the other. For example, if a child was unable to provide a plan, but was able to execute a successful action, then he or she was awarded a score of 1 on the action dimension and a score of 0 on the planning dimension.

The first dimension we analyzed was children's ability to provide a plan. First, to determine whether these tasks were appropriate for children in the 3-year-old age range, we required that at least 50% of the older 3-year-olds provide a plan on any given task. The percentage of younger and older children who planned across the eight tasks is shown in Table 7.2. Older 3-year-olds did not reach a planning criterion of 50%

TABLE 7.2
Percentage of Younger and Older Children Who Provided a Plan

Age	Trial							
	Bell	Bucket	Bunny	Frog	Box	Tube	Water	Ball
Younger	22	44	28	22	28	22	28	22
Older	72	78	39	39	50	67	72	50

TABLE 7.3
Percentage of Younger and Older Children Who Succeeded

Age	Trial					
	Bell	Bucket	Box	Tube	Water	Ball
Younger	50	39	100	78	89	50
Older	94	50	94	100	100	89

in either of the two tool tasks, and so we did not include these in any of the remaining analyses.

To determine if there was an age effect in children's planning, we conducted a 2-way repeated measures analysis of variance (ANOVA age by task). This analysis revealed a main effect of age only, such that across the six tasks older children provided a significantly greater number of plans than did younger children, $F(1, 34) = 14.56$, $p = .001$. The percentage of younger and older children who were successful in achieving the goal across the six tasks is shown in Table 7.3. A repeated measures ANOVA revealed significant main effects of age, $F(1, 34) = 11.86$, $p = .022$, in the expected direction; and of task, $F(1, 34) = 12.24$, $p < .001$; but these were qualified by a significant Age by Task interaction, $F(1, 34) = 2.72$, $p = .022$. The Age by Task interaction suggests that the younger children may have had difficulty achieving the goal in some of the tasks and thus were precluded from providing a plan. However, it is important to note that on the box, tube, and water tasks the younger children's success rates were 100%, 78%, and 89%, respectively. Thus, it is arguable that, at least on these tasks, younger children were evidencing difficulty in their planning per se, even when they were able to successfully achieve the goal. This difficulty is less pronounced in the older children. It appears that the older 3-year-olds in this study were often able to provide plans and, more important, were able to do so in contexts that were not completely familiar to them (i.e., were not script based). Thus, it appears that children's planning abilities are showing some improvement during the fourth year of life, although this claim must be qualified by the fact that, in some of the tasks, younger children evidenced more difficulty achieving the goal than did the older children.

In terms of language ability, older 3-year-olds obtained significantly higher scores on the TELD–2 than did the younger 3-year-olds, $F(1, 34) = 6.48$, $p = .016$. Younger children's mean score was 44.7, whereas the mean score of the older children was 49.3. To examine if a relation existed between children's language ability and their planning abilities, we computed correlations, with age partialed out, for each of the six tasks. Planning scores for four of these tasks (box, tube, ball, and water) were significantly correlated with children's scores on the TELD–2 (see Table 7.4). This indicates that children's ability to provide a plan was related to

TABLE 7.4
Correlations Between TELD–2 and Planning Scores, Controlling for Age

Task	TELD–2
Bell	.30
Bucket	.15
Box	.38*
Tube	.44*
Water	.43*
Ball	.33*

Note. TELD–2 = Test of Early Language Development–2; *p < .05.

their language abilities but was not solely governed by this factor. In fact, we argue that there were at least two reasons why it was not the case that children were limited in their planning because the language that was necessary to convey a plan was beyond their grasp. First, as a group, 94% of the younger 3-year-olds, and 83% of the older 3-year-olds, scored above average on the TELD–2. Second, the verbal plans that children were required to produce in order to score a 1 on this dimension did not need to be linguistically complex. For example, simply providing the word *feet* for the bucket task was sufficient for a child to obtain a score of 1. Rather, we believe that additional cognitive factors may have played a role in children's ability to provide a plan. We speculate as to the nature of these factors later.

We compared planning and success scores across the six tasks, and the results indicate that both younger and older 3-year-olds were more likely to successfully achieve the goal than they were to provide the corresponding plan. So, were children's planning scores related to their success scores, or were these two variables somewhat independent one from the other? To address this question, we looked at several conditional probabilities, which determine the probability that one event will occur given that some other event has also occurred. The probability that a child succeeded across the six tasks, given that he or she had not provided a plan, was .67. Thus, it is clear that planning cannot be viewed as the cause of a child's success, because children succeeded two thirds of the time when they had not provided one. Likewise, it was not the case that being able to achieve the goal was sufficient in allowing children to provide a plan. Across tasks, the probability that a child had provided a plan, given that he or she had succeeded, was .54. Were being able to achieve the goal all that was required to provide a plan, then we would expect this probability to be 1. Why, then, were children who were able to achieve the goal unable to provide a plan? In the context of our tasks, these children may have been able to exhibit their knowledge by successfully acting to obtain the goal but were unable to reflect on the current situation and project themselves the necessary one step into the future to explicitly represent the means to the goal—that is, children may not have needed to draw on the future self to succeed in our tasks. However, was it the case that children *did* need to do so in order to provide a plan?

To answer this question, it is important to consider the processes that may underlie children's ability to provide a plan. Because our tasks required only one step to obtain the goal, we believe that children may have relied on either of two processes in formulating what we coded as a plan. First, children may have looked one step into the future to contemplate an action that would achieve the goal and then provided the corresponding plan. Second, children may simply have "seen" this same action without looking one step ahead, akin to having the solution "pop into mind." In each case, the outcome is the same: Children provide what appears to be a plan and then go on to obtain the goal. What is important to note, however, is that these two *processes* are different: The first requires looking ahead to formulate a plan, whereas the second does not. One could argue that in the latter instance the child is not providing a true plan but rather an atemporal verbal solution. These two processes fit well with Searle's (1983) notion of a prior intention versus an intention-in-action, respectively (for a review of others who have made this similar type of distinction, see Astington, 1999). In the first case, an action is caused by a prior intention, such that one thinks and then acts. On the other hand, within Searle's notion of intention-in-action, the action need not be caused by a prior intention; one can simply act intentionally without having planned the act. Related to this latter instance, children in our study, for example, need not have formulated a prior intention, or plan, but may simply have had a solution pop into their minds. Thus, it is only the action itself that can be labeled intentional.

There are also linguistic data that support the distinction between a prior intention and an intention-in-action. First of all, early in development, children use terms such as *will* and *gonna* to mark their own and others' future actions (Astington, 1999), which fits well with the notion of a prior intention. However, Gee (1985) looked more closely at 3- and 4-year-old children's use of these terms and provided evidence that they are not used in the same way. Gee found that children used the term *gonna* to refer to temporally distant future events for which they had formed a mental representation. In fact, it was often the case that the event in question did not get fulfilled. Gee suggested that the use of *gonna* served to "organize certain experiences for the self by projecting them as plans" (p. 206) and that it is this activity-type of planning that functions to separate the intention (plan) from the ensuing action. It is in this sense that one can consider the intention as divorced, or dissociated, from the proposed action. This dissociation between action and intention was not found by Gee to be as marked in children's use of *will*. In fact, children's use of *will* appears to be more similar to Searle's (1983) notion of intention-in-action. Finally, this proposed dissociation between intention and action also was noted by Wellman (1990), who claimed that it is between 3 and 6 years of age that children begin to conceive of people as mentally constructing an intention, separate from the intentional act itself. In light of this distinction between a prior intention and an intention-in-action, is there any evidence in our data that children's plans were reflective of a prior intention?

To address this question we examined the linguistic constructions of children's plans. Each plan was analyzed to determine whether children had used future-oriented language. The future-oriented terms *gonna*, *will*, *can*, *have to*, and *if* appeared in children's plans. Younger children's plans included these terms 40% (12/30) of the time, whereas older children's did so 29% (20/70) of the time. More important though, is that only 20% (6/30) of the younger children's plans and 13% (9/70) of the older children's plans included the term *gonna*. This linguistic analysis does not provide compelling support for the claim that children were projecting themselves into the future in their plans. Instead, it appears that children's stance when formulating these plans may have been relatively atemporal in nature.

There are several reasons why our tasks may have, unfortunately, fostered plans that reflected only intention-in-action. First, because they involved only one step, it may have been possible for children to "see" the answer without having to look ahead to formulate a plan. It is clear that this process would not reflect Searle's (1983) notion of a prior intention, or Gee's (1985) notion of creating a mental representation of a future event. Second, a number of our tasks may have prompted such an automatic solution to the problem (e.g., box = open up) that children may have been prevented from taking the time to contemplate the action before providing their "plan."

This may imply that in order to tap children's ability to state a plan with a prior intention it is necessary to present children with situations in which the end state cannot simply be obtained by seeing the solution or by relying on an automatic response. However, this must be accomplished while remaining in the realm of one-step actions, because multistep sequences are outside of a 3-year-old's capability. To achieve this, it may be necessary to have children plan for remote, hypothetical events. We discussed elsewhere (Atance & O'Neill, 2001) a task in which children are required to anticipate future needs that are both hypothetical and remote. Because in this case the action does not get carried out, children's plans are more likely to reflect prior intentions. We believe that planning for an event that is both hypothetical and remote may be more conducive to the child formulating a mental representation of it, in a manner that precludes, for example, simply "seeing" a solution, wherein no clear boundary between intention and action may exist.

Another context in which children may find it easier to dissociate intention and action, by virtue of the social environment in which the activity is set, is drawing. For example, from early on, children are given experience stating an intention, or a plan, before they begin to draw (Gearhart & Newman, 1980). This is part of a social routine in which children's parents, teachers, and even peers solicit this type of information from them. This is in sharp contrast to the context of the one-step tasks. In the latter case, it is unlikely that children in their everyday lives are asked about their plans for such actions as opening boxes, placing balls into buckets, or tipping over tubes to obtain stickers. In fact, we are currently assessing children's planning behavior in a drawing context in the hope that this may shed some light on the development of the future self.

At this point we return to Tulving's patient, N.N., to speculate about how he would perform in the one-step tasks. We hypothesize that if N.N is able to "see" the solution to a given task, then it would be possible for him to provide this plan verbally, as this process can be achieved atemporally. In doing so, we would not expect that N.N. would use future-oriented terms such as *gonna*, but rather would provide solutions that resemble the one-word solutions that children provided (e.g., he might say "dump it out," but not "I'm gonna dump it out"). On the other hand, if N.N. does not see the solution to a given task, then we believe that he would not be able to provide a plan, as this would require him to look into the future—an ability that N.N., of course, does not possess.

At this point, Haith's (1997) statement "imagine an individual who has no comprehension of the future, and you have imagined a person who is unable to plan" (p. 28) must be qualified. In one-step planning tasks it may be possible to provide what appears to be a plan without necessarily having a corresponding understanding of the future. As we have argued, children who provided one-word solutions, such as "feet," may fit this description. Because of this, using planning tasks as a window to reveal children's understanding of the future, and of the future self in particular, is a tricky enterprise. At one extreme, multistep sequences prove too difficult for this age group, whereas at the other extreme, one-step actions may not be tapping any understanding of the future self. Although 3-year-old children may indeed have a conception of the future self, one-step planning tasks of the kind we used do not appear to be able to reveal this understanding. However, as we outlined earlier, there appear to exist several other promising methods that may successfully tap children's notion of the future self, and these are where we are currently directing our focus.

ACKNOWLEDGMENTS

This research was supported in part by a Natural Sciences and Engineering Research Council (NSERC) doctoral scholarship to Cristina M. Atance and an NSERC operating grant to Daniela K. O'Neill. We thank the parents and the children who participated in this research at the Centre for Child Studies at the University of Waterloo, Waterloo, Ontario, Canada.

REFERENCES

Anglin, J. M., Ward, L., & White, M. (1999, April). *Displaced language in mother–child discourse: Developmental and contextual effects.* Poster presented at the annual meeting of the Society for Research in Child Development, Albuquerque, New Mexico.

Astington, J. W. (1999). The language of intention: Three ways of doing it. In P. D. Zelazo, J. W. Astington, & D. R. Olson (Eds.), *Developing theories of intention: Social understanding and self control* (pp. 295–315). Mahwah, NJ: Lawrence Erlbaum Associates.

Atance, C. M., & O'Neill, D. K. (2001). *Thinking about real and pretend possibilities: Preschoolers' developing notion of the future.* Manuscript in preparation.

Bauer, P. J., & Thal, D. J. (1990). Scripts or scraps: Reconsidering the development of sequential understanding. *Journal of Experimental Child Psychology, 50,* 287–304.

Benson, J. B. (1994). The origins of future orientation in the everyday lives of 9- to 36-month-old infants. In M. M. Haith, J. B. Benson, R. J. Roberts, Jr., & B. F. Pennington (Eds.), *The development of future-oriented processes* (pp. 375–407). Chicago: University of Chicago Press.

Benson, J. B. (1997). The development of planning: It's about time. In S. L. Friedman & E. K. Scholnick (Eds.), *The developmental psychology of planning: Why, how, and when do we plan?* (pp. 43–74). Mahwah, NJ: Lawrence Erlbaum Associates.

Eisenberg, A. R. (1985). Learning to describe past experiences in conversation. *Discourse Processes, 8,* 177–204.

Friedman, W. J. (1990). Children's representations of the pattern of daily activities. *Child Development, 61,* 1399–1412.

Gardner, W., & Rogoff, B. (1990). Children's deliberateness of planning according to task circumstances. *Developmental Psychology, 26,* 480–487.

Gauvain, M., & Rogoff, B. (1989). Collaborative problem solving and children's planning skills. *Developmental Psychology, 25,* 139–151.

Gearhart, M., & Newman, D. (1980). Learning to draw a picture: The social context of an individual activity. *Discourse Processes, 3,* 169–184.

Gee, J. (1985). An interpretive approach to the study of modality: What child language can tell the linguist. *Studies in Language, 9,* 197–229.

Haith, M. M. (1997). The development of future thinking as essential for the emergence of skill in planning. In S. L. Friedman & E. K. Scholnick (Eds.),

The developmental psychology of planning: Why, how, and when do we plan? (pp. 25–42). Mahwah, NJ: Lawrence Erlbaum Associates.

Haith, M. M., & Benson, J. B. (1992). *Development of future-oriented processes questionnaire.* Unpublished instrument, University of Denver.

Hresko, W. P., Reid, D. K., & Hammill, D. D. (1991). *The Test of Early Language Development (TELD–2).* Austin, TX: Pro-Ed.

Hudson, J. A., & Fivush, R. (1991). Planning in the preschool years: The emergence of plans from general knowledge. *Cognitive Development, 6,* 393–415.

Hudson, J. A., Fivush, R., & Kuebli, J. (1992). Scripts and episodes: The development of event memory. *Applied Cognitive Psychology, 6,* 483–505.

Hudson, J. A., Shapiro, L. R., & Sosa, B. B. (1995). Planning in the real world: Preschool children's scripts and plans for familiar events. *Child Development, 66,* 984–998.

Klahr, D., & Robinson, M. (1981). Formal assessment of problem-solving and planning processes in preschool children. *Cognitive Psychology, 13,* 113–148.

Moore, C. (Chair). (1997, April). *The development of a temporally extended self.* Paper symposium conducted at the biennial meeting of the Society for Research in Child Development, Washington, DC.

Nelson, K. (1989). *Narratives from the crib.* Cambridge, MA: Harvard University Press.

Nelson, K. (1991). Remembering and telling: A developmental story. *Journal of Narrative and Life History, 1,* 109–127.

O'Connell, B. G., & Gerard, A. B. (1985). Scripts and scraps: The development of sequential understanding. *Child Development, 56,* 671–681.

Perner, J., & Ruffman, T. (1995). Episodic memory and autonoetic consciousness: Developmental evidence and a theory of childhood amnesia. *Journal of Experimental Child Psychology, 59,* 516–548.

Povinelli, D. J. (1995). The unduplicated self. In P. Rochat (Ed.), *The self in infancy: Theory and research* (pp. 161–192). Amsterdam: Elsevier.

Sachs, J. (1983). Talking about the there and then: The emergence of displaced reference in parent–child discourse. In K. Nelson (Ed.), *Children's language* (Vol. 4, pp. 1–28). Hillsdale, NJ: Lawrence Erlbaum Associates.

Searle, J. R. (1983). *Intentionality: An essay in the philosophy of mind.* Cambridge, England: Cambridge University Press.

Thompson, C., Barresi, J., & Moore, C. (1997). The development of future-oriented prudence and altruism in preschoolers. *Cognitive Development, 12,* 199–212.

Tulving, E. (1985). Memory and consciousness. *Canadian Psychology, 26,* 1–12.

Tulving, E., Schacter, D. L., McLachlan, D. R., & Moscovitch, M. (1988). Priming of semantic and autobiographical knowledge: A case study of retrograde amnesia. *Brain and Cognition, 8,* 3–20.

Wellman, H. M. (1990). *The child's theory of mind.* Cambridge, MA: MIT Press.

Wellman, H. M., Fabricius, W. V., & Sophian, C. (1985). The early development of planning. In H. M. Wellman (Ed.), *Children's searching* (pp. 123–149). Hillsdale, NJ: Lawrence Erlbaum Associates.

8

Extending Self-Consciousness Into the Future

John Barresi
Dalhousie University

As adults we have little difficulty thinking of ourselves as mental beings extended in time. Even though our conscious thoughts and experiences are constantly changing, we think of ourselves as the same self throughout these variations in mental content. Indeed, it is so natural for adults to think this way that it was not until the 18th century—at least in Western thought—that the issue of how we come to acquire such a concept of an identical but constantly changing self was first recognized as a problem that required an explanation. Philosophical discussion of this issue was initiated when John Locke (1694/1975) proposed a notion of personal identity and selfhood based on consciousness:

> For since consciousness always accompanies thinking, and 'tis that, that makes every one to be, what he calls *self*; and thereby distinguishes himself from all other thinking things, in this alone consists *personal Identity*, i.e. the sameness of a rational Being: And as far as this consciousness can be extended backwards to any past Action or Thought, so far reaches the Identity of that *Person*; it is the same *self* now it was then; and 'tis by the same *self* with this present one that now reflects on it, that that Action was done. (p. 335)

According to this view, we are the same self insofar as we can consciously accept as our own not only those mental and physical acts that we perform *now* but also those acts done in the *past*, that we can

141

recollect as our own. This Lockean view of self based on consciousness was an advance beyond Descartes's (1641/1984) notion that the self was an immaterial soul or mind, whose identity was guaranteed not by being conscious of itself but by being a substance distinct from the body. However, Locke's (1694/1975) more empirical approach to personal identity and self raised a new question: How do we come to form the notion of this conscious self that is extended in time? Some progressive followers of Locke—such as Hume (1739/1888)—believed that our notion of an *identical* extended self is, in fact, a fiction. On this view there is no *actual* mental self that is identical through time, merely an *illusion* of such an identical self. Although this suggestion was an important advance toward a strictly psychological account of the origins of our concept of self, Hume did not focus on the developmental problem of how or when this fictional notion of an identical but extended mental self is formed. It was not until 1805, when William Hazlitt, the well-known English Romantic critic, published *An Essay on the Principles of Human Action* (Hazlitt, 1805/1969; Martin & Barresi, 1995, 2000), that a truly developmental account of the formation of the concept of an extended self was first proposed.

Unlike Locke, who focused his account of the extended self on our self-conscious recollection of the past, Hazlitt was more interested in our relation to the future. Why should we be concerned about a self, whom we might become in the future? In what sense is this future self, with its different motives and goals, the *same* self that we are now and have been in the past? And how do we come to believe that it is the same self as the present and past self? In other words, how do we form a notion of a changing mental self that extends not only into the past but also into the future?

In attempting to answer these questions, Hazlitt (1805/1969) put forward a fascinating hypothesis concerning the development of the concept of a self that extended into the future. Hazlitt felt that, unlike our relationship to our present and past selves, which depend on causal relations of sensation and memory, our relationship to our future selves can depend only on *imagination*, because we can have no causal relations working backward from our future to our present selves. For Hazlitt, an important consequence that follows from this assumption is that we can have no *necessary* interest in *any* future self. All interest in our future selves must be mediated by imagination, which is our only connection with the future. However, imagination, which connects us to the future interests or motivations of ourselves, can operate no differently, *at least initially*, when imagining our *own* future interests than it can when imagining the future interests of *another* person. Hence, he concluded that, insofar as we make voluntary choices and reflect on future interests or desires, we are not "naturally" self-interested. All self-interestedness involving our future selves must be acquired through experience. Before such self-interest is acquired we have no more present concern about the interests or desires of our future selves than about those of any other person.

In addition to his hypothesis about the origins of a future-oriented *extended self* Hazlitt also recognized, as a developmental problem, the issue of how we come to know ourselves as selves *at all*. He believed that one could know one's self as a self only if one could discriminate one's own thoughts or mental states from those of another and that making this discrimination required knowing that another individual was also a *self*. Learning to distinguish one's own emotions, motives, and other mental states is an achievement that implies forming a distinction between self and other, where previously no such distinction was made.

Hazlitt's ontogenetic perspective on the origins of self-concepts has found a parallel in recent developmental studies. His suggestion about the origin of the concept of the self receives support from some recent theories that claim that infants become aware of shared mental states before distinguishing their own mental states from those of others (e.g., Barresi, 2000; Barresi & Moore, 1993, 1996). For instance, in the area of emotions it is only after the first year of life that infants begin to distinguish their own original emotions from those that they experience contagiously from others (Hoffman, 1976). Furthermore, evidence suggests that it is not until the end of the second year of life that the child begins to exhibit clear signs of self-consciousness (Barresi & Moore, 1996, for a review). This evidence includes self-recognition in a mirror task; self-conscious emotions, such as embarrassment, that imply a reflexive self-awareness; and linguistic differentiation of self and other. However, this acquired self-consciousness involves only the here and now. This suggests that the infant has achieved only a concept of a *present* or *now self*, which—because of the infant's lack of awareness of its temporal and changing properties—is treated as if it were an unchanging, or permanent, self.

It is not until children are past 3 and closer to 4 years old that they begin to show evidence of a self-consciousness that extends through time. Most of the research that provides evidence of this shift in self-consciousness has focused on the child's ability to remember past events in a serial fashion and to integrate the past with the present (cf. Gopnik & Slaughter, 1991; Nelson, 1992, chap. 2, this volume; Perner, 1992, chap. 10, this volume; Perner & Ruffman, 1995; Povinelli, 1995, chap. 5, this volume). For instance, the child at this time acquires the ability to recognize him- or herself in videotapes taken earlier in a way that indicates an understanding of how past events involving the self relate to one's self in the present. This videotape task is particularly interesting because of its analogy to the mirror recognition task. Povinelli has shown that 3-year-olds are perfectly competent at recognizing themselves in the replay of a recent video (Povinelli, 1995; chap. 5, this volume). However, young 3-year-olds fail to appreciate the relation between stickers placed on their heads in a recent video and the possibility that the stickers might still be there. If they remove the stickers on seeing a video of the stickers being placed on their heads, it does not seem to matter to them whether the video was taken a few minutes earlier or a week earlier. Older 3-year-olds are more sensitive to this variation in video timing and more likely overall to remove the sticker immediately on seeing the video. Although this task alone might not indicate the development of a temporally extended self-consciousness, it is during this same period that the child begins to show autobiographical knowledge of past events and becomes capable of recalling past mental states of self. Taken together, these results suggest that a shift in self-consciousness has occurred, from one involving a permanent "present" or "now" self to one involving a concept of a temporally extended, ever-changing self—what Neisser (1988) calls the *extended self*.

To date, the bulk of this research on the temporally extended self has focused on extensions of self into the past, much as Locke originally posed the problem of personal identity. It has not dealt with extensions of self into the future. In this chapter I describe some research that focuses on our relations to future selves. In this research we pursued Hazlitt's suggestion that the use of imagination with respect to future mental states of self and other is—at least initially—symmetrical, and that, as a result, future-oriented prudence and future-oriented altruism ought to develop concurrently. Furthermore, we took the position that Hazlitt's theory of imagination is analogous to current simulation accounts of theory of mind (e.g., Harris, 1991), which implies that the development of future-oriented prudence and altruism ought to emerge around 4 years of age. After briefly describing these experiments, which have been more fully reported elsewhere (Moore, Barresi, & Thompson, 1998; Thompson, Barresi, & Moore, 1997), I use some findings from these experiments as a basis from which to develop a theoretical account of the emergence of extended self-consciousness.

EXTENDING THE SELF INTO THE FUTURE

The basic paradigm that we used in this research was Mischel's delay-of-gratification choice procedure (Mischel, 1974; Thompson et al., 1997). However, the rewards were stickers that could be placed in a sticker book immediately or later, after the sticker choice activity was finished. Furthermore, the children who were tested were asked to make decisions that would affect another person as well as themselves.

On the basis of Hazlitt's view that imaginative projection into a future self and other are analogous, and that children have a natural sympathy toward others as well as toward self, we built the study design to measure how children would acquire concepts about the future, when both self and other were involved. The general hypothesis that we entertained in the first experiment was that younger children would prefer immediate rewards to delayed rewards and that this would occur for choices involving the self alone as well as involving self and other.

The four choice conditions about which the child had to make decisions were:

1. *Shared-gratification condition without cost*: The child had to choose between having one sticker for the self now, or one sticker for the other person as well as the self now.

2. *Shared-gratification condition with cost*: The child had to choose between having two stickers for the self now or one sticker for the other and one for the self now.

3. *Delay-of-self-gratification condition (or future-oriented prudence)*: The child had to choose between one sticker now for the self or two stickers later for the self.

4. *Delay-of-shared-gratification condition (or future-oriented altruism)*: The child had to choose between one sticker now for the self or one sticker each later for the self and the other.

Each child received three blocks of choices; each block had one of each of these four choice conditions.

We anticipated that all children (3-, 4-, and 5-year-olds) would prefer having both self and other receive rewards over the self alone because it has been shown that even 2-year-olds exhibit empathy toward others. However, this preference was expected to extend only to present sharing and not to future sharing for young children. We anticipated that only the older children would be willing to forgo a present reward for the self in favor of a larger reward in the future and that this preference would apply to conditions involving the self alone, thus implying prudence, as well as self and other, thus implying altruism.

As shown in Fig. 8.1, these hypotheses were confirmed by the results of the experiment. Out of three trials of the same type, all groups showed a preference for shared reward in the present over self-alone rewards in the present, and this did not vary as a function of age. More important, 3-year-olds, but not 4- or 5-year-olds, preferred present to future rewards, whether this involved increased future rewards for self alone or for self and other. Furthermore, there was a correlation of responses between these two delayed reward choice conditions for 3-year-olds, but not for the older children.

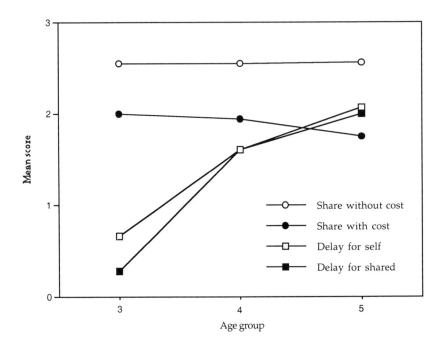

FIG. 8.1 Mean share or delay scores for different choices in sticker-choice task for three age groups in Experiment 1. The choice conditions are: share without cost (one sticker for self now vs. one sticker for each now), share with cost (two stickers for self now vs. one sticker for each now), delay for self (one sticker for self now vs. two stickers for self later), delay for shared (one sticker for self now vs. one each later).

These results support the hypothesis that it was the factor of delay that caused a problem for younger but not for older children. They suggest that 3-year-olds, although capable of dealing with the mental states of self and other in the present, are not able to make decisions that would be preferred by their own future self or the future self of another person. In terms of consciousness, the 3-year-olds show evidence of being conscious of their own immediate or present desires as well as of the supposed immediate desires of the other, but they fail to have any empathy for their own future self or the future self of the other. Apparently, they are not yet conscious of the self or other as extended in time, with desires that can conflict between selves from different times.

I want now to discuss two other experiments that my colleagues and I conducted (Moore et al., 1998) that bear on the issue of how 3-year-olds come to form a concept of a self that extends through time. It seemed to us that two mechanisms might be involved: First, children's ability to represent to themselves mental states of self and other that conflict with their own current mental states, and second, children's ability to engage in executive decision making that requires inhibition of responses based on the children's own current desires in order to make future-oriented choices. Both of these abilities have been shown to develop during the fourth year of life.

In both of the follow-up experiments we included the sticker-choice task, and replicated the two conditions from the first experiment that involved the future, but we varied the other two conditions. In the other two conditions of the second experiment the children were asked to make choices for the other person rather than for themselves, but this involved the same two future choice conditions—prudence and altruism—only now for the other person (see Choice Conditions column in Table 8.1). In addition, in this experiment we assessed the child's ability to perform on three theory-of-mind tasks (False Belief; Representational Change, and Desire Change). In all three tasks the children (old 3-year-olds and young 4-year-olds) were first exposed to a situation in which they initially believed or desired one thing about an object and, later, believed or desired a conflicting thing about the same object. In the self-change tasks (Representational Change and Desire Change) they were asked about their former belief or desire. In the other belief task (False Belief) they were asked to guess what another person naïve to the original situation would think. The critical aspect of all three tasks is that the children's own current mental states after they acquired knowledge of the object, or fulfilled their initial desire, would conflict with their prior mental states, which—in the case of belief—would be the normal naïve state of another person.

The results of this experiment replicated the findings showing a developmental change in children's ability, during the fourth year, to

TABLE 8.1
Experiment 2 Choice Conditions and Correlations With
Composite Measures of Theory of Mind

	Choice Condition	*Theory-of-Mind Tasks*
Self	One for self now vs. 2 for self later	
	One for self now vs. 1 for each later	Correlated with choice condition in 4-year-olds
Other	One for other now vs. 2 for other later	Correlated with choice condition in 4-year-olds
	One for other now vs. 1 for each later	Correlated with choice condition in 4-year-olds

deal with the future in the choice conditions involving the self. Again, we found a correlation between prudence and altruism choices involving the future in the group of old 3-year-olds tested in this experiment. We also found that all the children had trouble dealing with the choice task when it involved choices for another person rather than for the self. It is interesting, however, that we found that the young 4-year-old's performance on this task was correlated with their ability at theory-of mind-tasks (see Table 8.1, which shows a similar correlation for the future-oriented altruism condition).

What these results suggest is that the ability to do theory-of-mind tasks may be a necessary skill for children to be able fully to imagine another person's choice situation, when that involves the future. As I argue later, however, these results can also be interpreted as indicating that it is only 4-year-olds who have a sufficiently rich and stable concept of the extended self to be able to make choices requiring simulation of the point of view of the extended self of another person. By contrast, the ability to make such choices for the self, and the origins of the extended self, seems to develop at an earlier time and may even precede the development of a theory of mind. But how does the child come to form this concept of his or her own self as extended? And how might it contribute to the development of a theory of mind? I believe our third experiment (Moore et al., 1998) speaks to this issue.

In the third experiment we (Moore et al., 1998) again replicated the two future-choice conditions previously tested but added two new future choice conditions: a choice condition involving a decision between one for each now or two for the self later and another requiring a decision between two for the other now or one for the self later (see Table 8.2). The children (young 3-year-olds, old-3-year-olds, and young-4-year-olds) were also tested on the "windows" task, an executive function task that normal children learn to pass around the middle of the fourth year (Russell, Mauthner, Sharpe, & Tidswell, 1991). The windows

TABLE 8.2
Experiment 3 Choice Conditions and
Correlations With Executive Function Task

	Choice Condition	*Executive Function Task*
Old	One for self now vs. 2 for self later (conflict) One for self now vs. 1 for each later (conflict)	Correlated with choice condition in young 3-year-olds Correlated with choice condition in young 3-year-olds
New	One for each now vs. 2 for self later (conflict) Two for other now vs. 1 for self later (no conflict)	Correlated with choice condition in young 3-year-olds

task requires the child to learn a rule according to which they have to point to an empty box in order to acquire the reward in another similar box. Russell et al. (1991) showed that all children in this age range can learn the rule and follow it when the contents of the boxes are not visible at the time of pointing. When they are switched to boxes with windows, however, the younger children fail to generalize their performance. It seems that they cannot inhibit their natural tendency to point to the box with the visible reward, although they are able, verbally, to describe the rule requiring them to point at the empty box in order to obtain the reward.

We replicated these findings in the present experiment. Most young 3-year-olds, but few older children, failed at the windows task. More important, we found that only for the young 3-year-olds did performance on the windows task correlate with their performance on any of the sticker-choice tasks (see Table 8.2). For the three conditions in which the child had to make a choice involving conflict between current and future rewards for self, their preference for the delayed but larger future rewards correlated with their ability to point to the empty window in order to obtain rewards in the windows task. The one choice condition that didn't correlate with performance on the windows task was the condition in which the choice was between a current reward for the other and a future reward for self—a condition that did not produce conflict and in which most children chose the future reward for self.

EXTENDING SELF-CONSCIOUSNESS

The results of these three experiments provide evidence that children acquire the ability to deal with future mental states of self and other in choice situations involving prudence and altruism during the age-4 transition. These results also suggest the possibility that there are at least two independent skills involved in acquiring this ability to deal with future mental states of self and other. The first of these skills is an executive capacity that allows the child to inhibit responding to current desires in order to obtain future rewards. This skill, which appears to develop during the early part of the fourth year, directly affects all decisions involving conflict between current and future-oriented desires of self. The second skill is the ability to imagine or think about the future desires of another self or person as well as the ability to think about another person's decision processes in choice situations similar to those that the younger child can already handle for him or herself. This latter skill arises somewhat later—possibly as late as in young 4-year-olds. I would now like to speculate on the meaning of these results, in conjunction with other findings relating to the age-4 transition, for the development of an extended conception of self.

What is remarkable about the changes that occur around the fourth year of life with respect to the self is that children become able to treat their own past and future selves as if these selves were other persons, with points of view different from their current self. With respect to the past, children can now remember having had experiences that differ from those that they have at present. With respect to the future, as the present research suggests, they can anticipate having experiences that they do not have at present. As Hazlitt's (1805/1969) hypothesis suggests, this is not accomplished by imagining being the very same self that one is now but located in the past or future. Instead, it is accomplished by imagining being an altogether different self, who exists at a different time, with a different perspective on things. Hazlitt suggested that there is an asymmetry between past and future with respect to the present self, where the past involves memory and a causal relation, whereas the future requires imagination. But Hazlitt, who often mentioned the use of imagination with respect to the past as well as the future, was not always consistent in his view on how one relates to "other" selves in the past as well as in the future. Hence, a more detailed analysis than he presented is required.

Consider first the future. A person might anticipate having certain experiences in the future without having to consider possible differences between his or her current and future selves. In such a case the role of imagination is limited to simulating a future situation without changing one's attitude about that situation. For instance, in the present-choice task children might imagine what it would be like to make a choice that results in immediately receiving a sticker to place in their sticker book. In such a case the children's desire for the sticker will be immediately gratified, thus their imagining that gratification following the choice requires no adjustment in their desires—no imagining of different desires of future selves. On the other hand, they may try to imagine themselves in a future situation, where their own viewpoint is itself changed in that context from the viewpoint that they currently have. Thus, children in the choice task might try to imagine getting many stickers at the end of the sticker game if they make the delayed choices now. In this case it won't do to imagine making a choice that is immediately gratified with a sticker or several stickers to put in the book. They must imagine making a choice that leads immediately to no stickers and hence, not satisfy their immediate desire, but which nevertheless will eventually make them happy—but only after they, themselves, have changed. It is only in this latter kind of situation that one is truly imagining a future self as an "other." It is only in this situation that a person makes a distinction between his or her own current point of view, his or her *now* self, who will not be immediately gratified by the decision, and a *future* self, who will be so gratified yet with whom he or she might still be able to identify.

The same distinction applies to one's possible relations to the past. On the one hand, one can remember particular events and happenings as if one were there but as the same self that one is at the moment. For instance, children in the sticker task might remember getting stickers on previous occasions, after making a nondelayed choice, and of not receiving a sticker when they make a delayed choice. Now, if they are still in the midst of making choices, their attitude to these two types of situation won't have changed very much. They will remember the nondelayed choices followed by gratification with a more positive feeling than the delayed choices. On the other hand, one can recollect having had certain experiences, from the point of view of a past self, while at the same time having a distinct current personal viewpoint that differs from this past self. This could happen to some of the older children at the end of the sticker game, when they receive the delayed rewards. At that time, they might recall originally being unhappy about their delayed choices and happy about their nondelayed choices but now feeling happy about the delayed choices and unhappy about the nondelayed choices. In this situation the person or child distinguishes how things seem to him or her now from how they seemed to him or her in the past. Whereas in the past he or she had one attitude toward the situation, now he or she can recall having had that attitude but not currently feeling the same way about the situation.

To appreciate the processes involved in memory of past events it is important to consider several distinctions. One distinction is that between reliving an event and remembering it. In reliving an event, one re-experiences the past from the point of view of the past self, entirely forgetful of the present self. In the example just considered, this would involve re-experiencing the choice made in the past from the point of view that one had in the past but not noticing that this is a memory, rather than a re-experiencing, of the past event. In remembering it, one recalls what happened in the past, but one realizes that the event occurred in the past while also maintaining one's present point of view. However, remembering also takes several forms. One of these forms happens when one remembers the past event as an occurrence rather than as an experience. If children at the end of the game merely remembered that they previously made very few delayed choices, without remembering their experience of making those choices, they would have this kind of memory of the past. In this case they might now feel sorry about the choices they made then, without remembering that at the time they felt quite differently about the choices. When a person both remembers what happened and how he or she experienced that happening at the time, we say he or she recollects his or her past. This is the kind of self-conscious memory that Locke (1694/1975) described as essential to personal identity. In such a recollection of the past one distinguishes between how one experienced the event then and how it appears to one now, and one can appreciate both past and present points of view as distinct. Yet both viewpoints are conceived as phases in the personal history of the same temporally extended self. In a sense, recollection involves a kind of empathic re-experiencing of the past while not fully identifying with this past self (see Reed, 1994; also compare Lemmon & Moore, chap. 9, and Perner, chap. 10, this volume). One must distinguish the two selves and not collapse them into either the present self or the past self yet also appreciate that they both belong to the same person, or self, as extended in time. The same distinction holds true with respect to the present and future selves. Perhaps one can imagine being some future self, a sort of "living" this future self. However, for this future self to have an independent reality from one's current self one must distinguish the two, so that they are not confused with each other, yet both are conceived to represent phases of a temporally connected person. In the case of children thinking about future rewards, they must distinguish how they will feel then about their choice now and how they feel now in making that choice. Furthermore, they must identify sufficiently with the future self that they are willing to accept current dissatisfaction in order to gratify the desires of the future self. In effect, they must see the future self not as another conflicting self but as a temporal extension of the current self into the future.

As one sees here there is a perfect symmetry in what is required to distinguish a future and a past self from the self of the present. It should be noted, however, that there is a difference—one that is congruent with Hazlitt's (1805/1969) notion of asymmetry. In the case of the past self, the imagination of that self, although in a sense reconstructive, has prior experience on which to build this reconstruction. In the case of the future self, imagination has to do the work of construction in the absence of specific memorial content. It can use past selves to help imagine a future self, but it cannot use a specific past self to build this imagined future self. Hence, it is, in some sense, surprising that the abilities to deal with past and future selves seem to develop at the same time. As Hazlitt did, one would expect that the child's ability to extend to a past self would precede his or her ability to extend to a future self, but this appears not to be the case (see Lemmon & Moore, chap. 9, this volume). I consider shortly an explanation of why this symmetry may occur.

It might seem at this point that all that is required to form a conception of an extended self is to understand that past and future selves are different from one's present self. More is required, however, and, theoretically, what remains to be dealt with is probably the most crucial part. This is the requirement that one have a conception of the present self as also temporally located—in the now. One must be able to conceive that the present point of view is no different from one in the past or in the future in being a point of view with a temporal locus, with particular experiential properties. Without this differentiation, one's consciousness of a mental self that transforms through time cannot be conceptualized. As in the case of the past and future selves, to differentiate this now self from the present self one must not "live" in the experience but obtain some psychological distance from it. And, in accomplishing this psychological distance from the now self, one not only backs off from being embedded in the present but also makes possible a conception and consciousness of a self that is extended in time. From the point of view of this extended self-concept the current now self is seen as only a phase of a self that extends from the past through the present and into the future (cf. Nagel, 1970). In a very real sense, the child thus creates a new level of personal unity and self-consciousness, one where the immediate motives and points of view of past, present, and future selves are all treated on a par—each with a right to demand allegiance of the newly created extended self, but none with any special priority over the others.

THE DEVELOPMENT OF THE EXTENDED SELF

How does this conception of the origins of an extended self relate to the present research? One possible interpretation, depicted in Table 8.3, is that there are three phases in the development of an extended self. During the first phase the child must develop sufficient self-consciousness to separate him or herself from his or her current immediate motives and to inhibit responding to a potent stimulus based on immediate desires. What emerges here is an ability to distance oneself from one's immediate desires, by taking up the stance of a reflexively aware self rather than that of an impulse motivated self. During the second phase this reflexively aware self then develops more generally into an extended self and concurrently develops a general theory of

TABLE 8.3
Three Temporal Phases With Approximate Ages
in the Development of an Extended Self.

Young 3s	Old 3s	Young 4s
Becomes reflexively aware of current mental states in the process of learning to inhibit making responses based on immediate desires; acquires the ability to imagine mental states in conflict with current mental states	Can now use the ability to imagine mental states in conflict with own current states, to form a concept of self as extended, and becomes better at making future choices for self; also begins to form an abstract theory of mind	Becomes efficient at theory of mind and has abstract theory of an extended self, thus can now imagine the future-choice situation for the extended self of another person

mind. Children develop not only a distancing awareness of their own current point of view of reality but also the ability to compare this current point of view with other points of view, including those from their own past and anticipated future as well as those of others. Indeed, even the memory of past mental states may depend on first developing this capacity for reflexive awareness of current mental states as modes of experience or points of view of internal and external objects. These current states of reflective awareness then become the objects of memory, those objects of episodic memory, which tell us how we experienced things in the past (cf. Perner, chap. 10, this volume; Perner & Ruffman, 1995; Tulving, 1985; Wheeler, Stuss, & Tulving, 1997). The current states, from which the child has acquired some psychological distance, might also, through memory and imagination, provide the child with models for how he or she might feel in the future under changing circumstances. Because the development of such a reflexive awareness is a necessary condition for developing a more general notion of ourselves and others as mental beings extended in time, this reflexive awareness would develop somewhat earlier than the more general theory of a mental agent extended in time. The development of such a general theory of an extended mental self would then represent the third phase of development. In partial agreement with these speculations, delay choices were correlated in Experiment 3 with executive function only in young 3-year-olds, whereas delay choices involving others were correlated in Experiment 2 with theory-of-mind tasks only in young 4-year-olds.

However, it is important to note that the two processes—reflexive awareness and the ability to imagine alternative states of mind—that I represent here as being part of the first and second phases of development cannot develop entirely independently of each other. In order to gain some distance from one's current mental state to view it objectively, one must be motivated to reflect on it and have some means by which to begin to conceptualize it. If one attends to the situations in executive function tasks, such as the window task, and the choice task, we can get some idea of what motivates reflection and how "other" minds are sometimes implicated.

In the windows task it is probably an internal conflict within the child, rather than a conflict involving another self, that is at issue (Russell, Jarrold, & Potel, 1994). Even so, it can be understood as a conflict of two "minds" within the child that must become unified. The child has two dispositions to act: one that is habitual, and another that is not. What the child needs to "control" in this situation is his or her habitual response that tends to dominate over the new, nonhabitual, and correct response. To do this, the child must "reflect" on his or her own habit, become aware that there is this inclination to respond in a certain way, and inhibit this response in this particular case. In effect, the child is in two states of mind about how to behave. In one state of mind the child is reflectively aware of the rule that is to be followed and is prepared to follow it. In the other of state of mind the child is not yet reflectively aware of his or her disposition to act in a certain habitual way and is prepared only to give this habitual response. In order to be able to "follow" the rule, the child must become reflectively aware not only of the rule but also of the habitual response. The child must achieve a unity of mind—that is, a unity of self-consciousness—that can consider both alternatives at once and follow the rule while concurrently inhibiting the habitual response. In doing so the child must become able to reflect on the inclination to respond and to turn it into a choice situation between two possible responses, with the new rule being the choice that is made (cf. Zelazo & Sommerville, chap. 12, this volume).

Now consider the choice task and see how it compares to this process. In the choice task there is again a natural inclination on the part of the child: to request the current reward, regardless of long-term consequences. At least for young children, future rewards can have current value only when they are not in conflict with other current desires. In the third experiment this happened only in the sticker-choice condition in which the children were asked to make a choice between two stickers for the other person now versus one sticker for self. This is a complex choice for children to make, if they fully empathize with the viewpoint of the other person. It is likely, however, that the children take a simpler route in this situation. If they follow self-interest and ignore the interest of the other person they can choose the option for which they get some kind of reward, although a delayed one, over the option for which they get no reward. Probably as a result of such thinking, even young 3-year-olds tend to choose the option for which they will get a delayed reward. The issue of time is not important here for the child because there is no conflict between a present and future self. Both selves prefer getting a reward to getting none: The earlier self can anticipate getting the reward later without having to give up anything important in the present, and the later self can be gratified when he or she receives the reward. Having to wait is just a condition on gratifying the desire to get some kind of reward for the self, so there is no conflict between earlier and later versions of self—the imagined future self and the present self are at one.

However, in the remaining sticker-choice conditions in the third experiment the children must somehow both imagine a future self's point of view, which conflicts with their own current desires, and choose in favor of that future self. Suppose for the moment that the children can actually imagine what the future self's preference would be. Thus, in the future-oriented prudence condition they can imagine getting many stickers at the end of the sticker game if they make the delayed choices now. In doing this they must also imagine making a choice that leads immediately to no stickers, which is in conflict with their own immediate desire. As a result there is a true conflict between their present and future selves. How do they overcome the conflict and make the choice that will make the future self happy but not gratify the immediate desire? What is required is analogous to what happens in the windows task, but it adds a temporal dimension not found in that task. The children must inhibit their natural inclination to take what they can get now in order to get the reward later. They must give a response in support of the future self over the present self. However, in doing that they must clearly distinguish these two selves and identify with the future self over the present self. The children's task here is to conceptualize the self as a unified self extended in time, distinguishing current feelings from those that they will feel later and not allow their choice to be dominated by current motives alone.

According to current theorizing about the relation among *autonoetic* consciousness (Tulving, 1985), episodic memory, and the extended self, this is just the kind of situation that should promote the development of a conception of an extended self. It is a situation that requires the child to conceive of him- or herself in terms of a temporal dimension, with—in the current context—a present and a future, where the self differs or changes according to time. Thus it is similar to what occurs in episodic memory, which requires a distinction between a past self and a present self, who changed through time. Furthermore, evidence from experiments conducted by Lemmon and Moore (see chap. 9, this volume) shows that the development of the future-oriented extension of the self, and the past-oriented extension of self, are correlated in older 3-year-olds and 4-year-olds. Thus, the child seems to be developing a general abstract representation of his or her self extended in time from the past, through the present, and into the future. And it is here that one may find the reason for this symmetry between acquiring a conception of the self that extends into the past at the same time as a self that extends into the future. What often motivates the development of reflexive self-awareness is some possible reward in the future, but once one is reflexively self-aware of being in a particular state, it leads to a recollective memory of oneself in that state and of the future-oriented choice one made in that state. Thus, in the present-choice task the child at the end of the game can recollect desiring the immediate reward on earlier choice trials. Nevertheless, he or she can also recollect having chosen the delayed reward in order that his or her present—at that time future—self might gain a greater number of stickers, than his or her past—at that time present—self could have received.

Acquiring such a notion of an extended self is no minor accomplishment. It is the means by which children acquire a self-conscious personal identity. What is crucial here is that children begin to think of themselves each as beings with coherently connected mental lives that extend through time. They know how their past choices have resulted in their present situation, and they know how their present choices will result in their future situations. They no longer live just in the present. They are now persons with a past that they know and a future that they anticipate having, and they view themselves as abstract entities who live through these temporal phases of existence.

THEORY OF MIND AND THE EXTENDED SELF

At about the time that children form a concept of the self as an extended self they also begin to understand other humans as selves or persons extended in time. Indeed, it may be that fully acquiring a theory of mind requires this particular kind of concept of a self or person. In order to understand mental states as representational rather than as presentational of states of the world, or of the organism, it may be necessary to conceive of the individual mind as existing outside of a particular time. If this were the case, as indicated in Table 8.3, it could account for the delay found in the present research between the executive-function and theory-of-mind tasks in their respective correlations to delay choices in the sticker task.

To more clearly understand this possibility consider the actual structure of the theory-of-mind tasks used in the research described earlier and how its structure relates to the extended self. The child in the Belief Change and the Desire Change tasks is required to be able to conceive of him- or herself changing from one state to another state as a function of time and of the events that occur between these two states. A child who lives in the present, with only a sense of an immediate self, but not a sense of an extended self in time, cannot be expected to organize such information about him- or herself. There is an inherent contradiction between the self the child currently experiences him- or herself to be and the past self that the child is requested to describe. This proves to be a difficulty that the child cannot overcome until he or she has a concept of self that extends through time. With such a concept, the child can conceive of him- or herself as a being capable of such contradictions because changes in the self over time allow for them. However, what is at issue here is more than a change in the physical activities of the self, it is the self's nature as a changing mental agent with which the child must become acquainted. Until children can conceive of their mental states as different at different times and as a function of temporally changing situations, they do not actually have a self of which they are conscious, whose very essence is to exist outside of particular times and to change through them. So it is a necessary condition for passing these tasks that the child already has, or be on the way to having an extended self. The same applies to the False Belief task, which requires the child to think about contradictory mental states of another person. The other individual has to be conceived as having true and false knowledge of the same "fact"—for example, the content of a box of Smarties. What the other person believes to be true now was true at one time (for many other boxes of Smarties) but is now false (for this box). Only a self that can have true and false mental states about the same represented thing, but at different times, can remain the same while also having both of these mental states. So again the child is required to think of a self whose essence is a mental nature that changes as a function of time and situation.

In this research (Moore et al., 1998) the theory-of-mind tasks correlated with the choice task only for young 4-year-olds and, in particular, theory of mind related to the choice task only when the child needed this ability in order to take specific cognizance of another person's mind. Although in this research we did not collect theory-of-mind and executive-function measures in the same experiment, other research shows that theory of mind is correlated with executive function tasks in 3- and 4- year-olds (Carlson, 1997; Hughes, 1998a, 1998b). I think that these results, taken together, are congruent with the idea suggested earlier that theory of mind is an outgrowth of the processes involved in executive decision making (see Table 8.3, Phase 2). Furthermore, as indicated earlier, executive decisions, which require autonoetic processing, or self-conscious distancing from one's present self, also provide the ground for developing a conception of an extended self. I believe that the extended self is also required for, or develops concurrently with, the development of a theory of mind (again see Table 8.3, Phase 2). The evidence that older 3-year-olds are just acquiring the ability to do the delayed self-recognition task, and that this correlates with executive function and with the choice task, suggests that it is during this period that all these activities are going through concurrent development. By contrast, the third experiment seems to indicate that the primary effect of executive function on choice activity has already occurred, and from the second experiment, it appears that the primary effect of theory of mind has yet to appear. Thus it seems most reasonable to suppose that it is out of executive decisions involving a future self that children first come to think of themselves as extended in time. Furthermore, it is out of this forward-looking decision making activity that children eventually develop an abstract conception, or theory, of a temporally extended mind that can be applied to others as well as to the self.

HAZLITT AND THE EXTENDED SELF

Hazlitt (1805/1969) made two important contributions toward understanding the child's development of the concept of an extended self. The first was his realization that the only way for one to connect to the future was through imagination—what today is called *simulation*—and that the use of the imagination to represent future selves applies equally well to the future selves of other people as to one's own future self. Thus, insofar as sympathy with a future self involves the capacity to represent that self, and to identify with it, both future-oriented prudence and future-oriented altruism should, at least initially, be on par with each other. He realized that there is no necessary preference for one's own future over that of another person, because both depend on an imagination and sympathy—or identification—that takes one out of one's current point of view so that one can adopt the point of view of another temporally distinct self. Research conducted on the basis of this insight of Hazlitt provides some support for this view of the concurrent development of future-oriented prudence and altruism.

Hazlitt's second contribution was his suggestion that one must learn to give preference to one's own future self over that of another and that this learning involves treating one's future self in a way that one does not treat the future self of another. Thus far, I have not specifically considered this aspect of Hazlitt's view, but it is a significant one for appreciating the transformation that occurs in the child's conception of self during the age-4 transition. What develops at this time is a way of thinking about the future—and also about the past—that treats temporally distinct selves in a new way. These selves, which one can imagine, and remember, are partitioned into those that belong together and those that do not. The ones that belong together are those that form phases in the life of a single, continuing, thinking being, a self-conscious being with a past, present, and future, a being with a sense of personal identity through time. The self of the present comes to appropriate as his or her own those past and future states that are viewed as connected through consciousness to the present self and at the same time reject as other those past, present, and future states connected through consciousness to another person. Whereas a younger child knew only of a distinction between the present self and present other, and might be able to imagine other "present" selves distributed in space and time, the child now conceives of the self not as present but as extended. In doing so, he or she not only makes stronger connections to his or her own past and future but also builds a new barrier between one person and another, between a self as temporally extended and other temporally extended selves. Whether this new barrier should be seen as an unfortunate one because it facilitates self-interested thinking over altruism, as Hazlitt thought, or instead be seen as a fortunate one because it extends the range of activities of an integrated self, including moral activities, is one that cannot be answered here. In any event, the acquisition of the concept of a temporally extended self is an important event in human development, one with enormous implications for the type of existence we have as a species. For it is through this concept of a temporally extended self that one can rise above the present self and can live in an abstract realm not localized in space and time as a rational being in communion with other rational beings.

ACKNOWLEDGMENTS

This chapter was prepared with support from the Social Sciences and Humanities Research Council of Canada (Grant 410-97-0767). I thank Chris Moore for very helpful comments on earlier versions of this chapter.

REFERENCES

Barresi, J. (2000) Intentional relations and divergent perspectives in social understanding. *Arob@se: Journal des Lettres et Sciences Humaines, 4,* 74–99.
Barresi, J., & Moore, C. (1993) Sharing a perspective precedes the understanding of that perspective. *Behavioral and Brain Sciences, 16,* 513–514.
Barresi, J., & Moore, C. (1996). Intentional relations and social understanding. *Behavioral and Brain Sciences, 19,* 107–122.
Carlson, S. M. (1997, April). *Individual differences in inhibitory control and children's theory of mind.* Poster presented at biennial meeting of Society for Research in Child Development, Washington, DC.
Descartes, R. (1984). Mediations on first philosophy. In J. Cottingham, R. Stoothoff, & D. Murdoch, (Trans.), *The philosophical writings of Descartes,* II (pp. 1–62). Cambridge, England: Cambridge University Press. (Original work published 1641)
Gopnik, A., & Slaughter, V. (1991). Young children's understanding of changes in their mental states. *Child Development, 62,* 98–110.
Harris, P. (1991). The work of the imagination. In A. Whiten (Ed.), *Natural theories of mind* (pp. 283–304). Cambridge, MA: Basil Blackwell.
Hazlitt, W. (1969). *An essay on the principles of human action and some remarks on the systems of Hartley and Helvetius.* Gainesville, FL: Scholars' Facsimiles & Reprints. (Original work published 1805)
Hoffman, M. L. (1976). Empathy, role-taking, guilt, and development of altruistic motives. In T. Lickona (Ed.), *Moral development and behavior* (pp. 124–143). New York: Holt, Rinehart, and Winston.
Hughes, C. (1998a). Executive function in preschoolers: Links with theory of mind and verbal ability. *British Journal of Developmental Psychology, 16,* 233–253.
Hughes, C. (1998b). Finding your marbles: Does preschoolers' strategic behavior predict later understanding of mind? *Developmental Psychology, 34,* 1326–1339.
Hume, D. (1888). *Treatise of human nature* (L. A. Selby-Bigge, Ed.). Oxford, England: Clarendon. (Original work published 1739)
Locke, J. (1975) *An essay concerning human understanding* (P. H. Nidditch, Ed.). Oxford, England: Clarendon. (Original work published 1694)

Martin, R., & Barresi, J. (1995). *Hazlitt on the future of the self.* Journal of the History of Ideas, 56, 463–481.

Martin, R. & Barresi, J. (2000). *Naturalization of the soul: self and personal identity in the eighteenth century.* London: Routledge.

Mischel, W. (1974). Processes in delay of gratification. In L. Berkowitz (Ed.), *Advances in experimental social psychology* (Vol. 7, pp. 249–292). New York: Academic.

Moore, C., Barresi, J., & Thompson, C. (1998). The cognitive basis of future-oriented prosocial behavior. *Social Development, 7,* 198–218.

Nagel, T. (1970). *The Possibility of Altruism.* Oxford, England: Clarendon.

Neisser, U. (1988). Five kinds of self. *Philosophical Psychology, 1,* 35–59.

Nelson, K. (1992). Emergence of autobiographical memory at age 4. *Human Development, 35,* 172–177.

Perner, J. (1992). Grasping the concept of representation: Its impact on 4-year-olds' theory of mind and beyond. *Human Development, 35,* 146–155.

Perner, J., & Ruffman, T. (1995). Episodic memory and autonoetic consciousness: Developmental evidence and a theory of childhood amnesia. *Journal of Experimental Child Psychology, 59,* 516–548.

Povinelli, D. J. (1995). The unduplicated self. In P. Rochat (Ed.), *The self in infancy: Theory and Research* (pp. 161–192). Amsterdam: Elsevier.

Reed, E. S. (1994). Perception is to self as memory is to selves. In U. Neisser & R. Fivush (Eds.), *The remembering self* (pp. 278–292). Cambridge, England: Cambridge University Press.

Russell, J., Jarrold, C., & Potel, D. (1994). What makes strategic deception difficult for children—the deception or the strategy? *British Journal of Developmental Psychology, 12,* 301–314.

Russell, J., Mauthner, N., Sharpe, S., & Tidswell, T. (1991). The "windows task" as a measure of strategic deception in preschoolers and autistic subjects. *British Journal of Developmental Psychology, 9,* 331–349.

Thompson, C., Barresi, J., & Moore, C. (1997). The development of future-oriented prudence and altruism in preschoolers. *Cognitive Development, 12,* 199–212.

Tulving, E. (1985). Memory and consciousness. *Canadian Psychology, 25,* 1–12.

Wheeler, M. A., Stuss, D. T., & Tulving, E. (1997). Toward a theory of episodic memory: The frontal lobes and autonoetic consciousness. *Psychological Bulletin, 121,* 331–354.

9

Binding the Self in Time

Karen Lemmon
Chris Moore
Dalhousie University

A standard claim in the growing literature on the temporally extended self is that this form of self-understanding or self-awareness spans the past, present, and future states and activities of the self (see, e.g., Nagel, 1970; Neisser, 1988; Povinelli, 1995; Suddendorf, 1999; Tulving, 1985; Wheeler, Stuss, & Tulving, 1997). With the development of the temporally extended self the child becomes able not only to think about his or her own personal history but also to imagine possible futures in which he or she might be involved. In the developmental literature, however, research on the temporally extended self has concentrated on the child's representation of either the past or, less commonly, the future.

The bulk of the research on the past has focused on how children start to represent their personal histories in autobiographies that take narrative form (see Fivush & Hudson, 1990; Howe & Courage, 1993, 1997; Nelson, 1992, 1993). Studies of autobiographical memory have tended to focus on memory for personally experienced events and how those events are represented. Recently, considerable interest has been shown in the social environmental conditions for the representation of events from the personal past (see, e.g., Welch-Ross, 1997). Although it is clear that children younger than 4 years can recall earlier events, these events do not appear to be connected to the self in the sense of being part of a personal narrative or autobiography. Such an autobiographical memory appears to develop at about 4 years of age (Nelson, 1993). In addition to the work on autobiographical memory, there has been significant recent interest in the use of the delayed self-recognition procedure, introduced by Povinelli and colleagues (Povinelli, Landau, &

Perilloux, 1996; Suddendorf, 1999; Zelazo, Sommerville, & Nichols, 1999; see also Povinelli, chap. 5, this volume) to assess children's ability to link past events to the present. As Povinelli (chap. 5, this volume) argues, the delayed self-recognition procedure may well index children's understanding of the causal connection between previous states of the self and the current state of the self.

In the last few years, researchers have started to recognize the importance of examining children's ability to imagine and plan for future scenarios (e.g., Atance & O'Neill, chap. 7, this volume; Benson, 1994; Hudson, chap. 4, this volume; Hudson, Shapiro, & Sosa, 1995). For example, Hudson et al. (1995) investigated young children's ability to provide a plan for the familiar event of grocery shopping. However, this research does not clearly require children to have a sense of self extended into the future, because it is about a routine event that may rely more on present knowledge about grocery shopping than future planning. More recently, Atance and O'Neill (chap. 7, this volume) examined younger and older 3-year-olds' ability to plan one-step actions to achieve a goal in a novel circumstance. They suggested that planning may involve imagination of the self being involved in this future event. Their results showed that the ability to plan on these tasks increased with age. However, the authors recognize that children may have succeeded on these tasks without necessarily identifying with self in the future. Again, it is not clear that children needed to represent the link between future and present events in these tasks.

Another area of research that may require the ability to connect future and present is the work using a modified delay-of-gratification paradigm (Moore, Barresi, & Thompson, 1998; Thompson, Barresi, & Moore, 1997; see Barresi, chap. 8, this volume). In this procedure, children make a series of choices between a materially inferior reward now and materially superior reward later. As such, the task can be said to measure future-oriented prudence, which Nagel (1970) argued reflects awareness of a temporally extended self. He suggested that "failure to be susceptible to prudence entails radical dissociation from one's future, one's past, and from oneself as a whole, conceived as a temporally extended individual" (Nagel, 1970, p. 58).

Thus, although researchers have examined children's ability to link past and present and to link present and future, no research of which we are aware has explicitly addressed the issue of whether these two components of the temporally extended self develop together as is typically assumed. That is the topic of this chapter. We report two studies designed to investigate the links among past, present, and future. Our general strategy has been to test the same children on tasks that assess the understanding of the link between past and present and between present and future. In addition, because we are interested in the possibility that the development of the episodic neurocognitive system, coincident with autonoetic consciousness (Tulving, 1985), accompanies the acquisition of the temporally extended self, we have also used a measure that we suggest best represents the essence of the operation of autonoetic consciousness in memory.

LINKING THE PAST AND PRESENT

For our measure of the understanding of the link between past and present we adopted Povinelli's delayed self-recognition task (see chap. 5, this volume). Povinelli (1995) theorized that around 4 years of age, children develop a "proper self" that "holds the self-concept together as an enduring entity through time with a past and a future" (p. 168). To test this idea, Povinelli et al. (1996) investigated young children's ability to realize that the past can influence the present by developing a delayed self-recognition task that is analogous to the mirror self-recognition test for infants. Instead of wiping rouge onto a child's face and showing her a mirror (Amsterdam, 1972), a sticker was surreptitiously placed onto the child's head during a game that was being videotaped or photographed. At the end of the game, children viewed their past activities, and those who reached up to remove the sticker from their heads at this point were credited with delayed self-recognition. The compelling aspect of Povinelli et al.'s results was that children around 4 years of age reached up to remove the sticker, whereas younger children did not. Moreover, younger children's difficulty with the task was limited to the delay component and not to the video or photo medium (although see Zelazo et al., 1999; Zelazo & Sommerville, chap. 12, this volume).

In subsequent work, Povinelli and his colleagues (Povinelli, Landry, Theall, Clark, & Castille, 1999; Povinelli & Simon, 1998) found that 4- and 5-year-olds, but not 3-year-olds, differentiated the relevance for the present self of different lengths of delay and of whether the viewed events from the past actually involved the children themselves. Taken together, the experiments by Povinelli and his colleagues indicate that 3-year-olds have little understanding that the past self is causally connected to the present self. In contrast, older preschoolers do seem to be aware that their past can influence their present.

LINKING THE PRESENT AND FUTURE

For our task assessing children's link between future and present we chose the modified delay-of-gratification procedure that measures future-oriented prudence (Thompson et al., 1997; see Barresi, chap. 8, this volume). We selected this task because it focuses on the child's ability to identify with his or her own future interests. Children who opt for a greater but delayed reward in preference to an immediate reward appear to be able to identify with their future selves. Previous results using this procedure have indicated that, in general, there is significant developmental change over the period from 3 to 5 years, with 3-year-olds experiencing particular difficulty making choices in favor of their future interests compared to their immediate interests (Moore et al., 1998; Thompson et al., 1997). By age 5, children appear to be able to take account of their future interests in making choices between immediate and delayed rewards, and they tend to opt for the greater future reward.

AUTONOETIC CONSCIOUSNESS AND THE EPISODIC NEUROCOGNITIVE SYSTEM

In addition to the two tasks assessing the links between current and noncurrent representations of self, we included a task aimed at examining the idea that autonoetic consciousness is connected to the ability to construct these links. Wheeler et al. (1997) argued that one must be autonoetically aware of the present self to remember the past and to imagine the future. Moreover, they argued that "the possessor of autonoetic consciousness is capable of considering the past in relation to the future and making up action plans and ambitions for the anticipated future based on past experiences" (p. 346). Autonoetic consciousness is therefore not limited to memory for previous subjective experiences but includes the imagination of potential future experiences as well.

Building on Tulving (1985), Wheeler et al. (1997) suggested that the emergence of autonoetic consciousness coincides with the development of the episodic neurocognitive system, which includes memory for previous subjective experiences. Studies of memory have shown that when recalling a personally experienced event one relies on both the episodic and semantic systems, but it is the episodic system that is linked to the self (Wheeler et al., 1997). Memory of an event is often factual and likely involves the semantic memory system as well. However, memory about less central details of the event may rely more on the episodic system than the semantic. Instead of asking someone to report the facts about what happened, one may tap the episodic system by asking about the order in which parts of an event occurred (provided the sequence was not based on logic or general knowledge). Another method of tapping the episodic system may be to ask about the context of events, for example, who told you a certain fact or where you learned it.

Perner and Ruffman (1995) investigated this link between episodic remembering and autonoetic consciousness in young children. Participants were shown 12 pictures and then asked to recall them after delays of 1 hour and 1 week. The authors' results revealed that free recall of the pictures was related to the ability to succeed on tasks that measured understanding the source of knowledge, which they argued is a form of autonoetic consciousness. Perner and Ruffman concluded that free recall of an episode relies on having encoded the source of one's knowledge about that episode and, therefore, is accompanied by autonoetic consciousness (see also Perner, chap. 10, this volume).

On the basis of research on memory abilities, Wheeler et al. (1997) suggested that the level of awareness for episodic remembering does not develop until around 4 years, although autonoetic consciousness may be present around 3 years of age. It would follow from this that the ability to identify with future interests would also not develop until about 4 years of age even though autonoetic consciousness may be present earlier.

In our work we included an episodic memory task about a hide-and-seek game that required children to remember the order in which they had discovered their stickers. In designing our memory measure we capitalized on the structure already provided by the delayed self-recognition task. As described earlier, to provide a context for the surreptitious marking procedure, children participated in a series of trials in which they were asked to find stickers hidden under one of three cups. A different sticker was concealed on each trial, and the child was allowed to place the found stickers in a sticker book. At the end of the trials, the child was asked to remember the order in which he or she had discovered the stickers, and it was this measure of memory for order that served as the assessment of episodic memory.

We should emphasize that the to-be-remembered order of sticker presentation during the delayed self-recognition task was random (i.e., there was no necessary reason for any one particular sticker to be hidden after another particular sticker). As Tulving (1972) argued, recalling a random order of events necessarily involves the episodic memory system because one can rely only on one's phenomenal experience as a guide. Conversely, with recall of a logical order of events one may rely on general knowledge to reconstruct the sequence without actually remembering it. Indeed, preschoolers' memory for a logical sequence of three events surpassed their memory for those same events in random order (Brown, 1975). Moreover, recent work by McCormack and Russell (1997) showed that in memory judgments for recency, 4-year-olds relied on remembering, not knowledge, to distinguish item order.

Finally, we should note that our memory tasks tested incidental memory. That is, children were not told beforehand that they would be asked to remember what stickers they found or the order and context of finding stickers. We followed this approach because incidental tasks exclude the use of deliberate memory strategies, which increase with age (Bjorklund, 1995). This was consistent with our goal of eliminating potential variability due to strategy implementation while measuring children's episodic memory.

EXPERIMENT 1

The purpose of our first experiment was to determine whether children who appreciated the connection between past and present self also appreciated the connection between future and present self. Thirty-nine preschoolers (18 male, 21 female) between the ages of 3;6 and 4;0 participated in this study. Children had a mean age of 46.5 months (SD = 1.4). They were given the delayed self-recognition task, the order memory task, and the future-oriented prudence choice task, although not all children completed all of the tasks. Half of the children were administered the future-oriented choice task before the delayed self-recognition task.

For the delayed self-recognition and order memory tasks, the sequence of events was (a) playing the hide-and-seek sticker game, (b) completing the order memory task, and (c) watching the video playback. In the delayed self-recognition procedure the experimenter hid a yellow dot (2 cm in diameter) on the child's head while he or she was playing a hide-and-seek sticker game that was being videotaped. Five different stickers were sequentially hidden under one of three colored cups. After each sticker was found the child was patted on the head in congratulatory fashion. After the child found the third sticker, the yellow dot was surreptitiously placed on his or her head. At the end of the game, the child viewed the video playback and watched the experimenter putting a sticker on his or her head. During the playback, children who did not remove the dot approximately 30 s after it was placed on their heads in the video were asked a sequence of questions. First, the experimenter pointed to the image of the child on the television and asked the identity question ("Who is that?"). Children who did not answer this question correctly were not informed that the image was in fact them. Next, the experimenter asked "What is that?" while pointing to the image of the dot on the child's head. If children did not answer or responded incorrectly, then they were told "That's a yellow dot. That's a yellow sticker." The final two questions were: "Where is that yellow dot really?" and "Can you find where that yellow dot really is?" Answers to these last two questions were not corrected. If children did not remove the dot after the last question, then they were shown a mirror. Following the coding procedure of Povinelli and Simon (1998), two trained coders recorded the point at which each child appeared to reach for the sticker on his or her head during the video playback: before the first question, during the questions, and not during the video. During the video playback of the hide-and-seek game, children who appeared to reach for the sticker on their head before the first question received 2 points. Children who reached up during the questions were awarded 1 point, and children who did not reach up during the video playback received 0 points.

As noted earlier, the memory task required children to remember the order in which the stickers had been found during the hide-and-seek sticker game. We did not require the child to recall the name of the sticker but presented the children with the five stickers they had found and simply asked them to point to the sticker they had found on each trial in its proper sequence (i.e., "Which sticker did you find first?" through to "Which sticker did you find last?"). Participants were awarded 1 point for each correct answer on the order memory task, with total scores ranging from 0 to 5.

The procedure for the future-oriented sticker choice task was adapted from that used by Thompson et al. (1997). Children were offered a number of choices between a less desirable sticker reward now and a more desirable sticker reward at the end of the game. Sticker rewards that were chosen now were given to the child for immediate placement in a sticker book, whereas rewards chosen for later were saved in an envelope until the end of the game, at which point they were given to the child to take home. Both quantitative and qualitative questions were asked. Quantitative choices offered one sticker now versus two stickers at the end of the game, whereas qualitative choices offered a plain sticker now versus a shiny sticker at the end of the game. In addition, we included a game board with an arrow for the children to indicate their preferred choices. This game board was used because we had observed during pilot work that when choices were displayed some participants immediately began to point and reach for the sticker they most liked as if unable to inhibit this type of response. Adding a game board was thought to afford participants some control over this gesture by forcing them to choose by means of the board (see Carlson, Moses, & Hix, 1998). The game board consisted of a black rectangle with computer-generated replicas of a sticker book in one corner and an envelope in the other. A large red arrow was secured in the middle of the board which allowed the child to point the arrow to the envelope for delayed rewards or to the sticker book for immediate rewards. Participants received 1 point for choosing the delayed reward. Scores on this task ranged from 0 to 6.

Children scored a mean of 1.00 (SD = 0.8) on the delayed self-recognition task, a mean of 2.13 (SD = 1.4) on order memory, and a mean of 1.97 (SD = 2.2) on the choice task. We predicted that delayed self-recognition scores would correlate positively with future-oriented prudence scores, indicating an awareness of the self extended into both the past and future. Indeed, delayed self-recognition and future-oriented prudence scores correlated significantly (r = .465, p = .006 [N = 34]) with age in months partialed out. We also predicted that order memory scores would correlate positively with the other two tasks, suggesting that the episodic neurocognitive system may play a role in the development of the temporally extended self. Controlling for age in months, order memory scores correlated significantly with delayed self-recognition scores($r = .350$, $p = .04$ [$N = 36$]) and with the number of future-oriented choices ($r = .327$, $p = .05$ [$N = 37$]). Thus, at this age, all three tasks were related to each other, as hypothesized.

These results seem to indicate that children's understanding of the connection between past and present and their understanding of the connection between future and present emerge simultaneously. Children who recognize the relevance of past states of self for the present state of the self also are more able to identify with the potential future self and act in the interests of that future self. These results provide empirical support for the notion that a self extending into the past develops with a self extending into the future. As such, we have evidence for previous assumptions regarding the temporally extended self, namely that it spans past, present, and future.

On the basis of our finding that order memory was related to the other two tasks, it is plausible to argue that the emergence of the temporally extended self coincides with developments in the episodic neurocognitive system, namely autonoetic consciousness (Tulving, 1985; Wheeler et al., 1997). Our order memory task was designed to tap this episodic system. Autonoetic consciousness may enable the child to connect the experienced past and potential future experiences to the present self. Children who lack this autonoetic consciousness in their episodic system may not have a sense of self for past and future experiences that is connected to the present. Indeed, Povinelli et al. (1996) suggested that children do not pass the delayed self-recognition task because they do not have a sense of "me" in their memories of the event. Instead of being autobiographical, then, memories would be strictly episodic such that nonrecognizers could still report certain aspects of the events that happened without being able to connect those events with a sense of self.

EXPERIMENT 2

The purpose of our second study was to replicate and extend the findings from the first experiment. To get a larger developmental picture of performance on these tasks, the age range was expanded to cover a span of approximately 18 months, from 3 to 4.5 years of age. Fifty-five children with a mean age of 45.6 months ($SD = 5.0$) completed the same three types of task as in the first study.

The procedure for the delayed self-recognition task was almost identical to that of Experiment 1. During the video playback we gave children the same first three prompts, but we changed the last question to "Can you touch that yellow sticker?" Children who reached up before the first question received 2 points, children who reached during the questions received 1 point, and children who did not reach during the video received 0 points.

For the future-oriented choice task we introduced a number of different trial types. The child was first given a practice trial in which he or she was asked to choose between one sticker now or two stickers now. Children who chose one sticker were told that in this game they could have two stickers for their sticker book. This initial trial was followed by three identical trials of choice between one or two stickers now to give children the opportunity to receive stickers for themselves now (simple present). This trial type also allowed an assessment of the extent to which individual children would choose two stickers over one when there was no delay involved. Although one might assume that the choice of two over one would be the rational decision, it is possible that other factors might be involved. For example, some children might choose one over two on some trials because they do not want to appear greedy. Such a strategy would contaminate the tendency to show future-oriented choices. The inclusion of the one versus two stickers now trials yielded a measure that could be used as an adjustment for the future-oriented measures on an individual basis.

After the simple-present choice trials, children received two types of future-oriented choice with three trials of each type. One type of trial was the same as the quantitative trials in Experiment 1. Here children were offered the choice between one sticker now or two at the end of the game (future-oriented prudence). In the other type of trial children chose between one or two stickers with both alternatives delivered at the end of the game (simple future). The latter trial type was included to determine whether children could make decisions about their future desires that did not involve a conflict with their present ones. We reasoned that if younger children were having difficulty with inhibiting the need for immediate rewards (as is possible in the case of prudence trials) then eliminating the choice of an immediate reward might enable children to demonstrate their future-oriented thinking abilities more easily. Moreover, the simple-future trials should allow younger children to express their future desires more easily than the prudence trials, given the difference in cognitive demands. Simple-future trials may be less demanding than future-prudence trials because the former choice is between two rewards at a *single* time (comparing one value with another), whereas the latter choice is between two rewards each at *different* times (comparing one current value with another future value). The simple-future trial is similar in this sense to the simple-present trial. Participants received 1 point for choosing the larger reward in the simple-present and simple-future questions and 1 point for choosing the delayed reward in the future-oriented prudence questions. Scores ranged from 0 to 3 for each trial type.

Before we conducted the analyses, we calculated adjusted scores for the future-oriented choice trials by subtracting simple-present scores from simple-future and future-oriented prudence scores. We used these adjusted scores to control for participants' tendency to choose their stickers for reasons other than identification with the future self; that is, we had expected children to choose two stickers over one in the simple-present trials. However, there was some variability in children's choices on these trials, suggesting that for some reason two stickers were not always preferable to one. As noted earlier, one possibility is that some children did not want to appear greedy and thus limited their choice to one sticker. By using a difference score we were able to control for children's tendency to base their sticker choice on reasons other than identification with the future self. Therefore, the adjusted measure arguably provides a more stringent measure of the orientation to the future self.

To improve the memory assessment portion of the experiment we modified the procedure for the order task and added two new memory tasks that involved other aspects of the task events. For the order memory procedure in Experiment 1 children responded by pointing to a sticker in their books. This may have presented unwanted contextual cues for the children as to the order of recovery, such as position in the book. To eliminate this possibility, we removed the context of the sticker book and presented the same five stickers on a card, at which point the children were given the order memory task. Our purpose here was to require the children to rely solely on their remembered personal experience of finding the stickers, without receiving potential clues from the sticker book. Moreover, if memory for the order of random event sequences truly requires remembering, as Tulving (1972) suggested, then this version of the order memory task should show a stronger relationship with delayed self-recognition than the version used in Experiment 1.

In addition to the order memory task, children were asked to recall the types of stickers they had found during the game and, because episodic remembering involves the context of a personally experienced event, children were asked to point to the color of the cup under which each sticker had been hidden. The recall task was used as a measure of general memory ability and was given first. We assessed recall by asking the children simply to name the five stickers they had found during the hide-and-seek game without any stickers being present as cues. In theory, children might perform well on this task by reporting images held in memory without these images necessarily being remembered as part of a personal past. We therefore used the simple recall task as a control measure of general memory ability to be partialed out during analyses. We also directly assessed memory for context by asking the children under which cup they had found each sticker. This task was considered to be another measure of episodic memory, as argued by Wheeler et al. (1997), and its use was exploratory. On the one hand, it could be argued that memory for context, like memory for the order of events, is more about how an event was experienced rather than what was experienced. In this sense, it might depend more on episodic memory and show an association with order memory and with delayed self-recognition. On the other hand, memory for context could also be considered to be more about knowing what had happened and thus might have more in common with recalling the particular stickers that had been found. For all three memory tasks, participants were given 1 point for each correct answer, with scores ranging from 0 to 5 on each task.

For analysis, correlations between age in months and each variable were first examined. Age correlated significantly with delayed self-recognition ($r = .337$, $p = .01$), and future-oriented prudence scores ($r = .281$, $p = .04$) but not with simple-future scores ($r = .222$, $p = .10$). Age also correlated significantly with order memory ($r = .313$, $p = .02$), but not with simple recall ($r = .228$, $p = .09$), or context memory ($r = .128$, $p = .35$). Given the significant age effects for the critical measures, the children were divided into two age groups for subsequent analyses: 3-year-olds ($N = 27$) with a mean age of 41.1 months (range: 3;1–3;9) and 4-year-olds ($N = 28$) with a mean age of 49.9 months (range: 3;10–4;6).

Mean scores for all the tasks for each age group in this experiment are presented in Tables 9.1 (in which unadjusted simple future and future-oriented prudence are provided) and 9.2. To determine relative performance on the episodic memory tasks, we subjected mean scores to a 2 (age) by 2 (task: order memory, context memory) mixed analysis of variance (ANOVA) with age in months and simple recall as covariates.

TABLE 9.1
Mean Scores (*SD*) on Past and Future Self Measures
for Each Age Group in Experiment 2

			Unadjusted		Adjusted	
Age Group	*Delayed S-R*	*Simple present*	*Simple future*	*Future prudence*	*Simple future*	*Future prudence*
3s (N = 27)	0.8 (0.9)	2.6 (0.6)	1.9 (1.0)	1.4 (1.0)	-0.7 (1.3)	-1.3 (1.1)
4s (N = 28)	1.3 (0.8)	2.4 (0.8)	2.1 (0.8)	1.7 (1.1)	-0.3 (1.2)	-0.6 (1.6)
Total (N = 55)	1.0 (0.8)	2.5 (0.7)	2.0 (0.9)	1.6 (1.1)	-0.5 (1.2)	-1.0 (1.4)

Note. S-R = Self-recognition

TABLE 9.2
Mean Scores (*SD*) on Memory Measures
for Each Age Group in Experiment 2

Age Group	Simple recall	Order memory	Context memory
3s (N = 27)	2.5 (1.2)	1.6 (1.6)	1.7 (1.2)
4s (N = 28)	2.6 (1.4)	2.7 (1.4)	2.0 (1.0)
Total (N = 55)	2.6 (1.3)	2.2 (1.6)	1.9 (1.1)

There was no effect of age, $F(1) = 0.86$, *NS*; no effect of task, $F(1) = 1.34$, *NS*; and no interaction, $F(1) = 2.12$, *NS*. Although performance did not differ on the context and order memory tasks, they were not significantly correlated ($r = .055$, *NS*, with age and simple recall partialed out). To determine whether children scored higher on simple-future trials than on future-prudence trials we compared their mean performances (adjusted scores) in a 2 (age) by 2 (trial type) mixed ANOVA with age in months as the covariate. There was no effect of age, $F(1) = 0.07$, *NS*, and no interaction effect, $F(1) = 0.28$, *NS*. However, the effect of trial type was significant, $F(1) = 9.45$, $p = .003$, indicating that children performed significantly better on simple-future trials. Despite this difference, the age-partialed correlation between simple future and future prudence was significant ($r = .598$, $p < .001$).

We then computed correlations among the delayed self-recognition and future-oriented tasks separately for each age group (see Table 9.3) with age partialed out. Delayed self-recognition correlated with future-oriented prudence for the older age group ($r = .432$, $p < .05$), but not the

TABLE 9.3
Age-Partialed Correlations Between Delayed Self-Recognition and Future Choice
Tasks for Each Age Group in Experiment 2

Age Group	Simple Future	Future Prudence
3s (N = 27)		
Delayed self-recognition	-.018	.255
Simple future		.602***
4s (N = 28)		
Delayed self-recognition	.276	.432*
Simple future		.589***

Note. * = p < .05; *** = p < .001

TABLE 9.4
Correlations Between Delayed Self-Recognition, Future Choice, and Episodic
Memory Tasks With Age and Simple Recall Partialed Out
for Each Age Group in Experiment 2

Age Group	Order Memory	Context Memory
3s (N = 27)		
Delayed self-recognition	-.014	.219
Adjusted simple future	-.085	-.035
Adjusted future prudence	.010	.395*
4s (N = 28)		
Delayed self-recognition	.624***	.453*
Adjusted simple future	.284	.479*
Adjusted future prudence	.363$^+$	.423*

Note. $^+$ = p < .07; * = p < .05; *** = p < .001

younger group. However, delayed self-recognition did not correlate significantly with simple future at either age. With the episodic memory tasks, delayed self-recognition correlated significantly with order and context memory for the 4-year-olds but not the 3-year-olds (see Table 9.4). Future-oriented prudence correlated with memory for context at both ages and, for the older children, future-oriented prudence was marginally related to order memory. Simple future did not correlate with either type of memory for the younger children, but it did correlate significantly with context memory for the 4-year-olds.

The results from this second experiment replicate what we found in the first experiment. To begin, as in Experiment 1, delayed self-recognition correlated significantly with future-oriented prudence. Thus, children who understand the relation between the personal future and present also understand the link between the personal past and present. These results are consistent, therefore, with the idea that children develop a sense of self that extends into the future as they develop one that extends into the past. Also in concert with the first experiment, the memory tasks hypothesized to assess the development of the episodic neurocognitive system with its corresponding autonoetic level of consciousness were related to the development of the temporally extended self. In Experiment 2 it was the task assessing memory for context that showed the strongest general relation with the measures of past and future orientation. The order memory task was correlated with future-oriented prudence at a level similar to that seen in Experiment 1 for the older age group only. Finally, the simple recall task, assumed to depend more on the semantic system, showed no relations with the tasks assessing the temporally extended self.

In general, the results from dividing up the age range into two groups put the target developmental changes closer to 4 years of age. It is not surprising that performance improved with age on delayed self-recognition, future-oriented prudence, and order memory. These results are consistent with those of Povinelli et al. (1996) and Zelazo et al. (1999) on delayed self-recognition and those of Thompson et al. (1997) and Moore et al. (1998) on future-oriented prudence. When the relations among measures were examined separately for older and younger children, we observed the majority of significant correlations, generally positive associations, in the older age group. Thus, developments in the temporally extended self tended to occur later in the fourth year.

This experiment also expands on our earlier research. In this study, we included two types of future-oriented choice trials. One type (future prudence) involved a conflict between immediate and future interests, whereas the other (simple future) did not. Performance on the two types of trial was highly correlated, indicating that they have something in common, presumably future-oriented thinking. However, future prudence was more difficult than simple future, and only prudence showed a significant improvement with age. These results suggest that the task demands of the simple-future trials may lie somewhere between the simple-present and the future-prudence trials. On the one hand, simple-future trials might be solved by imagining two noncurrent interests (a future desire for one item versus a future desire for two items) and choosing appropriately in the present. On the other hand, it is also plausible that children may make the simple future decision on the basis of current interests alone because no conflict between immediate and future interests exists. In short, children may opt for two stickers over one in the simple future trials without considering the temporal dimension at all. This explanation cannot be the whole story given the higher success on simple present over simple future. Nevertheless, we cannot rule out the possibility that simple-future choices were made on the basis of current desires.

We suggest that, in order to be certain that a task measures future-oriented thinking, the potential future state must be made distinct from the current state. For example, future-oriented thinking may be demonstrated by taking an umbrella to work in the sunshine (the umbrella is not needed now because it is not raining, but it may be needed on the way home, should it rain). The conflict in this example would be the current desire to leave the umbrella at home because one has too much to carry already versus the future desire to have the umbrella shield one from the rain on the walk home. In future research these considerations should be addressed. For now, although the 3-year-olds succeeded on the simple-future trials in this experiment, it is not clear that these results indicate an ability to engage in future-oriented thinking about the self in younger children.

CONNECTING SELF STATES ACROSS TIME

Our primary goal in this work was to investigate the development of the temporally extended self by examining children's performance on two tasks hypothesized to assess the ability to connect the current state of self with a noncurrent state of self. The delayed self-recognition task requires children to connect a previous state of self to the current state, and the future-oriented prudence task requires children to connect the present state of self with a future state. In order to pass the delayed self-recognition task, the child must be able to think about the connection of the prior self (the self with the sticker in the video image) with the current self so he or she can make the inference that there must still be a sticker on his or her head. To demonstrate future-oriented prudence, the child must be able to consider a current desire (have one now) as well as a future desire (have two later) in order to maximize benefit for the self. Our results showed that delayed self-recognition correlated with future-oriented prudence in two studies involving children at the end of the fourth year of life. We conclude, therefore, that these two forms of behavior share a common element. To be explicit, our suggestion is that both tasks require the child to be able (a) to represent both current and noncurrent states of self and (b) to recognize the link between current and noncurrent states of self.

The further suggestion from this work is that episodic memory and autonoetic consciousness are implicated in this ability to connect self states across time. Our memory measures showed significant correlations with both tasks requiring children to connect current and noncurrent states of self. These results are consistent with the idea that recognizing the connection of self states across time involves the ability to reflect simultaneously on one's own state both now and at some other point in time. In addition, for children to connect current and noncurrent states, these states must be represented with similar information properties. There are two sides to this achievement. First, children must be able to experience noncurrent states of self in the same way as they experience current states, namely from a subjective or first-person point of view. In effect this is the achievement of autonoetic consciousness. Second, and at the same time, the current self must be represented from an objective or third-person point of view so that the current state can be recognized to be just one in a continuing series of states of self. Only when both current and noncurrent states of self can be represented in the same way will the child be able to achieve temporal decentration (Nagel,

1970; see also chaps. 8 by Barresi, 11 by McCormack & Hoerl, and 12 by Zelazo & Sommerville, this volume).

CONCLUSION

In this chapter we have reported evidence that toward the end of the fourth year of life children develop a sense of self extended into the past as they acquire a sense of self extended into the future. In particular, recognition of the relevance for the current situation of past events involving the self is consistently related to the tendency to make current decisions for future benefit. This association also appears related to the development of episodic memory and autonoetic consciousness. The standard claim that the temporally extended self spans past, present, and future seems, then, to have support. By about 4 years, children have acquired a notion of self that includes the awareness that the present self is connected to other stages of self in a continuous sequence from past through to future.

ACKNOWLEDGMENTS

This work was supported by a grant from the Social Sciences and Humanities Research Council of Canada to Chris Moore.

REFERENCES

Amsterdam, B. (1972). Mirror self-image reactions before age two. *Developmental Psychobiology, 5,* 297–305.
Benson, J. B. (1994). The origins of future orientation in the everyday lives of 9- to 36-month-old infants. In M. M. Haith, J. B. Benson, R. J. Roberts Jr., & B. F. Pennington (Eds.), *The development of future-oriented processes* (pp. 375–407). Chicago: University of Chicago Press.
Brown, A. L. (1975). Progressive elaboration and memory order in children. *Journal of Experimental Child Psychology, 19,* 382–400.
Bjorklund, D. F. (1995). *Children's thinking: Developmental function and individual differences.* Monterey, CA: Brooks/Cole.
Carlson, S. M., Moses, L. J., & Hix, H. R. (1998). The role of inhibitory processes in young children's difficulties with deception and false belief. *Child Development, 69,* 672–691.
Fivush, R., & Hudson, J. A. (1990). *Knowing and remembering in young children.* New York: Cambridge University Press.
Howe, M. L., & Courage, M. L. (1993). On resolving the enigma of infantile amnesia. *Psychological Bulletin, 113,* 305–326.
Howe, M. L., & Courage, M. L. (1997). The emergence and early development of autobiographical memory. *Psychological Review, 104,* 499–523.

Hudson, J. A., Shapiro, L. R., & Sosa, B. B. (1995). Planning in the real world: Preschool children's scripts and plans for familiar events. *Child Development, 66,* 984–988.

McCormack, T., & Russell, J. (1997). The development of recency and frequency memory: Is there a developmental shift from reliance on trace-strength to episodic recall? *Journal of Experimental Child Psychology, 66,* 376–392.

Moore, C., Barresi, J., & Thompson, C. (1998). The cognitive basis of future-oriented prosocial behavior. *Social Development, 7,* 198–218.

Nagel, T. (1970). *The possibility of altruism.* Oxford, England: Clarendon Press.

Neisser, U. (1988). Five kinds of self-knowledge. *Philosophical Psychology, 1,* 35–59.

Nelson, K. (1992). Emergence of autobiographical memory at age 4. *Human Development, 35,* 172–177.

Nelson, K. (1993). The psychological and social origins of autobiographical memory. *Psychological Science, 4,* 1–8.

Perner, J., & Ruffman, T. (1995). Episodic memory and autonoetic consciousness: Developmental evidence and a theory of childhood amnesia. *Journal of Experimental Child Psychology, 59,* 516–548.

Povinelli, D. J. (1995). The unduplicated self. In P. Rochat (Ed.), *Self in infancy: Theory and research* (pp. 161–192). Amsterdam: Elsevier.

Povinelli, D. J., Landau, K. R., & Perilloux, H. K. (1996). Self-recognition in young children using delayed versus live feedback: Evidence of a developmental asynchrony. *Child Development, 67,* 1540–1554.

Povinelli, D. J., Landry, A. M., & Theall, L. A., Clark, B. R., & Castille, C. M. (1999). Development of young children's understanding that the recent past is causally bound to the present. *Developmental Psychology, 35,* 1426–1439.

Povinelli, D. J., & Simon, B. (1998). Young children's understanding of briefly versus extremely delayed images of self: Emergence of an autobiographical stance. *Developmental Psychology, 34,* 188–194.

Suddendorf, T. (1999). Children's understanding of the relation between delayed video representation and current reality: A test for self-awareness? *Journal of Experimental Child Psychology, 72,* 157–176.

Thompson, C., Barresi, J., & Moore, C. (1997). The development of future-oriented prudence and altruism in preschoolers. *Cognitive Development, 12,* 199–212.

Tulving, E. (1972). Episodic and semantic memory. In E. Tulving & W. Donaldson (Eds.), *Organization of memory* (pp. 381–403). New York: Academic.

Tulving, E. (1985). Memory and consciousness. *Canadian Psychology, 26,* 1–12.

Welch-Ross, M. (1997). Mother–child participation in conversation about the past: Relationships to preschoolers' theory of mind. *Developmental Psychology, 33,* 618–629.

Wheeler, M. A., Stuss, D. T., & Tulving, E. (1997). Toward a theory of episodic memory: The frontal lobes and autonoetic consciousness. *Psychological Bulletin, 121,* 331-354.

Zelazo, P. D., Sommerville, J. A., & Nichols, S. (1999). Age-related changes in children's use of external representations. *Developmental Psychology, 35,* 1059–1071.

10

Episodic Memory: Essential Distinctions and Developmental Implications

Josef Perner
University of Salzburg

TERMINOLOGICAL PREAMBLE

Memory is used in a quite inflationary way in contemporary cognitive science for any process that stores information over some period of time. *Episodic memory* is clearly more specific but may to many readers mean nothing more than a process that stores information about a particular episode. I use the term here with the even more specific meaning that Tulving (1972, 1985) has given it with reference to Ebbinghaus as "calling back into consciousness a seemingly lost state that is then 'immediately recognized as something formerly experienced' (Ebbinghaus, 1885, p. 1)" (Tulving, 1985, p. 3). In this use episodic memory is one kind of what James (1890) denoted *memory proper*: "Memory proper (or secondary memory) is the knowledge of an event, or fact .... with the additional consciousness that we have ... experienced it before." (p. 648).

The common locution that captures episodic memories best is "having a memory of something" or "remembering something." It stresses the directness of experience, whereas "remembering that something took place" can be used to express knowledge gained indirectly through being told without direct experience. I can say that I *remember that* there was a second world war (as I was told in school) but, as a postwar child, I cannot say that I remember (or have a memory of) the second world war.

I think it is intuitively clear what is meant by this kind of (episodic) memory. However its explicit definition in terms of "recognized as formerly experienced" requires further clarification. To this end I want to make four important points of clarification and then draw out some potential developmental implications. In particular, I discuss which of the characteristics of episodic memories may prevent young children from having genuine episodic memories and as a consequence are responsible for our difficulty in remembering early childhood events (infant amnesia).

CRITICAL DISTINCTIONS

Origin Versus Content of Knowledge

Let me introduce a simple example for making this distinction: I saw at some earlier time that an object was put into a box. Now, some time later, I know that the object is in the box. This is knowledge of the present location of the object, but it is knowledge that was formed on the basis of past information. This requires "memory" in cognitive science terms, and even in common sense terminology we speak of "remembering where the object is." The important thing to realize is that this knowledge is *not* memory or knowledge of a past event (knowledge of where the object was put), it is knowledge about the present (where the object is), and I can have this knowledge even though I have forgotten that it comes from observing the relevant past event (that the object had been put inside the box). Although we would call this knowledge a memory and speak of remembering, it is not an episodic memory.

The inverse case is also possible: I did not witness how the object was put inside the box, but I am now told by a reliable source that the object was put inside. Now I have knowledge of the past: I know that the object was put inside the box, but one would not call this knowledge a memory; it is knowledge of the past.

In sum, important constraints on what counts as episodic memory are that it represents the past and is based on information from the past. I discuss the first of these constraints in the next section; the other one will be elaborated in the ensuing two sections.

Individual Events, Individual Times

When we say that episodic memory is the memory of a past event, then we naturally mean that we represent a particular event of a certain kind and that this event took place at a particular time. That is, with reference to the example just discussed, we know that there was some event, which took the form of putting the object inside the box, and this took place at some particular time in the past. One might be tempted to identify that particular event with the details of its form, that is, the precise way the particular object was put into the particular box. This is inadvisable, however, because it would make it impossible to ask otherwise sensible questions about the precise form of *this event* or raise counterfactual considerations about how *this event* could have been different from how it really was. Moreover, we also need to keep the particular event and the particular time at which it occurred conceptually distinct, or else we could not discuss questions about whether two events took place at the same time or at different times.

In contrast to thinking in terms of a particular event having occurred at a particular time, there is another possible interpretation of the phrase "representing a past event" (of which only philosophers can think): We represent the event type, "object being put into the box," without representing that there was a particular event of this type at a particular time in the past at which this event took place. I indicated this by writing *being put* as a means of leaving individual occurrence and the "past-ness" of this event unspecified. Perhaps a more natural and clearer way of illustrating this point is to think of a case in which the perception of the event is encoded as a visual image. Now I am "remembering" the event by reactivating the visual image, then I can say with some justification that I am representing that particular past event. However the image represents only the form of the event, not the fact that there was a particular time at which this event took place. As Perner and Ruffman (1995; Perner, 2000) pointed out, infants' ability to imitate a particular event is potentially overinterpreted as a memory of a particular past event when, in fact, it may be no more than general knowledge of what can be done on the basis of observing a particular event.

The difference between these two interpretations of "representing a past event" can be captured by differentiating "representing a past event *as* a past event" (restricts it to the normal interpretation) and "representing an event (that happened in the past)." This distinction is important when looking at development, because one central constraint on children's ability to have episodic memory is their ability to represent the past, that is, events as having occurred at particular times, an issue also addressed by McCormack and Hoerl (chap. 11, this volume).

Directness of Information

A genuine memory requires more than representation that a particular event occurred in the past. This would still qualify as mere knowledge of the past. We need—in Tulving's (1985) words—to draw a distinction between *knowing* the past and *remembering* the past. Part of the basis of this distinction is the directness of information. Knowledge of the past can be acquired indirectly through testimony (being told) or by inferring what must have happened. A memory of a past event must result from directly perceiving (experiencing) that event.

We all immediately understand the difference between the directness of experience and indirect information through testimony, but there is no immediately obvious expression to capture exactly that difference in directness. *Experience* clearly has this meaning of directness, whereas *observation* and *perception* can be indirect (e.g., Dretske's entry in Honderich, 1995, pp. 261, 652). I can perceive that an oil tank is empty by looking at the pointer on the gauge pointing to zero, whereas I cannot say "I experienced the empty tank" after looking at the gauge. As a consequence, I cannot claim having a genuine (proper) memory of the empty oil tank.[1] In contrast, if I actually looked inside the tank I could say that I experienced the empty tank, and I could say that I have a memory of the empty oil tank.

By stipulating that the relevant knowledge be noninferential the required directness of episodic memories can be partially captured. Knowledge gained through inference is indirect and cannot be the basis of a proper memory. However, not every kind of indirect knowledge is inferential. Knowledge through testimony (or from observing a gauge or other indicator) is indirect as well, without being inferential (e.g., Millikan, 1984, p. 62). If you tell me that the tank is empty, I know that the tank is empty without going through an inferential chain of reasoning: "Oh, she says that the tank is empty, she tends to be a reliable informant and has no reason to be lying, therefore, the tank must be empty."

A different suggestion is that the required directness stems from the lack of initial truth evaluation of information (Perner, 2000). When I perceive something with my own eyes I immediately take it as a fact. I can later disown that fact. For instance, when I look at the two lines of the Müller–Lyer illusion I keep seeing them as different in length even after measuring them and having established that they are the same length (Crane, 1992)—that is, despite my better knowledge my visual experience consciously registers a "false" fact,[2] which is then annulled at

---

[1] At best, I could say that I remember the day the oil tank was empty, which expresses my direct experience of the consequences of the empty oil tank on that day.

[2] This observation produces an intriguing picture of different levels of information processing. There is evidence (e.g., Milner & Goodale, 1995) that perceptual information is processed dorsally unconsciously for direct action. This information tends to be veridical and not subject to illusion (e.g., Aglioti, DeSouza, & Goodale, 1995, for the Ebbinghaus/Titchener circle illusion).

a conscious level because of my knowledge to the better. In contrast, when I am told something that contradicts my existing knowledge, it does not register consciously as a fact. It is directly, subconsciously sifted through a filter of compatibility and, depending on how it fares in that filter, becomes conscious as trustworthy or untrustworthy. In the latter case this may be followed up by additional conscious tests of trustworthiness. True memories are made of this kind of direct information that is directly registered as a fact before it can be evaluated against existing knowledge.

For developmental considerations we can plausibly assume that infants from birth are able to have direct experiences and only later develop the ability to gain knowledge from communication or through inference. However, this question of how direct experience differs from indirectly gained knowledge becomes relevant for my next two points, which are that genuine episodic memory not only requires direct experience but also knowledge that the memory stems from a directly experienced event.

Causal Self-Reference

For something to be a genuine memory it is not sufficient that it originate from direct experience. The memory also has to reflect that fact; that is, if I know from direct experience that an object was put inside a box, but I have forgotten how I came to know this fact then it is not a genuine memory. In other words, a genuine memory of an event not only encodes the event but also encodes (this is perhaps too strong a term, as we will see) the fact that the memory of the event originated from direct experience. This coding of memories (and perceptions) of their own causal origin has been called *causal self-referentiality* by John Searle (1983), a term he also applied to intentional actions. A little thought experiment by Jérôme Dokic (1997) neatly illustrates why causal self-reference may be needed for genuine memories.

Let us assume I know of some event about my earliest youth but I am not sure whether I know it because I experienced it or because I was told it. I later tell my parents, and they assure me that this indeed happened and that no one could have told me. I must have known from experience. So now it is clear that I know of this childhood event through experience, and I have meta-knowledge about the causal origins of my knowledge; that is, I know that I know of this childhood event through experience. Yet this meta-knowledge with causal reference is not truly a genuine episodic memory. What it lacks is the following: Although there

---

Conscious perception follows a ventral processing path and is subject to the illusion. It would be in this processing path that illusory perceptions register first as a fact and are then, because of better knowledge, disowned as being veridical.

is meta-knowledge that the knowledge of the event was caused directly by experiencing the event, the meta-knowledge itself was not caused by experiencing the event but by being told (through testimony).

Dokic's (1997) example provides a counterexample to my meta-comment explication of episodic memory in Tulving's (1985) sense. My criterion was stated for the simple example of remembering an item, *pear* in a word list memory experiment (Perner, 1991, p. 163) in terms of "information." It can be rephrased and amended for present purposes more explicitly in terms of "knowledge":

(1) I have knowledge from my past experience of the list that ["pear" was on the list], and
    I have knowledge that [I have the knowledge that ["pear" was on the list] from my past experience of the list].[3]

This criterion is not sufficient because it leaves open the possibility—as in Dokic's (1997) example—that I do not remember seeing the item but that I found out about it by testimony (e.g., the experimenter assured me that I couldn't have come to know that *pear* was on the list except by having seen it on the list). Therefore, Dokic suggested that the criterion be sharpened by making it self referential:

(2) I have *experiential knowledge* that ["pear" was on the list and that I have *this knowledge* from my past experience of the list].

This is self-referential because the expression *this knowledge* in specifying the content of the experiential knowledge refers to itself, that is, the experiential knowledge that contains it. That has the effect that the causal connection ("from my past experience") expressed in the content applies not only to the knowledge that *pear* was on the list but also recursively to the knowledge about the causal connection. This elegant solution has the desired effect of excluding Dokic's (1997) example as a case of episodic memory, because in that example the knowledge of the origin of knowing about the list is not experiential itself (as required by criterion 2, above) but comes from testimony.

Searle (1983) made similar suggestions for memory, intentional action, and perception. For instance, the Intentional content of a visual experience of a yellow station wagon must also encode that it is the yellow station wagon there that causes the visual experience (p. 48).

---

[3] With the square brackets I want to differentiate clearly the attitude of knowing and the content of the knowing [given within brackets]. The lower part presents what I have been calling a *metarepresentational comment* (Perner, 1991, p. 163).

However, several authors have questioned how such a highly sophisticated condition as causal self-reference could be part of an intentional content of every ordinary perception or action. Armstrong (1991, p. 154), for instance, wondered whether a dog could have visual experiences if it needs concepts of causality and visual experience in order for its visual experiences to have the self-referential content of the experience itself being caused by the perceived object or event. Burge (1991, p. 198) shared this feeling that Searle's analysis attributes too complicated an Intentional content to visual experiences. In his reply to these commentaries Searle insisted that causal self-referentiality is internal to the content of intentions but pointed out that he was not arguing that the dog thinks to itself "I am having a causally self-referential visual experience" (1991, pp. 183-184). Rather, he argued that any visual experience is experienced by us *as caused by* its Intentional object.

This leaves the problem for cognitive psychologists of specifying the difference between contents that allow thinking to oneself as opposed to contents that are just experienced. One way of making sense of this difference is to assume that it is based on a functional difference. For instance, directly experienced information comes in through a different channel and is treated differently (taken as veridical without question, etc.) from information based on testimony or inference. The internal distinctions that constitute this functional difference can be said to implicitly represent (procedural knowledge that is not explicitly predicated on particular instances; Dienes & Perner, 1999) the causal self-reference of experiential knowledge, because only information that comes from direct experience is channeled in this way.[4] That is, the seeing dog experiences the causal self reference only in this way, whereas we (or some of us) can reflect on this causal self-reference, make it explicit by representing it declaratively, which allows "thinking about it to oneself." Although we can think about it, we seldom do, and dogs presumably never do.

For memory the same applies as for visual perception. The causal origins of our memories in direct perception are encoded only procedurally in that they are given corresponding status within our mental processes as something that constitutes—with no questions asked—past reality. When this distinction fails and doubt arises about the veridicality of the memory or even just its source, as in Dokic's (1997) example, then it loses its status as a proper memory.

In sum, a proper memory needs to encode not only the remembered event but also its status as having arisen from direct experience of this event. However, the causal origin does not need to be encoded explicitly,

---

[4] I have tried to provide a similar but much more extensive analysis for Searle's (1983) claim that the Intentional content of intentional action is causally self-referential (Perner, 1998, in press).

that is, that one thinks to oneself every time one has a memory of the past, "and it originates in direct experience of this event." Rather, this fact can be known implicitly, in the procedural distinctions of how memories of different origins are processed. However, once doubts do arise, then a child who does not have the conceptual resources for making explicit that a particular memory has its origin in direct experience has little means to resist repeated misleading suggestions about what had happened. As a consequence, children lacking these conceptual resources can be expected to be much more susceptible to the implanting of a false memory than an older child with such conceptual resources.

Subjective Sensations and the Re-Experiencing of Past Events

By arguing that a genuine episodic memory must preserve (encode) its origin in direct experience I have so far been emphasizing exclusively the directness of experience. However, besides its directness experience is also characterized by the subjective aspect of sensations as Fred Dretske, in his entry in the *Oxford Companion to Philosophy* (Honderich, 1995) pointed out:

> *Experience.* Direct, observational knowledge of the world. More narrowly, experience is sometimes restricted to the sensory basis (sensation) of this knowledge. In the first sense, one's experience includes whatever one has come to know or believe about the world by direct observation and without inference. In the second, narrower, sense, experience is distinguished from belief or knowledge. It refers to the sensory events. (p. 261)

Dretske's other entry reads: "*Sensation.* The subjective aspect of perception— ... One might hear—thus have a sensation caused by—a French horn without coming to know or believe that it is a French horn."(in Honderich, 1995, p. 821)

A genuine episodic memory must preserve both the directness of its experiential origins and its subjective sensations. Tulving (1985) emphasized both aspects of episodic memory, as expressed in his quote from Ebbinghaus as a process of calling something back into consciousness, which is then "immediately recognized as something formerly experienced." However, Tulving also pointed out that episodic memory is correlated with *autonoetic consciousness* which is necessary for the remembering of personally experienced events. When a person remembers such an event, he is aware of the event as a veridical part of his own past existence. It is autonoetic consciousness that confers the special phenomenal flavor to the remembering of past events, the flavor that distinguishes remembering from other kinds of awareness, such as those characterizing perceiving, thinking, imagining, or dreaming." (Tulving, 1985, p. 3)

"When autonoetically aware, an individual can focus attention directly on his or her own subjective experience" (Wheeler, Stuss & Tulving, 1997, p. 335). This also yields a particular "recollective experience" (Tulving, 1985, p 8) when recalling episodic events.

To make the point that preservation of subjective sensations is essential for a genuine memory, I now consider four different cases concerning my occasional trips home for lunch.

Case 1: Direct record rich of sensations (genuine memory). I remember having been home for lunch today. I know that I know it from direct experience, and I still can evoke specific sensations of sitting at the table, the food I had, and so on. I am able to reminisce about it.

Case 2: Direct record without sensations. I remember having been home for lunch the day before yesterday. I know that I know it from direct experience (unlike in Dokic's, 1997, example there is no doubt in my mind that this is so), but there are no specific sensations attached to that particular event.

Case 3: Indirect record. I know that I was home for lunch on a particular day because my diary tells me that I was.

Case 4: Imagined experience (daydream). My wife once promised me some special lunch. I started to imagine savoring these delights over lunch with candlelight. It never happened—and I know it—but I still can indulge in this daydream and savor my subjective sensations.[5]

---

[5] Here is a slight change in example. After some months or years of indulging in this pleasant daydream I come to feel that the imagined lunch actually might have happened, but I am not certain. Without this certainty, and without certainty that my sensations stem from direct experience (like in Dokic's, 1997, example) there is still no genuine episodic memory, despite phenomenal richness and suspected veridicality. It is only once I get (wrongly) convinced that it did happen and that my memory comes from direct experience that it turns into a genuine memory—albeit a "genuinely false memory."

The particularly interesting cases are 2 and 4. In Case 2 the criteria of experiential directness and of absence of any doubt about it are fulfilled, and yet it is difficult to speak in this case of a "genuine memory." In fact, we would say "I *just know* it; I was at home for lunch." Only when one can evoke subjective sensations of the remembered episode, as in Case 1, can we speak of a genuine memory. This means that the encoding of the experiential origins is not sufficient for being a genuine memory. The subjective sensations of the experience need also be available.

Conversely, Case 4 illustrates that the availability of subjective sensations in itself is not sufficient either. The origins in direct perception and their preservation are also necessary elements for a genuine memory because the mere ability to invoke the subjective sensations would leave open whether they are the re-experiencing of a past episode or the replay of an earlier imagination.

Case 1 also illustrates an important feature of genuine memories. In order to enjoy the desired subjective sensations in the right way one needs to somehow imagine oneself being in the original situation. It is such imagining of the remembered episode that makes for the intuition that one is "re-experiencing the episode" or "reliving the experience," which is seen as the definition of episodic memory: "Episodic memory … is the memory system that mediates mental time travel [in distinction of the possibility] for a person to know about events from the past, … without mentally traveling back to re-experience the retrieved event" (Wheeler et al., 1997, p. 332) and that may be a typical human ability (Suddendorf & Corballis, 1997).

It is not specifically the sensory detail of subjective experiences that separates knowledge of the past from memory. I may have seen a letter on the lunch table in an envelope of a peculiar shade of pink without being able to remember (re-experience the subjective sensation of perceiving that shade). Yet when shown different shades of pink I might be able to point to the sample closest to that of the letter. Although pure knowledge of such sensory details may be possible, it would not qualify as a case of genuine memory. Genuine remembering requires re-experiencing what the letter looked like. Usually, only such re-experiencing yields such sensory detail as the color shades of envelopes. It is this re-experiencing that makes episodic remembering distinct from purely conceptually knowing one's past as William James (1890) captured it using the term *remembrance*: "Remembrance is like a direct feeling; its object is suffused with a warmth and intimacy to which no object of mere conception ever attains" (p. 239).

The notion of re-experiencing is also reminiscent of the proposal that we understand other people's minds by a process of simulation (Gordon, 1986) or replication (Heal, 1986) in which we imagine ourselves being in the other person's situation and thereby vicariously experience the other person's plight by imaginative identification (Gordon, 1992). It has been suggested that we also understand our past mental life—for example, our old mistaken beliefs—in this way (Harris, 1992). One important feature of this process is that it is not sufficient to just identify imaginatively with the other person and then indulge in a process of simulative experiencing; rather, there needs to be concurrent awareness that the imaginative experiences are not what one oneself primarily experiences but what the other person is actually feeling (Perner, 1996).[6] Without this step the experienced emotions would be mere emotional contagion and not simulation. For this reason, simulation, or the re-experiencing of past events, introduces an important representational difference to the mere knowledge of a past event.

Knowledge consists of a representation of the past event. Imagining oneself in that situation consists of a representation of the image, and one has to understand how this image is related to the original event. This requires an understanding of "aboutness," namely that the image is an image *of* the original event. Without this understanding the re-experiencing of a past event would be indistinguishable from an imagined event.

Peacocke (1998) objected to Perner and Ruffman's (1995) claim that children cannot have genuine episodic memories until they can represent the origin of their knowledge of the past in their earlier experiences. He argued that

> someone can remember seeing something without having the concept of seeing or of experience. In describing the memory as one of seeing, we characterize the episodic memory as one of a certain subjective type, which is phenomenologically different from remembering hearing, remembering tasting, remembering feeling. The memory can be of one of these distinctive types without the rememberer having concepts of these types. (pp. 23–24)

This is certainly true in the sense that by replaying past experiences I can enjoy visual impressions as distinct from, for example, auditory and gustatory impressions without having to have a concept of these types. However, such enjoyment of different types of sensory information is not enough. There also needs to be an understanding of how the experienced image at the time of remembering relates to the bygone event that is thereby being remembered. Without this understanding, children from an early age can have experiences of different kinds and

---

[6] For primarily expository purposes I structured those different processes sequentially: a phase of imaginative identification followed by a phase of taking stock and attributing the imaginative experiences in an objective mode to the simulated person.

even replays of these experiences, but they cannot enjoy these replays *as* memories of an experienced event. As I outline next, this understanding emerges relatively late, around the age of 3–5 years.

Part of this understanding must concern the origin of the experienced image. A mere procedural distinction between factual and fictive information (as I considered for the case of keeping knowledge distinct from fiction) is implausible for images that are not themselves real but are *of* some real event. So, to enjoy these images as re-experiences of a past experience the child needs the conceptual tools for understanding the origin of knowledge in direct experience, which also develops around the age of 4 years. But I agree now with Peacocke (1998) that the prime reason for why young children cannot have genuine memories is not their failure to understand the origin of their knowledge. I now see it as primarily due to their inability to understand the relation between re-experiences of an event and the original experience of this event.

DEVELOPMENTAL IMPLICATIONS

From the analysis of what characterizes episodic memory there are two obvious factors that might pose a problem for young children for some years:

- •Relation between re-experience and original experience
  - •Understanding re-experience as being about original experience
  - •Explicit encoding of the causal origin of a re-experience
- •Individuation of past events and representing them as taking place at individual times

My claim is that the theory of mind development that takes place between ages 3 and 5 years makes re-experiencing possible with repercussions for children's ability to individuate past events.

Aboutness and the Causal Origin of Knowledge

One important development is children's appreciation of perspective (point of view, mode of presentation, Fregean sense) as something that is *about* something else. Converging evidence from different task paradigms points to the age of about 4 years. Before that age, children fail to understand false beliefs about the real state of the world (Wimmer & Perner, 1983) as recently summarized in a large meta-analysis by Wellman, Cross, and Watson (in press). These children fail to understand that a misleading appearance presents an object as being different than it really is (Flavell, Flavell, & Green, 1983) and that different visual vantage points create differences in perspective (Flavell, Everett, Croft, & Flavell, 1981).

There is also quite clear evidence that at the same age that children develop an understanding of perspective they also develop an understanding of the origins of their knowledge and other people's knowledge. For instance, Wimmer, Hogrefe, and Perner (1988) found that 3-year olds could not give reasons for their knowledge, for example, for knowing the contents of a box because they had seen what was put inside or because they had been told about it. Taylor, Esbensen, and Bennett (1994) found that between ages 4 and 6 years children become able to distinguish between words (e.g., animal or color names) that they have learned recently (e.g., *maroon*, a few minutes ago at an another table) and those they have known for some time (e.g., *red*).

One could further argue that the coordination of perspectives and the understanding of the causal origins of knowledge are not independent and both develop in synchrony. In fact, I have been claiming that around age 4 years children develop an understanding of representation, to capture that at this age they start to understand that there can be different modes of presentation (perspectives, senses) of one and the same state of affairs (referent) as the components of the representational content and that they start to understand the causal connections between the world and the carrier (representational vehicle) of these perspectives (Perner, 1991, 1995). Because of this developmental synchrony it is not possible to tell whether concurrent memory changes that have been documented in children at this age are due to the emergent understanding of perspective, the understanding of informational origin, or both (or some other development at this age).

Several studies document a marked increase between ages 3 and 5 years in children's resistance to misleading suggestions (decrease in suggestibility). Children's ability to pass false-belief and appearance–reality tasks correlates negatively with children's suggestibility (Welch-Ross, 1999b; Welch-Ross, Diecidue, & Miller, 1997). In particular, children's understanding of false belief makes them resistant against misleading suggestions by naïve interviewers (Welch-Ross, 1999a). Leichtman (1996) and Welch-Ross (1999b) reported that suggestibility declines significantly with children's understanding of experience as the source of knowledge. Several other studies have reported that susceptibility to misleading suggestions decreases strongly between ages 3 and 5 years (e.g., Ceci, Ross, & Toglia, 1987; Goodman & Reed, 1986; Leichtman & Ceci, 1995). One reason for this decline in suggestibility could be children's ability to relate their re-experiences of experienced events to the original experience and explicitly encode these re-experiences as resulting from real experiences. This should help make their knowledge of the past more resistant to false suggestions, especially when these suggestions are seen to be given by ignorant, uninformed interviewers.

It is also instructive to look at the closely related abilities that 3-year-olds do have. Woolley and Bruell (1996) showed that 3-year-old children can remember fairly well (although not perfectly) whether they were *told* what was in a box or had *seen* the object in the box. However, this is not the same as understanding that one knows something *because* one has seen it or was told it (Wimmer et al., 1988). The ability to remember in Woolley and Bruell's study can be based on the factual distinction between there being a toy in the box (direct visual experience) and someone speaking and saying that there is a toy inside. Moreover, the mention of the toy and the box may actually cause a perceptual image (like in a re-experience) of the event when the toy and the box were experienced, and this may help the child to decide correctly between "being told" and "having seen" without, however, the child understanding the evoked image as a re-experience of the original experience. Without this understanding, the image is not a re-experience of the original event but just an image associated with the target objects.

Individuating Past Events

Children's conceptual advance between ages 3 and 5 years in understanding perspective and the origins of mental states not only provides them with firmer memory traces, making them less suggestible, but it also may have repercussions for how they conceptualize the past in the first place. McCormack and Hoerl (1999; chap. 11, this volume) have discussed this link between understanding perspective and conceptions of the past extensively, emphasizing many points other than the two on which I focus here.

One such link can be seen in Campbell's (1997) argument about the origins of a linear conception of time in autobiographical memory. Insofar as episodic memory also involves the self as the experiencer of the remembered events, it is also autobiographical.[7] Campbell argued that in order to have autobiographical memory it is not enough to have a

---

[7] Although episodic memory has autobiographical aspects, I like to keep autobiographical and episodic memory conceptually distinct. In alignment with the meaning of *autobiography* as a work that reports one's own life, I think that autobiographical memory contains knowledge about one's own life as the central feature. Thus, an episodic memory of a football match that I personally experienced one would not call autobiographical, as one would not call a sports reporter's anthology of great football matches (which he personally experienced) his autobiography. By making a clear distinction between *autobiographical* and *episodic* I do not want to dispute that most episodic memories are probably also autobiographical.

picture of or narrative about self in some past episode. It is critical to see that person in the narrative as spatiotemporally connected with one's present self. It is that spatiotemporal continuity of a single self that forces a linear conception of time, that is, that the single self must have lived through and experienced the remembered narratives at particular times, one after the other. Evidently, one cannot see a single self experiencing remembered narratives without the 3- to 5-year-olds' acquisition of a conception of memories originating in the experienced events.

That younger children have no clear linear conception of causally connected times seems to be indicated in a recent finding by Povinelli, Landry, Theall, Clark, and Castille (1999, Experiment 4). As children were playing a game, a puppet was surreptitiously hidden in one of two containers. Then children were given two pieces of information about past events. They were told that while they had been playing the puppet was put inside Box A and that when some other child had been playing this game the puppet had been hidden in Box B. Five-year-old, but not 3-year-old, children understood that the puppet must, therefore, be now in Box A, not B. The 3-year-olds apparently seemed incapable of understanding that the hiding that had just happened was more relevant to where the object is now than a hiding that had taken place at some unspecified earlier occasion. Welch-Ross (chap. 6, this volume) reports that a similar procedure developed by Povinelli, Landau, and Perilloux (1996) correlates substantially with children's recall.

There is yet another argument one can make in favor of the link between a conception of individual past events and the understanding of how these states affect our knowledge on which Perner and Ruffman (1995, pp. 542–543) once briefly speculated. Campbell (1995) identified two principles that justify one's concept that the world is inhabited by concrete objects beyond the properties that these objects carry. One is that the properties and their causal effects tend to cluster because they are properties of a particular individual, and the other principle is the potentiality for propagating causal influence over time. Events (episodes), unlike objects, do not persist over time for very long. Hence the reason for individuating events must primarily lie in their clustering of causal effects. Some events (e.g., winning a race, an award, or a war) clearly have memorable causal effects on the subsequent series of events. If I had not won the race I would not have the trophy at home. But many events (e.g., having had lunch at home) have no effect worth mentioning except for their effect on our mind. What would be different if I had not had lunch at home today? Only one answer comes readily to mind: I could not know of it and have a memory of it. So, there is another compelling reason for why an understanding of the causal effects on one's mind (the causal origins of knowledge) play a critical role in forming a concept of individual past states. One's phenomenal experience of re-experiencing past events suggests that this understanding is not based on a pure (theoretical) encoding of causal origins but, as pointed out earlier, on (at least partly) a simulation (Gordon, 1986) or replication (Heal, 1986) of the original experience.

To have a notion of individual events has important consequences. It gives additional coherence to all the aspects of the event that are otherwise only linked by association, and one can linguistically refer to the event (a defining feature of direct tests of memory, in particular, free recall; e.g., Reingold & Merikle, 1988; Richardson-Klavehn & Bjork, 1988). Moreover, free recall depends especially strongly on an understanding of the event having been experienced, because the identifying description tends to be in terms of experience; for example, "What was on the list that I've just shown you?" In support of these contentions Perner and Ruffman (1995) found that between age 3 and 5 years children's free recall depends to a much larger degree on their understanding of how knowledge is acquired than on their cued recall, in which content cues are provided and access to the memory content can be obtained without the notion of an experienced event.

Several other findings fit this pattern. For instance, as emphasized by Fivush and Hamond (1990; Fivush, Hamond, Harsch, & Singer, 1991), recall in early childhood is principally structured by the semantic cues provided by the interrogator, and the information retrieved on different occasions will differ because different questions may be asked or different associations be triggered, whereas after the age of 6 years experienced events have a coherent identity, which allows free recall of such events and coherence of recall over repeated interrogations. For instance, in the case of an emergency school evacuation during a fire alarm, 4-year-olds remembered the causal and temporal sequence of the event 2 weeks after the evacuation much better than 3-year-olds did (Pillemer, Picariello, & Pruett, 1994). Almost all of the older, but only about half of the younger, children remembered that they were inside the building when the alarm rang. Seven years later only some of those who had been over age 4 at the time of the alarm, but none of the younger group, produced a narrative memory, indicating that the event had gained a coherence beyond the description of its components.

A colleague and I recently tried to disrupt the coherence that one gets from simulating, re-experiencing, a direct experience by giving some of the information indirectly (Gornik, 2001; Perner & Gornik, 2001). The free recall of children (aged 3–6 years) was assessed with 20 cards depicting common objects. Each child was shown all 20 pictures and had to name each object. Then 10 of these pictures had to be put one by one into a box. In the *direct experience* condition children looked at each picture as they put each card into the box. In the *indirect knowledge* condition they looked at the back side of each card as they put it into the box and were afterward shown a video of the pictures on each card. After a 10-min delay they were asked which cards they had put into the box. In the indirect condition a simple simulation of the original experience should be difficult, because one can only imagine oneself putting blank cards into the box. One can also re-experience the watching of the video, but one cannot re-experience putting particular pictures into the box. Indeed, adults and children older than 5 years show much better recall for directly experienced items than in the indirect condition. Four-year olds show no such difference—even a hint of a slight difference in the opposite direction. Children were assessed for their understanding of how (Wimmer et al., 1988) and when (Taylor et al., 1994) they have come to know something and for their understanding of which sense modality to use to find out particular properties (eyes for color, hand for weight; O'Neill, Astington, & Flavell, 1992). It seems that the children who have no awareness of how their senses relate to the different aspects of the world seem unable to take advantage of episodic encoding, that is, re-experience their original direct experiences, which is considered particularly helpful for free recall (Tulving, 1985).

Conclusion: Infant Amnesia

I have emphasized three important criteria for episodic memory: Remembered events need to be conceived of as particular events that happened at some particular time, the memory of these events has to be seen (treated if not explicitly encoded) as originating in one's direct experiences, and they must be available for re-experience. I have put forward arguments that these conceptual criteria are not independent and that children acquire the necessary conceptual competence between ages 3 and 5 years. Before that age children have knowledge of past events, and perhaps mental reruns of these experiences, but no genuine episodic memories (proper memories/remembrances in James' sense), because they cannot appreciate their mental experiences as re-experiences of, and originating in, their original experiences.

The developmental timing of the onset of episodic memory suggests that it might account for the phenomenon noted by Freud (1963) as "infantile amnesia," namely, that most adults are unable to remember their early childhood. Systematic investigations by, for example, Waldfogel (1948/1982) and many others (e.g., Dudycha & Dudycha, 1941) across a variety of methods, suggest that very few people remember anything that happened before their third birthday. Then the number of memories sharply increases for events that happened between 3 and 5 or 6 years. For events that occurred after age 5 or 6 there is no distinctly greater "amnesia" than expected by normal forgetting (Wetzler & Sweeney, 1986).

Most traditional explanations of this phenomenon assume that the actual content of early experiences fails to register in long-term memory or gets essentially lost. My current suggestion (theory-of-mind explanation of childhood amnesia; Perner, 1990) sees the problem in infants' inability to encode personally experienced events as personally experienced. My emphasis here is on the fact that the understanding of something having been personally experienced does not consist of a mere conceptual encoding but involves a process of re-experiencing the original experience in a kind of simulation (replication). Also, it is important to note that the process of re-experiencing (re-evoking the original sensations in imagination) needs to be linked to the knowledge of the original event. Infants' inability to make this link creates two problems for adults trying to remember their infancy. One problem is direct: Even though a representation of the experienced event may still exist, the event cannot be remembered *as* an experienced (directly observed) event, that is, as a genuine memory rather than as mere knowledge about some autobiographical fact, or as a mere experience (subjective sensations) without grounding in the real course of events. The other problem is indirect: Without understanding of the mental effects of experienced events there is only weak representation of them as particular events (that generated these rich sensations), and these representations are prone to interference from similar events. Hence, they are unlikely to survive into adulthood as representations of individual events. The developmental data from theory-of-mind investigations (as outlined earlier) locate the critical change within the age range of 3–6 years. This provides a good fit to the age at which infant amnesia ends (e.g., Sheingold & Tenney, 1982; Wetzler & Sweeney, 1986, and most other studies that looked at adults' memory for childhood events).

ACKOWLEDGMENTS

I thank Jerome Dokic, Chris Moore, Teresa McCormack, Christoph Hoerl, and Christopher Peacocke for guidance to relevant literature and helpful comments on an earlier draft, and Chris Moore and Karen Lemmon for their tremendous patience with a tardy author.

REFERENCES

Aglioti, S., DeSouza, J. F., & Goodale, M. A. (1995). Size-contrast illusions deceive the eye but not the hand. *Current Biology, 5,* 679–685.
Armstrong, D. M. (1991). Intentionality, perception, and causality: reflections on John Searle's *Intentionality*. In E. Lepore & R. Van Gulick (Eds.), *John Searle and his critics* (pp. 149–158). Oxford, England: Basil Blackwell.

Burge, T. (1991). Vision and intentional content. In E. Lepore & R. Van Gulick (Eds.), *John Searle and his critics* (pp. 195–213). Oxford, England: Basil Blackwell.

Campbell, J. (1995). The body image and self-consciousness. In J. Bermúdez, A. Marcel, & N. Eilan (Eds.), *The body and the self*, (pp. 29–42). Cambridge, MA: MIT Press.

Campbell, J. (1997). The structure of time in autobiographical memory. *European Journal of Philosophy, 5*, 105–118.

Ceci, S. J., Ross, D. F., & Toglia, M. P. (1987). Suggestibility of children's memory: Psycholegal implications. *Journal of Experimental Psychology: General, 116*, 38–49.

Crane, T. (1992). The nonconceptual content of experience. In T. Crane (Ed.), *The contents of experience: Essays on perception* (pp. 136–157). Cambridge, England: Cambridge University Press.

Dienes, Z., & Perner, J. (1999). A theory of implicit and explicit knowledge (target article). *Behavioral and Brain Sciences, 22*, 735–755.

Dokic, J. (1997, August). *Two metarepresentational theories of episodic memory*. Paper presented at the annual meeting of the European Society of Philosophy and Psychology, Padua, Italy.

Dudycha, G. J., & Dudycha, M. M. (1941). Childhood memories: A review of the literature. *Psychological Bulletin, 38*, 668–682.

Ebbinghaus, H. (1885). *Über das Gedächtnis [On memory]*. Leipzig, Germany: Duncker und Humblot.

Fivush, R., & Hamond, N. R. (1990). Autobiographical memory across the preschool years: Toward reconceptualizing childhood amnesia. In R. Fivush & J. A. Hudson (Eds.), *Knowing and remembering in young children* (pp. 223–248). New York: Cambridge University Press.

Fivush, R., Hamond, N. R., Harsch, N., & Singer, N. (1991). Content and consistency in young children's autobiographical recall. *Discourse Processes, 14*, 373–388.

Flavell, J. H., Everett, B. A., Croft, K., & Flavell, E. R. (1981). Young children's knowledge about visual perception: Further evidence for the Level 1–Level 2 distinction. *Developmental Psychology, 17*, 99–103.

Flavell, J. H., Flavell, E. R., & Green, F. L. (1983). Development of the appearance–reality distinction. *Cognitive Psychology, 15*, 95–120.

Freud, S. (1963). Introductory lectures on psychoanalysis. In J. Strachey (Ed.), *The standard edition of the complete psychological works of Sigmund Freud* (Vol. 7, pp. 135-243). London: Hogarth Press. (Original work published 1916-1917)

Goodman, G. S., & Reed, R. S. (1986). Age differences in eyewitness testimony. *Law and Human Behavior, 10*, 317–332.

Gordon, R. M. (1986). Folk psychology as simulation. *Mind & Language, 1*, 158–171.

Gordon, R. M. (1992). The simulation theory: Objections and misconceptions. *Mind & Language, 7*, 11–34.

Gornik, E. (2000). Die entwicklung des episodischen Gedächtnisses: Die Rolle der direkten Erfahrung [The development of episodic memory: The role of direct experience]. Unpublished master's thesis, University of Salzburg, Salzburg, Austria.

Harris, P. L. (1992). From simulation to folk psychology: The case for development. *Mind & Language, 7*, 120–144.

Heal, J. (1986). Replication and functionalism. In J. Butterfield (Ed.), *Language, mind, and logic* (pp. 135–150). Cambridge, England: Cambridge University Press.

Honderich, T. (Ed.). (1995). *The Oxford companion to philosophy.* Oxford, England: Oxford University Press.

James, W. (1890). *The principles of psychology.* London: Macmillan.

Leichtman, M. D. (1996, July). *What gets remembered? Patterns of memory and reminiscence in early life.* Paper presented at the International Conference on Memory, Padua, Italy.

Leichtman, M. D., & Ceci, S. J. (1995). The effects of stereotypes and suggestions on preschoolers' reports. *Developmental Psychology, 31,* 568–578.

McCormack, T., & Hoerl, C. (1999). Memory and temporal perspective: The role of temporal frameworks in memory development. *Developmental Review, 19,* 154–182.

Millikan, R. G. (1984). *Language, thought and other biological categories.* Cambridge, MA: MIT Press.

Milner, D. A., & Goodale, M. A. (1995). *The visual brain in action.* Oxford, England: Oxford University Press.

O'Neill, D. K., Astington, J. W., & Flavell, J. H. (1992). Young children's understanding of the role that sensory experiences play in knowledge acquisition. *Child Development, 63,* 474–490.

Peacocke, C. (1998, May). *Theories of concepts: a wider task.* Paper presented at the Lisbon Expo Conference, Lisbon, Portugal.

Perner, J. (1990). Experiential awareness and children's episodic memory. In W. Schneider & F. E. Weinert (Eds.), *Interactions among aptitudes, strategies, and knowledge in cognitive performance* (pp. 3–11). New York: Springer-Verlag.

Perner, J. (1991). *Understanding the representational mind.* Cambridge, MA: MIT Press.

Perner, J. (1995). The many faces of belief: Reflections on Fodor's and the child's theory of mind. *Cognition, 57,* 241–269.

Perner, J. (1996). Simulation as explicitation of predication-implicit knowledge about the mind: Arguments for a simulation–theory mix. In P. Carruthers & P. K. Smith (Eds.), *Theories of theories of mind* (pp. 90–104). Cambridge, England: Cambridge University Press.

Perner, J. (1998). The meta-intentional nature of executive functions and theory of mind. In P. Carruthers & J. Boucher (Eds.), *Language and thought: Interdisciplinary themes* (pp. 270–283). Cambridge, England: Cambridge University Press.

Perner, J. (2000). Memory and theory of mind. In E. Tulving & F. I. M. Craik (Eds.), *The Oxford handbook of memory* (297–312). New York: Oxford University Press.

Perner, J. (in press). Dual control and the causal theory of action: The case of nonintentional action. In N. Eilan & J. Roessler (Eds.). *Agency and self-awareness.* Oxford, England: Oxford University Press.

Perner, J. & Gornik, E. (2001, April). The role of direct experience in the development of episodic memory. Paper presented at the biennial meeting of the Society for Research in Child Development, Minneapolis, MN

Perner, J., & Ruffman, T. (1995). Episodic memory an autonoetic consciousness: Developmental evidence and a theory of childhood amnesia. *Journal of Experimental Child Psychology, 59,* 516–548.

Pillemer, D. B., Picariello, M. L., & Pruett, J. C. (1994). Very long-term memories of a salient preschool event. *Applied Cognitive Psychology, 8*, 95–106.

Povinelli, D. J., Landau, K. R., & Perilloux, H. K. (1996). Self-recognition in young children using delayed versus live feedback: Evidence of a developmental asynchrony. *Child Development, 67*, 1540–1554.

Povinelli, D. J., Landry, A. M., Theall, L. A., Clark, B. R., & Castille, C. M. (1999). Development of young children's understanding that the recent past is causally bound to the present. *Developmental Psychology, 35*, 1426–1439.

Reingold, E. M., & Merikle, P. M. (1988). Using direct and indirect measures to study perception without awareness. *Perception & Psychophysics, 44*, 563–575.

Richardson-Klavehn, A., & Bjork, R. A. (1988). Measures of memory. *Annual Review of Psychology, 39*, 475–543.

Searle, J. (1983). *Intentionality*. Cambridge: Cambridge University Press.

Searle, J. (1991). Response: Perception and the satisfactions of intentionality. In E. Lepore & R. van Gulick (Eds.), *John Searle and his critics* (pp. 181-192). Oxford, England: Basil Blackwell.

Sheingold, K., & Tenney, Y. J. (1982). Memory for a salient childhood event. In U. Neisser (Ed.), *Memory observed* (pp. 201–212). San Francisco: Freeman.

Taylor, M., Esbensen, B., & Bennett, R. T. (1994). Children's understanding of knowledge acquisition: The tendency for children to report they have always known what they have just learned. *Child Development, 65*, 1581–1604.

Suddendorf, T., & Corballis, M. C. (1997). Mental time travel and the evolution of the human mind. Genetic, *Social, and General Psychology Monographs, 123*, 133–167.

Tulving, E. (1972). Episodic and semantic memory. In E. Tulving & W. Donaldson (Eds.), *Organization of memory* (pp. 381–403). New York: Plenum.

Tulving, E. (1985). Memory and consciousness. *Canadian Psychology, 26*, 1–12.

Waldfogel, S. (1982). The frequency and affective character of childhood memories. In U. Neisser (Ed.), *Memory observed* (pp. 73–76). San Francisco: Freeman. (Original work published 1948)

Welch-Ross, M. K. (1999a). Interviewer knowledge and preschoolers' reasoning about knowledge states moderate suggestibility. *Cognitive Development, 14*, 423–442.

Welch-Ross, M. K. (1999b). Preschoolers' understanding of mind: Implications for suggestibility. *Cognitive Development, 14*, 101–132.

Welch-Ross, M. K., Diecidue, K., & Miller, S. A. (1997). Young children's understanding of conflicting mental representation predicts suggestibility. *Developmental Psychology, 33*, 43–53.

Wellman, H. M., Cross, D., & Watson, J. (in press). Meta-analysis of theory of mind development: the truth about false-belief. *Child Development*.

Wetzler, S. E., & Sweeney, J. A. (1986). Childhood amnesia: An empirical demonstration. In D. C. Rubin (Ed.), *Autobiographical memory* (pp. 191–201). Cambridge, England: Cambridge University Press.

Wheeler, M. A., Stuss, D. T., & Tulving, E. (1997). Toward a theory of episodic memory: The frontal lobes and autonoetic consciousness. *Psychological Bulletin, 121*, 331–354.

Wimmer, H., Hogrefe, J., & Perner, J. (1988). Children's understanding of informational access as source of knowledge. *Child Development, 59*, 386–396.

Wimmer, H., & Perner, J. (1983). Beliefs about beliefs: Representation and constraining function of wrong beliefs in young children's understanding of deception. *Cognition, 13,* 103–128.

Woolley, J. D., & Bruell, M. J. (1996). Young children's awareness of the origins of their mental representations. *Developmental Psychology, 32,* 335–346.

11

The Child in Time: Temporal Concepts and Self-Consciousness in the Development of Episodic Memory

Teresa McCormack
Christoph Hoerl
University of Warwick, UK

One interesting aspect of recent research on long-term memory and its development has been the exploration of possible links between memory and self-consciousness (Fivush, 1997; Howe & Courage, 1993, 1997; Perner, 2000; Perner & Ruffman, 1995; Wheeler, Stuss, & Tulving, 1997). In this chapter we distinguish between two different ways of linking memory and self-consciousness. According to some theorists, types of long-term memory differ primarily in the degree to which they involve or are associated with self-consciousness, although there may be no substantial differences in the kind of event information that they deliver (e.g., Wheeler et al., 1997). One of the difficulties with such a view is that it is not obvious what motivates introducing self-consciousness as the decisive factor in distinguishing between types of memory and what role it is supposed to play in remembering. In this chapter we argue in favor of the alternative view that distinctions between different kinds of memory should be made initially on the basis of the ways in which they represent events. In particular, we suggest that the way in which remembered events are located in time provides an important criterion for distinguishing between different types of memory. According to this view, if there is a link between memory development and self-consciousness, it is because some temporal concepts emerge developmentally only once certain self-conscious abilities are in place.

THE EPISODIC–SEMANTIC DISTINCTION

Tulving's (1972) distinction between episodic and semantic memory has been highly influential in shaping research on long-term memory over the last 30 years. However, the basis of this distinction remains controversial, particularly in the light of Tulving's more recent attempts to characterize it in terms of the *phenomenology* (i.e., subjective experience) associated with each type of memory (Tulving, 1985). Thus, although both episodic and semantic memory are described as species of conscious memory (as opposed to unconscious or implicit memory), episodic remembering involves a distinctive kind of subjective experience whose "phenomenal quality is not mistaken for any other kind of conscious awareness" (Tulving & Markowitsch, 1998, p. 202). This subjective experience is described as that of "re-experiencing something that has happened before in one's life" (Wheeler et al., 1997, p. 349).

Thus, according to Tulving's definition, it becomes necessary to consider the phenomenology of memory experiences when exploring empirically episodic and semantic memory. One way in which this has been attempted is by explicitly asking participants in memory experiments to report on their subjective experiences in recall (Gardiner & Java, 1993; Tulving, 1985). There is some controversy as to whether different responses in these tasks should indeed be interpreted in terms of the different states of awareness that Tulving discussed (Donaldson, 1996; Hirshman & Master, 1997; Inoue & Bellezza, 1998; though see Gardiner & Gregg, 1997). At the very least, however, the fact that participants can readily make sense of the instructions in such tasks suggests that Tulving's distinction captures an important ingredient of our common sense understanding of memory and memory experiences. Furthermore, Tulving's description of episodic memory as involving re-experiencing or reliving the past has close similarities to the notion of *experiential memory* that is central to some philosophical debates on memory (Wollheim, 1984).

A further claim that Tulving makes is that episodic recollection essentially involves *self-consciousness*, in the sense of a reflection on one's experiences at different times and on one's own identity across time. According to Tulving, the rememberer must represent the fact that "the self doing the experiencing now is the same self that did it originally"

(Wheeler et al., p. 349). In other words, episodic recollection is thought to involve a representation of oneself as the subject of certain experiences both in the past and in the present, and thus the self is represented in episodic recollection as an entity that persists over time and is in different mental states at different times.

It is important to be clear about the relation between the claim that episodic recollection involves self-consciousness and the claim that it has a distinctive phenomenology. The claim that episodic recollection involves reflecting on one's past and present mental states does not follow from the idea that when a person remembers episodically, he or she is in some sense re-experiencing or reliving the past. Indeed, attempts have been made to describe the notion of re-experiencing the past without introducing self-consciousness in this sense (e.g., see Conway & Rubin, 1993; Martin, 2001). Some theorists have used the notion of re-experiencing primarily to capture the idea that in episodic remembering one's recollection shares some features with one's original sensory or perceptual experience. Having memories of this character may be a matter of having available particular types of memory images (Hoerl, 2001), or what Conway (2001) has referred to as *phenomenological records*.

Thus, the claim that episodic recollection has a distinctive phenomenology and the claim that it involves self-consciousness are separable theoretically, and it is at least possible to make either of these claims without the other. However, in characterizing episodic memory Tulving seems to have had in mind William James' (1890/1950) notion of "memory proper" as "the knowledge of an event ... *with the additional consciousness* [italics added] that we ... have experienced it before." Moreover, his claim seems to be that it is this kind of self-conscious reflection that "provides the characteristic phenomenal flavor of the experience of remembering" (Tulving, 1985, p. 1).

Self-Consciousness and Episodic Memory

From a developmental standpoint, an implication of Tulving's view is that episodic memory can emerge only once a certain type of self-consciousness has developed. Indeed, Perner (1991, 2000, chap. 10, this volume) has argued for just such a developmental claim. Our aim in this chapter is to explore in more detail the way self-consciousness and episodic memory might be related in development. One important issue is the nature of the self-consciousness that is thought to be linked to episodic memory. Specifically, we need to consider whether the involvement of self-consciousness in episodic memory should be spelled out in terms of the ability to reflect on one's own mental states at different times (so-called theory-of-mind abilities) or in terms of a grasp of one's persistence over time (Povinelli, Landau, & Perilloux, 1996; Povinelli & Simon, 1998) or some more primitive grasp of one's own identity (e.g., as measured in mirror self-recognition studies; Howe & Courage, 1993).

More generally, however, we think it is important to distinguish between two different ways in which a link could be made between episodic memory and self-consciousness:

1. The *constitutive view*: There is a constitutive connection between episodic memory and self-consciousness because what episodic recollection is has to be spelled out in terms of the idea that the self is represented in certain ways in episodic memory.

2. The *causal view*: The ability to represent oneself in certain ways plays a role in the development of the concepts used in episodic memory. However, episodic recollection itself need not involve representing oneself.

Both Tulving and Perner seem to subscribe to the first type of view, the constitutive view. As we discuss later, Perner defends a particular version of this view, according to which episodic memory has a metarepresentational structure in which one's current mental state is represented as resulting from one's previous experience. However, in this chapter we defend a version of the causal view. In particular, we argue that episodic memory requires the ability to conceptualize the past in a certain way and that the development of the necessary concept of the past depends on the ability to engage in certain forms of self-conscious reasoning. In the section entitled 'Episodic Memory and Time' we defend the view that episodic memory differs from other types in memory in virtue of the way in which the concept of the past is used in episodic recollection. In particular, we identify two ingredients in the ability to think about remembered events as events that have happened in the past: (a) the ability to integrate nonperspectival and perspectival representations of time and (b) the ability to think of events as unrepeatable and thus as happening at unique points in time. In the section entitled 'Episodic Memory and Perspective Taking' we argue that having a concept of the past, in this sense, requires grasping that there are systematic temporal relations between different points in time and that this is a matter of being able to engage in a particular form of reasoning that we describe as temporal perspective taking. Finally, we explore the extent to which the ability to engage in temporal perspective taking requires self-consciousness.

Before turning to our positive claims regarding temporal concepts and episodic memory we first discuss Perner's proposal regarding episodic memory and self-consciousness in more detail. We do this because we see Perner's theory as one of the most fully articulated versions of what we have called a *constitutive view*.

Perner's Metarepresentational Theory of Episodic Memory

Perner (1991, 2000) has argued that although both episodic and semantic memory involve retrieval of information about events, episodic memory also involves grasp of an additional fact about this event information; namely, that it concerns an event that was personally experienced. Representing this kind of fact is importantly different from representing other types of information about the event, because it involves representing one's own mental states: On Perner's analysis, it involves *metarepresentational* abilities. Thus, Perner (2000, p. 300) gave the following example of the kind of representation involved in episodic memory: "I have information (that 'pear' was on the list and that I have *this information* because I have seen 'pear' on the list)."

Note that this involves metarepresentational abilities in two different senses. First of all, the rememberer has to represent her previous mental state (the seeing of the word *pear*). Second, however, she must also represent her current mental state (the bearer of "this information"). Not just any information about having been in a certain mental state in the past will do, as the rememberer can acquire such information through, say, the testimony of others who tell her that she experienced a certain event. It is the fact that her current mental state itself derives directly from her past mental state, and is represented as such, that Perner has taken to be the defining characteristic of episodic memory. Taking up a suggestion from Dokic (1997, after Searle, 1983), Perner has therefore called episodic memory "causally self-referential."

The claim is that in episodic memory one's current mental state refers not just to a past event but also to one's past experience of that event as the cause of that mental state. This seems to imply, though, that there might be a more primitive way of remembering the past, that is, a case in which one simply has a memory of a past event, without being aware that one's memory stems from one's own experience of that event. Indeed, in his 1991 book Perner argued that it is possible to switch from representing the present to representing the past *before* he believes that metarepresentational abilities are intact (i.e., before age 4 years). For example, he described a 2-year-old as remembering something that happened last winter by switching to a representation of a past event, claiming that the child is not confused about the difference between past and present, because she can mark off representations of different situations by a process described as *quarantining*. This would seem to be compatible with the abilities of 2- and 3-year-olds who are beginning to use past-tense morphology (Weist, 1989). It is also consistent with numerous reports in the literature of children of this age verbally recalling at least some information about specific past events (see Nelson, 1993; Pillemer, 1998, chap. 4). The crucial question is why one should view this way of remembering past events as falling short of episodic memory. In other words, why does Perner insist that we can speak of genuine episodic memory only once metarepresentational abilities have emerged?

As far as we understand his position, what has motivated Perner's claim is the idea that memories count as truly episodic only if they come with a particular phenomenology, and, crucially, he believes that what "confers the special phenomenal flavor to the remembering of past events" (Perner & Ruffman, 1995, p. 517) is precisely its special metarepresentational or self-referential structure. However, questions have been raised about the connection Perner draws between phenomenology and self-consciousness at this stage. One objection to Perner's account has run as follows. The fact that a certain memory originates from past visual perception, say, might *in and of itself* explain why this memory is of a type that is phenomenologically different from memories originating in some other way (e.g., why remembering a visually experienced event is different from retrieving information about an event about which one has merely been told). On this alternative view, what would explain the phenomenological difference is not the rememberer's ability to think about the experiential origins of her memory; rather, the difference can be explained in terms of the very fact that the memory derives from a past experience, and the particular kinds of information that have been encoded and retained (Peacocke, 2000). Such a claim is consistent with accounts that explain the notion of "re-experiencing" in episodic recollection in terms of the retrieval of certain kinds of sensory records or memory images (Conway, 2001; Martin, 2001).

Although Perner (chap. 10, this volume) allows for such differences in phenomenology between memories that have different origins, he does not believe that they are the ones that are relevant for distinguishing episodic memory from other types of conscious states. Rather, he claims that the distinctive phenomenological flavor that defines episodic memory is due to the involvement of metarepresentational abilities. However, it is difficult to see how metarepresentational abilities are supposed to explain the kind of difference in phenomenology that Perner envisages. Intuitively, it is not one's grasp of the fact that one's present mental state originates from a past experience that explains the subjective experience that one has when one is in that mental state. Rather, the reverse seems to be true: If one thinks about one's present mental state as originating from a past experience, one's reason for doing so is normally because of the particular kinds of conscious information one has about the past—that is to say, one's mental state must *already have* a certain phenomenology that makes it reasonable to think that it originates in past experience. Thus, we have to turn to features of the mental state itself, and the way in which it represents things, to explain the nature of the subjective experience one has when one is in that mental state, rather than introducing a higher order state to do this job.

Taking the conscious nature of episodic memory seriously means discussing its distinct phenomenology within the context of overall cognitive and representational capacities rather than taking that phenomenology to be merely epiphenomenal. No psychologically useful category is captured by defining episodic memory purely in terms of a subjective experience that does not make any difference to the kind of information that can be retained or to how that information can be used. If our interpretation of Perner's claims is correct, the connection he has drawn between episodic memory and self-consciousness can be seen, in part, as an attempt to make good this idea. He has tried to elucidate Tulving's (1985) claim—that episodic memory can be distinguished from other forms of memory in virtue of its distinct phenomenology—in terms of the involvement of a certain representational capacity, namely, metarepresentation. Yet, if what we have been saying is right, this attempt cannot succeed. Reflection on the nature and origin of a certain mental state is something that comes in over and above one's being in that mental state, and we have to appeal to the fact that this mental state has a certain phenomenology to explain what makes such reflection possible in the first place.

If one is to argue for a connection between episodic memory and self-consciousness, what needs to be shown is why the emergence of certain abilities for self-conscious reasoning should be thought of as making available a new type of memory. Perner tries to do so by adopting what we have called a *constitutive* view. In other words, he distinguishes between episodic memory and other forms of memory by arguing that episodic recollection itself involves metarepresentation. However, what Perner talks about is arguably not an emergence of a new type of memory but rather a new ability to reflect on memory itself and to think about different ways in which one's present mental states may derive from the past. (Of course, it would not be surprising if a new ability to reflect on memory facilitates performance on memory tasks, such as the free-recall task used by Perner & Ruffman, 1995. For example, the emergence of encoding or retrieval strategies may depend on such an ability, as earlier work on metamemory would suggest [Flavell & Wellman, 1977]. This in itself may explain the relation that Perner and Ruffman found between performance on memory tasks and performance on theory-of-mind tasks.)

According to the view we put forward in this chapter, episodic memory is first and foremost a matter of being conscious of past events in a certain way, rather than being self-consciously aware of one's own current mental state and its connection with experiences one has had in the past. However, being conscious of past events in the particular way in which we are when we episodically recollect events may involve the use of certain conceptualizing abilities. What this suggests is that if there is still a sense in which episodic memory requires self-consciousness, a more fruitful approach may be to ask why the required concepts could not be available before the development of certain self-conscious abilities. In the next section we develop the suggestion that having episodic memories is in part a matter of being able to conceptualize the past in a certain way. In the last part of the chapter, we argue that there are good reasons to doubt whether one could possess the requisite concept of the past without being able to reflect on one's own persistence through time and involvement with certain past events. Thus, if there is a connection between self-consciousness and episodic memory, it lies in the fact that the ability to engage in certain forms of self-conscious reasoning plays a crucial role in the development of the temporal concepts used in episodic recollection. Self-consciousness, in this picture, could have a substantive *causal* role in the emergence of episodic memory rather than being a necessary component of episodic recollection as such.

EPISODIC MEMORY AND TIME

Although Tulving's focus on phenomenology and self-consciousness has been influential recently, there are other aspects of his conception of episodic memory that should not be overlooked. Tulving and Markowitsch (1998) pinpointed two other less controversial features of episodic memory: First, it involves memory for specific past events, and second, the rememberer is thought to be "oriented, at the time of retrieval, to the past." It is crucial to consider these two points in parallel: If one does so, it is clear that to demonstrate episodic memory it is not enough to show that specific past experiences have simply had an influence on behavior. Rather, the second feature suggests that, in addition, in episodic memory the mental state of the rememberer must be directed toward the past. This seems to capture some of the difference between retrieving a fact from semantic memory that one learned on a single occasion versus remembering the episode in which one learned the fact. Only in the latter case need the rememberer be thinking about the past at all.

There are numerous studies that show that young children are capable of remembering information that stems from a single past event.

Studies of memory in very young infants demonstrate that they can reproduce a response, such as activating a mobile by kicking their feet, that has been acquired in a single learning session (see Rovee-Collier, 1997, for review). A large number of studies of deferred imitation have also demonstrated that even after long delays, 1- or 2-year-olds can reproduce a sequence of novel actions that they observed on a single occasion (e.g., Bauer & Mandler, 1989, 1992; Mandler & McDonough, 1995). There are a number of features of deferred imitation that suggest that it involves a relatively sophisticated kind of memory: It is intact even when different props are provided at retrieval (Bauer & Dow, 1994), it survives shifts in context (Herbert & Hayne, 1999; Meltzoff, 1999), and amnesic patients have difficulties with deferred imitation tasks (McDonough, Mandler, McKee, & Squire, 1995). However, we can still ask whether children engaged in deferred imitation are oriented toward the past. The crucial issue here is how remembered events are represented in recall or, more specifically, the way in which their temporal location is specified.

The Concept of the Past

As should become clear, we think that the crucial developmental question is when children become capable of representing events as having happened at particular times in the past. In this section, we also hope to make clear that this is not a developmentally primitive ability. We have argued elsewhere that although young children have ways of representing the temporal locations of events, these early frameworks fall short of the ability to locate events at particular times in the past (McCormack, 1999; McCormack & Hoerl, 1999). But in what does such an ability consist, and why should we believe that young children do not yet possess it? We address these questions by providing a more detailed analysis of two aspects that seem central to conceptualizing an event as having happened at a particular time in the past.

Perspectival and nonperspectival representations of time. Not all kinds of temporal thought need involve a concept of the past. Some kinds of temporal information about events may simply represent the relations in which they stand to each other: That is, one could represent Event B as coming before Event C but after Event A, and so on. Representing the order in which meals happen each day could be of this form (breakfast, then lunch, then dinner, then supper). Although this involves representing some kind of temporal information, what is represented are the temporal relations between the events in the sequence rather than the location of the events relative to one's current position in time. An analogy can be made with spatial representations: It is possible to represent the spatial location of an object with respect to a set of other objects (e.g., as in between the table and the bookcase), or with respect to a fronted object (e.g., as behind the TV set) without also representing where any of these objects are located relative to one's own spatial position. The fundamental difference here is captured in the distinction between allocentric (nonperspectival) and egocentric (perspectival) spatial representations. However, it would seem that a nonperspectival representation can tell one about where an object is actually located only if one has some means of combining it with a perspectival representation (e.g., one needs to combine the information that the object is behind the TV set with one's knowledge of where the TV set is relative to one's own location). Similarly, in order for a nonperspectival representation of events within a sequence to tell one something about their actual temporal location, one would also need to have a way of locating the sequence itself with respect to one's current temporal perspective. For example, events could be represented as being in the past or as just about to happen. Thus, like a mature concept of space, a mature concept of time has both perspectival and nonperspectival ingredients (see also Miller & Johnson-Laird, 1976).

The claim is that children may be able to represent the location of an event relative to other events in a sequence without in addition representing where it is located with respect to their own perspective on time. One way of interpreting deferred-imitation studies is that they are measuring children's ability to represent temporal information in this limited sense, that is, their ability to extract and remember the relative order of events in an event sequence. Typically, performance is scored not simply in terms of the number of component events remembered but also in terms of whether the events are reproduced in the correct order. Thus, such studies measure some kind of basic ability to remember temporal–sequential information. However, simply being able to reproduce a sequence one has previously encountered does not seem to require thinking of the sequence as a sequence that happened in the past, that is, identifying a particular occurrence of the sequence as being in the past with respect to one's current temporal perspective.

Specific past times. It is interesting that we can also turn to an observation made by Tulving to elucidate further the difference between children's early abilities to represent the relative order of events within a sequence and the mature understanding of time involved in episodic memory. Speaking of the reasoning that led him to develop his theory of episodic memory, Tulving (1983) mentioned how he came to realize the crucial importance of something that "many wise philosophers from Heraclitus on had known all the time: events do not repeat themselves, there is never another event exactly like a given one" (p. 19). The basic point is that part of what it is to represent a event as having occurred in the past is to think of it as unrepeatable (see also Hoerl, 1999). There is, of course, also a sense in which one can speak of certain events as reoccurring at different times, but each occurrence is distinct from the others in virtue of the particular, unique, position in time when it happens. Thus, it is not clear whether young children's ability to retain the relative order of events within a sequence also involves an ability to distinguish between, say, different occurrences of the same sequence.

It is important that, to show that someone has grasped the unrepeatability of events, in the sense described by Tulving, requires more than showing that he or she possesses knowledge that, as a matter of fact, derives from a single event. For example, one could acquire "script-like" knowledge about an event sequence (Schank & Abelson, 1977), such as what happens when you visit a restaurant, on the basis of a single visit. Subsequently, one need not remember the visit *as* a specific, unique event: one may simply remember what usually happens during restaurant visits.

A considerable amount of research suggests that young children are very good at remembering everyday event sequences in this way (Fivush & Hudson, 1990; Nelson, 1986). Children's scripts are fairly sophisticated in that they allow for a flexible way of representing event sequences and for the integration of newly encountered events into a representation of an already-familiar sequence (see McCormack & Hoerl, 1999, for more details). For example, when the child encounters a novel event occurring at a certain point in the nursery school day, she can encode its temporal location with respect to her script of the school day (e.g., as happening "before lunch break" or "after nap time"). As other theorists have emphasized, representations of such sequences have good practical purposes, because knowing what normally happens at such and such a point in a sequence can have many implications for action. Nelson (1990, p. 308) argued that

> the most basic general function for memory ... is to provide guidance for action. What has happened is used as the basis for predicting what will come next. For this purpose the most useful type of evidence comes from events that are frequently repeated, and thus the most useful ... type of memory is that for familiar routine events, the type of generalized event memory realized as scripts.

However, the restricted use to which scripts are put may still mean that the temporal information they can represent may fall short of adults' abilities for representing time. Encoding the temporal location of events within familiar event sequences is importantly different from the way in which we as adults think of the time of events we remember episodically. The temporal representations in question are representations of repeated events, of "what usually happens," and thus encoding an event in terms of a location within a script does not involve assigning it a unique location in time. If, as has been suggested, episodic memory involves locating events in the past, then an ability to assign events an unique location in time is crucial. Otherwise, it is difficult to see how the rememberer can be described as thinking about the past at all rather than as thinking of potentially reoccurring events. Thus, even though research suggests that young children can and do recall information that stems from a specific past event, in considering whether this is episodic memory one needs to consider whether the child is representing the remembered event as unrepeatable.

The Concept of the Past and Perspective Taking

The claim is that episodic memory differs from semantic memory in terms of the kind of information about events that must be represented. Episodic memory involves representing events as specific occurrences in the past, whereas this is not the case in semantic memory. This requirement raises key developmental issues. It implies that in giving an account of episodic memory development what needs to be considered are the particular type of temporal framework in which remembered events can be located and the development of such frameworks. As adults, our most common way of locating events in time (i.e., our most familiar temporal framework) is the conventional clock and calendar system. Our clock and calendar system is only one example of a mature temporal framework, but we introduce it here to bring out some features of a framework that assigns events a unique location in time.

We argued earlier that locating events in the past involves integrating nonperspectival and perspectival ways of representing temporal locations. Although, of course, the clock and calendar system provides a nonperspectival way of representing temporal locations (e.g., specifying the date at which an event occurred need not involve bringing in one's current temporal location), when we actually make use of the system we are typically sensitive to our own position within it. For example, we think of Christmas as being "2 months ago" when it is February.

This kind of temporal framework differs in crucial ways from the scriptlike frameworks described earlier. First, it is a *unified* temporal framework: All temporal locations are represented within the same system. By contrast, scriptlike frameworks may be localized insofar as different, unrelated, frameworks may be used in different contexts. For example, a different script may function for weekends versus school days. Thus, although young children may have extensive knowledge of everyday sequences in the form of scripts, and be able to use these representations in flexible ways, such representations do not provide them with a unified way of encoding temporal locations.

The second, related, property of the conventional clock and calendar system is that it allows one to *distinguish between repetitions*. For example, there is a sense in which times "repeat" (e.g., 4:00 comes around every day). However, the system provides a way of distinguishing between such repetitions such that every possible time can actually be specified uniquely. An important consequence of these properties is that the system allows one to specify the temporal relations between *any* two events, because each has a unique location within a unified temporal framework. Even if two occurrences of events are virtually identical (e.g., any two occurrences of the event of eating one's breakfast might be very similar), it is possible to specify the temporal relations between the events (e.g., eating breakfast on Monday happened before eating breakfast on Tuesday).

Of course, often one cannot remember accurate temporal information about events: One remembers an event, but one does not know how long ago it occurred, or one cannot decide which of two events happened longer ago. However, even under these circumstances one knows that there is a fact of the matter as to which of two remembered events, for example, happened first. One may find it difficult to uncover the fact, and may have to engage in further memory retrieval and complicated inferential reasoning (Friedman, 1993), but one is not in any doubt that there is such a fact. Thus, a hallmark of being able to think of events as having happened at unique past times seems to be that one is able in principle to reason about the temporal relations between *any* events (see Campbell, 1997, for a related point). In other words, one grasps that there are *systematic relationships* between different events in virtue of the points in time at which they are located.

We should emphasize that we do not believe that grasping the systematic relations between points in time depends on being competent at using the clock and calendar system. Rather, the reverse is more likely: This kind of understanding emerges developmentally earlier than the ability to use such a system, and it underpins subsequent competence with the conventional time system. Indeed, there is already evidence to suggest that by at least age 4 or 5 years, children do grasp that there are systematic relations between points in time (i.e., well before the age at which competence with conventional time systems is intact; Friedman, 1982). One way to measure this understanding is to ask children to make judgments about the temporal relations between past events. For example, Friedman (1991) asked children which of two events "happened a long time ago." The events in question had occurred at the children's school and had been created by the experimenter. In one experiment (Experiment 3), the first event consisted in children being introduced to a new kind of game, and the second event was a science demonstration. The events were separated by a period of 6 weeks, and the testing session took place a week after the second event. Friedman found that nursery school children were able to judge which of the two events occurred most recently.

In other studies, Friedman and his colleagues have examined children's ability to order events such as birthday and Christmas (Friedman, Gardner, & Zubin, 1995) and to judge the relative distances from the present of a number of holidays (Friedman & Kemp, 1998). Although accurate responding in such tasks clearly loads heavily on memory processes, it also depends on the children making sense of the question regarding the temporal relations between arbitrary and unrelated events, that is, events that do not fall within one sequence for which they have a script. Thus, many years before children are competent at using conventional temporal frameworks, such as the clock and calendar system, they seem to be able to reason about the objective temporal relations between events.

How does this understanding of the systematic temporal relations between events emerge from the more primitive abilities to represent event sequences? Consider a case in which Event A happened before Event B, and both of these happened before the current time, C. The issue is: What is involved in understanding the temporal relations between these events? One basis for this understanding might be grasping that Events A and B differ in terms of the temporal distance in which they stand to the present, for example, A stands X units from the present, and B stands X – N units. What might be thought to recommend this picture is evidence of "distance-based" processes in memory, and thus a primitive way of recording the time that has elapsed since a particular event happened, which allows us to make judgments about which of two different events happened earlier (Friedman, 1993, 1996, 2001). However, there is still a problem with seeing this as the basic way in which we conceive of the order of events in the past. The problem, in short, is that it begs the question as to how one can think about the temporal relations in which past events stand to each other. For instance, it is not at all clear that someone who represents Event A as being X units in the past and Event B as being X – N units in the past has all that is needed to represent the temporal distance between the two events as N units. What seems to be needed is a grasp of the *transitivity* of temporal relations: that is, an understanding that given the relation between A and C and the relation between B and C, it is possible to specify the relation between A and B.

How, then, must someone be able to think of two past events in order to have a conception of the way in which they are related to each other? Elsewhere (McCormack & Hoerl, 1999), we have suggested that the necessary form of reasoning involves perspective taking abilities. Understanding the transitivity of these temporal relations involves understanding that Event A stands in the same type of relation to Event B as both events stand to C; that is, what needs to be grasped is that when B was present, A was past, in the same way as at C, the current time, A and B are both past. Thinking of Event A as having been past when B was present requires imaginatively taking up a perspective corresponding to the time of B. From that perspective, A will be in the past while B is in the present. Thus, temporal perspective taking can be thought of as a specific kind of imaginative exercise, in which one envisages events and their relations to each other from a different temporal perspective while keeping track of the relation between one's actual temporal point of view and the alternative one adopted in imagination. It is the ability to engage in this kind of reasoning that may be seen as being at the heart of our understanding of events as happening at unique points in time.

We have argued that episodic recollection is not just a matter of retrieving information that stems from specific past events but representing remembered events as specific past events—as unique and unrepeatable and thus as having occurred at particular times in the past. We have suggested that representing the temporal locations of events in this way involves a grasp of the systematic temporal relations that obtain between events happening at different points in time and the transitive nature of such relations. We have also described the reasoning that this involves as a particular form of perspective taking. In short, therefore, the argument is that the ability to engage in this type of perspective taking is at the heart of our conception of events as having happened at particular unique points of time in the past.

EPISODIC MEMORY AND PERSPECTIVE TAKING

Although the notion of temporal perspective taking may be an unfamiliar one, we are using the term to capture a type of understanding that is obviously available to mature thinkers. As adults, we realize, for instance, that an event that happened yesterday is now past, but was present then, was still in the future 2 days ago, and so on. Indeed, the idea that mature temporal thought involves temporal perspective taking (or temporal decentering) is one that has occurred previously in the area of language acquisition (Cromer, 1971; Smith, 1980; Weist, 1986). There, it has been used in order to describe what is involved in mastering complex tenses (Reichenbach, 1947; although see Nelson, 1996). Our claim concerns conceptual development and is (arguably) a stronger one than that which has usually been made in the language acquisition literature. We argue that the ability to engage in this form of reasoning is central to possessing the concept of the past that is used in episodic memory and that children do not possess this concept until they are capable of engaging in this type of reasoning. Also, insofar as episodic memory requires such a concept of the past, its development involves the ability to engage in temporal perspective taking.

We began this chapter by considering previous claims regarding the link between self-consciousness and episodic memory, and we now return to this issue in the light of our discussion of temporal perspective taking. There already is a tradition in developmental psychology of linking perspective taking abilities to the development of self-consciousness (see Perner, 1991) and, to anticipate, our basic claim is that temporal perspective taking is developmentally grounded in the ability to engage in certain types of self-conscious reasoning. We elaborate this basic claim in two ways. The first issue to which we turn is the nature of the self-conscious abilities that are invoked here. Previous claims regarding memory development and self-consciousness have differed greatly in terms of the types of self-consciousness on which they have focused (Howe & Courage, 1993; Perner 1991; Povinelli et al., 1996). We believe a promising way to assess some of the claims that have been made in this context is by considering the particular kind of self-conscious reasoning required for temporal perspective taking.

The second, and final, issue that is discussed is the sense in which our claim is what we have termed a *causal* claim regarding the link between episodic memory and self-consciousness, rather than a *constitutive* claim. We argue that it is a causal claim in that self-consciousness is required for the requisite concept (a concept of the past) to develop. We are not making a constitutive claim, because we do not view episodic recollection itself as always involving a representation of the self.

Self-Consciousness and Temporal Perspective Taking

As we have said, temporal perspective taking can be thought of as a certain kind of imaginative exercise, in which one envisages events and their relations to each other from a different temporal perspective while keeping track of the relation between one's actual temporal point of view and the alternative one adopted in imagination. For example, consider your last day at school and your first driving lesson. As mature thinkers, we can grasp that from the perspective of our last day at school, taking our first driving lesson was still in the future, or vice versa, while keeping track of the fact that both of these events are actually in the past from our current point of view. In other words, we can conceive of the times when these events happened as affording alternative temporal perspectives on the order of events in time. It is this kind of ability that is at the heart of our grasp of the systematic temporal relations that obtain between events that have happened at different times in the past.

We want to distinguish between two respects in which this kind of perspective taking might be thought to involve self-conscious reflection or reasoning. First, it would seem that envisaging events and their relations to each other from alternative temporal perspectives, in the way we have described, entails the ability to think of one's *current* temporal perspective as but one of many perspectives. For instance, in order to grasp that your last day at school was once in the present, you must also have some grip on the fact that you consider it to be in the past only because of where you are now located in time. In other words, to think of finishing school as the very same event that was once present and is now past, you must have a conception of your present perspective as one perspective among others. It is in this sense that we can think of temporal perspective taking as involving a certain form of self-conscious reflection on one's own temporal point of view. In short, the claim is that the capacity to engage in temporal perspective taking involves a conception of oneself as being located at a certain position in time and as having a certain perspective onto time due to being at that position rather than another.

However, in the example we have used, temporal perspective taking also involves self-consciousness in a stronger sense, insofar as it seems to rely on a conception of oneself as persisting through time and occupying different temporal points of view at different times (or what Povinelli et al., 1996, referred to as a conception of the *temporally extended self*). In other words, we have used an example in which a person considers events that have, as a matter of fact, happened to him or her and can think of them as, say, "my last day at school" and "my first driving lesson." Here, temporal perspective taking involves more than the ability to think of one's current position in time as affording just one temporal perspective among others. It also involves the ability to think of oneself as the kind of entity that traces a certain path through time and that is involved with different events at different times, and we suggest that the ability to think about past events in this way, as events with which one was involved oneself, plays a crucial role in the development of temporal perspective taking abilities.

The claim, in other words, is that the ability to consider different temporal perspectives is tied up with the ability to think of one's own perspective as changing as one's life unfolds through time. Temporal perspective taking, as we have described it, is a way of understanding what it is for a past event to have happened at a particular time by considering it as having been present at that time in the past when other events had already happened or were still to come. But how does this kind of grasp of the systematic temporal relations between past events develop? A plausible developmental claim is that children first develop such an understanding by considering that what they could or could not do at one point in time in the past depended on what had or had not already happened at that time, or, similarly, by considering how what they did at one point in time had an effect on what they have been able to do since. One example of this type of reasoning in adults would be the way in which someone might grasp that her last day at school and her first driving lesson must have happened in a particular order, in virtue of remembering that she was able to drive to school on her last day there.

When thinking about how children first come to engage in these forms of reasoning, we could, for instance, turn to connections that other theorists have drawn between memory development and joint reminiscence. Previous research suggests that children come to a new understanding of past events and their significance through talking about the past with parents and other adults and that particular parental narrative styles promote such understanding (Fivush & Reese, 1991; Haden, Haine & Fivush, 1997; Reese, Haden & Fivush, 1993). One way of interpreting this research might be that the narrative style adopted by parents makes particularly salient how, for instance, the outcome of certain events in the child's past depended on what had happened previously. Similarly, we may think that part of parent–child discourse about the past consists in considering the reasons why it is correct to think of them as having happened in a certain order rather than another. It is in this sense that parent and child can be though of as jointly reconstructing the order in which events happened rather than simply recalling events in a particular sequence. For instance, Fivush and Fromhoff (1988) give the example of a mother talking to her 31-month-old child about the birth of her brother: Although the child recalls little about the event, the mother seems to draw the child's attention to the fact that certain things led up to the birth of the baby ("Mommy had a really big tummy") and that the baby came home from hospital together with her (correcting the child, who was maintaining that the baby stayed with the child while the mother was in hospital). What the mother makes salient, in other words, are the reasons why events in the child's own past happened in a particular order.

In short, the kind of temporal reasoning we have described as temporal perspective taking might be thought to be developmentally grounded in the ability to reflect on the fact that certain events in one's own past had to take place before one could do certain things or before certain other events could happen. Thus, if self-consciousness, in the sense of a grasp of one's own persistence through time, is required for temporal perspective taking, it is because such reflection brings in the thought of oneself as having been involved with different events at different times in the past.

Perspective Taking as a Causal Requirement for Episodic Memory

Where does this leave the idea that there is a link between the emergence of episodic memory and the development of self-consciousness? The arguments we have put forward would seem to support the view that the ability to represent oneself in certain ways plays a causal role in the development of episodic memory. Specifically, if what we have been saying is right, the ability to engage in certain forms of self-conscious reflection and reasoning can be seen to play a crucial role in the development of the temporal concepts used in episodic memory. To recap, our approach has been to look at the particular way the past is represented in episodic memory and to elucidate the sense in which episodic memory can be said to involve an orientation toward the past not involved in other forms of remembering. We have argued that possessing the concept of the past that is used in episodic memory is in part a matter of being able to engage in temporal perspective taking. Thinking of an event one remembers as an event that happened at a particular, unique time in the past requires the ability to grasp that events that happened at other times were already in the past or still in the future when it happened. Furthermore, we have suggested that this ability to engage in temporal perspective taking involves certain forms of self-conscious reflection and reasoning. In particular, it would seem to require the ability to think of one's current temporal perspective as but one of many perspectives on time and the ability to think of oneself as an entity that persists through time.

It is in this sense that certain forms of self-consciousness must be in place for the concepts used in episodic memory to develop. However, this type of causal claim has to be distinguished from a constitutive claim, according to which what it is to remember episodically has to be spelled out in terms of the idea that the self is represented in certain ways in episodic memory. That this is only a causal developmental claim, rather than a constitutive one, is clear if we consider whether one really goes through the modes of reasoning we have described as temporal perspective taking every time one remembers specific past events. It seems implausible that episodic recollection always involves going through such a reasoning process. Intuitively, when one remembers a particular past event one does not first have to reflect on and reason about one's own temporal perspective and how it has changed over time, by considering, for instance, how what one did at that point in time might have depended on what had happened previously, or might have had an effect on what one has been able to do since. Rather, what is before our mind in episodic memory is simply the event itself, as it happened at a particular time in the past.

How do our claims relate to other claims that have been put forward in favor of a connection between episodic memory and consciousness? It might be helpful to summarize some of the implications of the account that we have put forward by comparing it specifically with aspects of Perner's theory that we discussed earlier in this chapter.

Our account differs from Perner's in two ways. First, and most important, according to Perner, episodic remembering is constitutively dependent on self-consciousness insofar as each act of episodic recollection involves representing the fact that one's own present mental state was caused by a certain past experience. Thus, his claim is that episodic remembering is essentially a matter of metarepresentation, that is, of representing one's own past and present mental states. In our account there is instead a causal dependency between self-consciousness and episodic memory. Thus, even if there may be a sense in which the kinds of metarepresentational abilities Perner discusses must be in place for episodic memory to develop, individual occurrences of episodic recollection need not involve representing oneself as being or having been in certain mental states, over and above having a particular past event before one's mind.

Second, however, it should also be pointed out that the notion of metarepresentation may not be best suited for capturing the particular forms of self-conscious reflection and reasoning that we have associated with possession of the temporal concepts used in episodic memory. Elsewhere, we have suggested that temporal perspective taking may involve an understanding of the perspectival nature of one's mental states and hence theory-of-mind abilities (McCormack & Hoerl, 1999). This suggestion is analogous to claims linking spatial perspective taking and theory of mind (e.g., see Perner, 1991), and it was made in the light of previous work relating theory of mind and memory development (e.g., Welch-Ross, 1996, 1997). However, if what we have been saying in this chapter is right, one might think that the primary way in which temporal perspective taking is connected with self-consciousness is that it is developmentally grounded in the ability to reflect on one's own persistence through time. Furthermore, in spelling out what it is to reflect one's own persistence through time we have not specifically talked about the ability to think about one's own mental states. Indeed, a grasp of one's persistence through time would seem to be presupposed in the ability to think of oneself as having had different experiences at different times rather than being made available by one's ability to conceptualize these mental states.

Instead, in spelling out what it is to grasp one's own persistence through time we have appealed, for instance, to the ability to reason about how certain events in our own past had to happen before we could do certain things, or how things we did at certain points in time have had an effect on what we have been able to do since. Thus it is arguable that the specific kind of self-consciousness we have described is at least as much a matter of being able to think of oneself as an agent whose possibilities for action are determined by one's own past as it is a matter of being able to conceptualize one's own mental states at different times.

CONCLUSIONS

In his book *Elements of Episodic Memory* Tulving (1983) speculated that there is a relation between children's representations of temporal information and the development of episodic memory: "The absence of episodic memory in young children may be related to their inability to keep track of the order of events in their personal past. The difficulty that children have with the temporal organization of their memories has been described by Piaget" (p. 50). More recently, there has in fact been a general revision of the Piagetian picture of young children as unable to represent and remember temporal sequential information (see Mandler, 1986, for a discussion of this point). However, there is an important sense in which Tulving's basic intuition is correct: We have argued that although young children may be competent at learning ordered event sequences, they cannot represent events as happening in at unique temporal locations in their past. There is an important sense in which children's memories are not temporally organized like those of adults, because they lack a unified temporal framework that can be used to represent the systematic relations that obtain between past events in virtue of the particular times at which they happened.

The claim we have made is that the subsequent development of episodic memory is linked to the development of temporal perspective taking abilities. We have argued that the ability to engage in temporal perspective taking is a crucial ingredient in the possession of the temporal concepts that are used in episodic memory. However, we have also tried to show that temporal perspective taking requires the ability to engage in certain types of self-conscious reflection and reasoning. It is in this sense that the development of self-consciousness can be seen to play a central role in the emergence of episodic memory.

ACKNOWLEDGMENTS

This research was supported by a grant from the Medical Research Council (G9608199), to Teresa McCormack, and an institutional fellowship from the British Academy Humanities Research Board, awarded to Christoph Hoerl. We are grateful to Christopher Peacocke and to Chris Moore and Karen Lemmon for their helpful comments on a previous draft of this chapter.

REFERENCES

Bauer, P. J., & Dow, G. A. (1994). Episodic memory in 16- and 20- month-old children: Specifics are generalized but not forgotten. *Developmental Psychology, 30,* 403–417.

Bauer, P. J., & Mandler, J. M. (1989). One thing follows another: Effects of temporal structure on 1- to 2-year-olds' recall of events. *Developmental Psychology, 25,* 197–206.

Bauer, P. J., & Mandler, J. M. (1992). Putting the horse before the cart: The use of temporal order in recall of events by one-year-old children. *Developmental Psychology, 28,* 441–452.

Campbell, J. (1997). The structure of time in autobiographical memory. *European Journal of Philosophy, 5,* 105–118.

Conway, M. A. (2001). Phenomenological records and the self-memory system. In C. Hoerl & T. McCormack (Eds.), *Time and memory: Issues in philosophy and psychology* (pp. 235-255). Oxford, England: Oxford University Press.

Conway, M. A., & Rubin, D. C. (1993). The structure of autobiographical memory. In A. F. Collins, S. E. Gathercole, M. A. Conway, & P. E. Morris (Eds.), *Theories of memory* (pp. 103–137). Hillsdale, NJ: Lawrence Erlbaum Associates.

Cromer, R. F. (1971). The development of the ability to decentre in time. *British Journal of Psychology, 62,* 353–365.

Dokic, J. (1997, August). *Two metarepresentational theories of episodic memory.* Paper presented at the annual meeting of the European Society of Philosophy and Psychology, Padua, Italy.

Donaldson, W. (1996). The role of decision processes in remembering and knowing. *Memory & Cognition, 24,* 523–533.

Fivush, R. (1997). *A self in time.* Paper presented at the Biennial Meeting of the Society for Research in Child Development, Washington, DC.

Fivush, R., & Fromhoff, F. A. (1988). Style and structure in mother–child conversations about the past. *Discourse Processes, 11,* 337–355.

Fivush, R., & Hudson, J. A. (1990). *Knowing and remembering in young children.* Cambridge, England: Cambridge University Press.

Fivush, R., & Reese, E. (1991). The social construction of autobiographical memory. In M. A. Conway, D. C. Rubin, H. Spinnler, & W. A. Wagenaar (Eds.), *Theoretical perspectives on autobiographical memory* (pp. 115–132). Dordrecht, the Netherlands: Kluwer.

Flavell, J. H., & Wellman, H. M. (1977). Metamemory. In R. V. Kail & J. W. Hagen (Eds.), *Perspectives on the development of memory and cognition* (pp. 3–33). Hillsdale, NJ: Lawrence Erlbaum Associates.

Friedman, W. J. (1982). Conventional time concepts and children's structuring of time. In W. J. Friedman (Ed.), *The developmental psychology of time* (pp. 171–208). New York: Academic.

Friedman, W. J. (1991). The development of children's memory for the time of past events. *Child Development, 62,* 139–155.

Friedman, W. J. (1993). Memory for the time of past events. *Psychological Bulletin, 113,* 44–66.

Friedman, W. J. (1996). Distance and location processes in memory for the times of past events. *Psychology of Learning and Motivation: Advances in Research and Theory, 35,* 1–41.

Friedman, W. J. (2001). Memory processes underlying humans' chronological sense of the past. In C. Hoerl & T. McCormack (Eds.), *Time and memory: Issues in philosophy and psychology* (pp. 139-167). Oxford, England: Oxford University Press.

Friedman, W. J., Gardner, A. G., & Zubin, N. R. E. (1995). Children's comparisons of the recency of 2 events from the past year. *Child Development, 66,* 970–983.

Friedman, W. J., & Kemp, S. (1998). The effects of elapsed time and retrieval on young children's judgments of the temporal distances of past events. *Cognitive Development, 13,* 335–367.

Gardiner, J. M., & Gregg, V. H. (1997). Recognition memory with little or no remembering: Implications for a detection model. *Psychonomic Bulletin and Review, 4,* 271–276.

Gardiner, J. M., & Java, R. I. (1993). Recognising and remembering. In A. F. Collins, S. E. Gathercole, M. A. Conway, & P. E. Morris (Eds.), *Theories of memory* (pp. 163–188). Hillsdale, NJ: Lawrence Erlbaum Associates.

Haden, C., Haine, R., & Fivush, R. (1997). Developing narrative structure in parent–child conversations about the past. *Developmental Psychology, 33,* 295–307.

Herbert, J., & Hayne, H. (1999, April). *Deferred imitation during the first year of life: More evidence for declarative memory.* Poster presented at the biennial meeting of the Society for Research in Child Development, Albuquerque, New Mexico.

Hirshman, E., & Master, S. (1997). Modeling the conscious correlates of recognition memory: Reflections on the remember–know paradigm. *Memory & Cognition, 25,* 345–351.

Hoerl, C. (1999). Memory, amnesia and the past. *Mind & Language, 14,* 227–251.

Hoerl, C. (2001). The phenomenology of episodic recall. In C. Hoerl & T. McCormack (Eds.), *Time and memory: Issues in philosophy and psychology* (pp. 315-335). Oxford, England: Oxford University Press.

Howe, M. L., & Courage, M. L. (1993). On resolving the enigma of infantile amnesia. *Psychological Bulletin, 113,* 305–326.

Howe, M. L., & Courage, M. L. (1997). The emergence and early development of autobiographical memory. *Psychological Review, 104,* 499–523.

Inoue, C., & Bellezza, F. (1998). The detection model of recognition memory using know and remember judgments. *Memory & Cognition, 26,* 299–308.

James, W. (1950). *The principles of psychology.* New York: Dover. (Original work published 1890)

Mandler, J. M. (1986). The development of event memory. In F. Klix & H. Hagendorf (Ed.), *Human memory and cognitive capabilities: Mechanisms and performance.* Amsterdam: Elsevier.

Mandler, J. M., & McDonough, L. (1995). Long-term recall of event sequences in infancy. *Journal of Experimental Child Psychology, 59,* 457–474.

Martin, M. (2001). Out of the past: Episodic recall as retained acquaintance. In C. Hoerl & T. McCormack (Eds.), *Time and memory: Issues in philosophy and psychology* (pp. 257-284). Oxford, England: Oxford University Press.

McCormack, T. (1999). Temporal concepts and episodic memory: A response to Hoerl. *Mind and Language, 14,* 252–262.

McCormack, T., & Hoerl, C. (1999). Memory and temporal perspective: The role of temporal frameworks in memory development. *Developmental Review, 19,* 154–182.

McDonough, L., Mandler, J. M., Mckee, R. D., & Squire, L. R. (1995). The deferred imitation task as a measure of declarative memory. *Proceedings of the National Academy of Sciences, 92*, 7580–7584.

Meltzoff, A. N. (1999, April). *Infant memory development: Contributions from the deferred imitation paradigm.* Paper presented the Biennial Meeting of the Society for Research in Child Development, Albuquerque, New Mexico.

Miller, G. A., & Johnson-Laird, P. N. (1976). *Language and perception.* Cambridge, England: Cambridge University Press.

Nelson, K. (1986) *Event knowledge: Structure and function in development.* Hillsdale, NJ: Lawrence Erlbaum Associates.

Nelson, K. (1990). Remembering, forgetting and childhood amnesia. In R. Fivush & J. A. Hudson (Eds.), *Knowing and remembering in young children* (pp. 223–248). Cambridge, England: Cambridge University Press.

Nelson, K. (1993). The psychological and social origins of autobiographical memory. *Psychological Science, 4*, 7–13.

Nelson, K. (1996). *Language in cognitive development: Emergence of the mediated mind.* Cambridge, England: Cambridge University Press.

Peacocke, C. (2000). Theories of concepts: A wider task. *European Journal of Philosophy, 8*, 298-321.

Perner, J. (1991). *Understanding the representational mind.* Cambridge, MA: MIT Press.

Perner, J. (2000). Memory and theory of mind. In E. Tulving & F. I. M. Craik (Eds.), *The Oxford handbook of memory* (pp. 297–312). Oxford, England: Oxford University Press.

Perner, J., & Ruffman, T. (1995). Episodic memory and autonoetic consciousness: Developmental evidence and a theory of childhood amnesia. *Journal of Experimental Child Psychology, 59*, 516–548.

Pillemer, D. B. (1998). *Momentous events, vivid memories.* Cambridge, MA: Harvard University Press.

Povinelli, D. J., Landau, K. R., & Perilloux, H. K. (1996). Self-recognition in young children using delayed versus live feedback: Evidence for a developmental asynchrony. *Child Development, 67*, 1540–1554.

Povinelli, D. J., & Simon, B. B. (1998). Young children's understanding of briefly versus extremely delayed images of the self: Emergence of the autobiographical stance. *Developmental Psychology, 34*, 188–194.

Reese, E., Haden, C. A., & Fivush, R. (1993). Mother–child conversations about the past: Relationships of style and memory over time. *Cognitive Development, 8*, 403–430.

Reichenbach, H. (1947). *Elements of symbolic logic.* New York: Macmillan.

Rovee-Collier, C. (1997). Dissociations in infant memory: Rethinking the development of implicit and explicit memory. *Psychological Review, 104*, 467–498.

Schank, R. C., & Abelson, R. P. (1977). *Scripts, plans, goals, and understanding.* Hillsdale, NJ: Lawrence Erlbaum Associates.

Searle, J. (1983). *Intentionality.* Cambridge, England: Cambridge University Press.

Smith, C. S. (1980). The acquisition of time talk: Relations between child and adult grammars. *Journal of Child Language, 7*, 263–278.

Tulving, E. (1972). Episodic and semantic memory. In E. Tulving & W. Donaldson (Eds.), *Organization of memory* (pp. 381–403). New York: Academic.

Tulving, E. (1983). *Elements of episodic memory*. Oxford, England: Oxford University Press.

Tulving, E. (1985). Memory and consciousness. *Canadian Psychology, 25*, 1–12.

Tulving, E., & Markowitsch, H. J. (1998). Episodic and declarative memory: Role of the hippocampus. *Hippocampus, 8*, 198–204.

Weist, R. M. (1986). Tense and aspect. In P. Fletcher & M. Garman (Eds.), *Language acquisition: Studies in first language development* (2nd ed., pp. 356–374). Cambridge, England: Cambridge University Press.

Weist, R. M. (1989). Time concepts in language and thought: Filling the Piagetian void from two to five years. In I. Levin & D. Zakay (Eds.), *Time and human cognition: A life-span perspective* (pp. 63–118). Amsterdam: Elsevier.

Welch-Ross, M. K. (1996). An integrative model of the development of autobiographical memory. *Developmental Review, 15*, 338–365.

Welch-Ross, M. K. (1997). Mother–child participation in conversation about the past: Relationships to preschoolers' theory of mind. *Developmental Psychology, 33*, 618–629.

Wheeler, M. A., Stuss, D. T., & Tulving, E. (1997). Toward a theory of episodic memory: The frontal lobes and autonoetic consciousness. *Psychological Bulletin, 121*, 331–354.

Wollheim, R. (1984). *The thread of life*. Cambridge, England: Cambridge University Press.

12

Levels of Consciousness of the Self in Time

Philip David Zelazo
University of Toronto

Jessica A. Sommerville
University of Chicago

In order to have a genuine temporal awareness, a being must be able to distinguish between the history of the world and the history of its *encounters* with this world. And the continuously changing temporal perspective ... is nothing but the continuous process of connecting these two series of events within a representation of one unified time. — Bieri (1986, p. 266)

As the chapters in this book likely make clear, questions concerning the self in time have recently been raised in the context of several overlapping research literatures, including those on episodic and autobiographical memory, theory of mind, and self-control. By identifying consciousness and two of its most important properties—namely, that it is both personal and temporally extended—as core concerns, these questions reveal more precisely the way in which these different literatures overlap: They arguably all address cognitive and behavioral consequences of age-related changes in children's consciousness. In this chapter we characterize these changes in consciousness in terms of the Levels of Consciousness (LOC) model of the role of consciousness in reasoning and intentional action (P. D. Zelazo, 1999, 2000b; P. R. Zelazo & Zelazo, 1998) and attempt to show how this model contributes to an understanding of the self in time by making fine distinctions among several levels of self-awareness. In particular, we address differences among (a) past and future orientation in behavior, (b) a subjective experience of self continuity in time, and (c) two levels of conceptual understanding of the self as a nexus of particular subjective experiences that are ordered in time. We argue that explicit understanding that the self persists in time is not required for a subjective experience of self-continuity in time and that this experience of continuity is manifested relatively early in development (e.g., in planning and intentional action late in the second year of life).

THE LOC MODEL OF THE SELF IN TIME

According to the LOC model, there are four major age-related increases in the highest level of consciousness that preschool children are able to muster in response to situational demands. These increases are brought about by a functional process of recursion whereby the contents of consciousness are fed back into consciousness so that they can become available to consciousness at a higher level, with important consequences for (a) the qualitative character of experience, (b) the potential for recall, and (c) the conscious control of behavior.

Consider each of these consequences in turn. First, recursion adds depth to subjective experience because more details can be integrated into the experience before the contents of consciousness are replaced by new intero- and exteroceptor stimulation. Second, each degree of recursion causes information to be processed at a deeper, less superficial level (Craik & Lockhart, 1972), which increases the likelihood of retrieval (Craik & Tulving, 1975). Third, recursion moves consciousness farther away from the exigencies of environmental stimulation in what might be called *psychological distance* (cf. DeLoache, 1993; Dewey, 1931/1985; Sigel, 1993), and this allows for the formulation and use of more complex knowledge structures to be maintained in working memory (P. D. Zelazo & Frye, 1997). The complexity of these knowledge structures, which is measured in terms the number of degrees of embedding in the structures (e.g., an "if X then if Y then Z" rule is more complex than an "if Y then Z" rule), determines the scope of one's cognitive control of thought and action because greater complexity allows for the integration of incompatible pieces of knowledge. If incompatible pieces of knowledge are not integrated into a single, more complex system, behavior can become perseverative. In addition, it can be characterized by abulic dissociations between knowledge and action, which occur because the particular conscious knowledge that controls behavior is determined by relatively narrow considerations. For example, the rules that are selected and stored in working memory may depend on the way in which a test question is asked or on what one has previously done in a particular situation.

The main features of the LOC model are depicted graphically in Fig. 12.1. Minimal consciousness (abbreviated as minC) is meant to be the simplest, but still conceptually coherent, kind of consciousness that we can imagine. When an object in the environment (objA, which appears in the lower left hand corner of the figure) triggers an intentional representation of that object (IobjA) from semantic long-term memory (LTM), the IobjA can become the content of minC, where it will be causally connected (cc) to a bracketed objA. The contents of minC can then trigger an associated action program stored in procedural LTM. When the entire contents of minC are fed back into minC via a recursive loop, a higher level of consciousness is achieved, namely recursive consciousness (recC). The contents of this level of consciousness can be related to a corresponding description (descA) or label, which can then be decoupled from the experience described and deposited into working memory (WM) where it can serve as a goal (G1) to trigger an action program (stored in procedural LTM). Self-consciousness involves

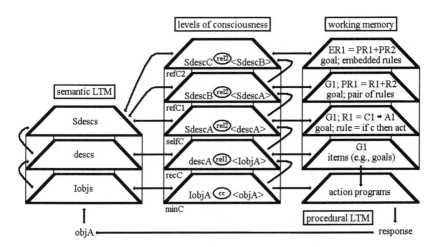

FIG 12.1.   The Levels-of-Consciousness (LOC) model of the role of consciousness in reasoning and action. (From "Children's Rule Use: Representation, Reflection, and Cognitive Control" by P. D. Zelazo and S. Jacques, 1996, in R. Vasta (Ed.), *Annals of Child Development*, Vol. 12, p. 163). Copyright 1997 by Jessica Kingsley Publishers. Reprinted by permission.

another degree of recursion and makes possible the use of conditionally specified self-directed speech (i.e., rules). Additional degrees of recursion (Reflective Consciousness 1 and 2) yield additional levels of consciousness, and each new level of consciousness affords a new degree of self-regulation by allowing the formulation and use of rules of greater complexity.

In subsequent sections of this chapter we highlight key aspects of each level of consciousness identified in the LOC model and, for each level, describe the implications for children's experience of time and the self in time. The current account focuses on development during infancy and early childhood, although children's understanding of the self in time undoubtedly continues to develop during the school-age years (e.g., Fraisse, 1982; Friedman, 1993; Piaget, 1946).

Minimal Consciousness

According to the LOC model, consciousness prior to the end of the first year of life can be described as *minimal consciousness* (cf. Armstrong, 1980). As argued elsewhere (P. D. Zelazo, 1996), minimal consciousness must be intentional in Brentano's (1973) sense (i.e., it is about something), but it is unreflective. Thus, a minimally conscious infant will be conscious of what he or she perceives, but he or she will not be conscious of experiencing it. Therefore, he or she could not remember perceiving what he or she perceived.

Because it mediates responding to the environment, minimal consciousness plays a functional role in the production of behavior. However, behavior at a minimally conscious level is necessarily stereotypical. The presence of a rattle, for example, elicits an habitual stereotypical response—the infant puts the rattle into his or her mouth, assimilating it to the intentional object "suckable thing," which is (reflexively) associated with a sucking schema. Although sensorimotor schemata are modified through practice and accommodation (i.e., learning can occur, including learning of spatiotemporal event sequences; Haith, Hazan, & Goodman, 1988), and coordinated into higher order units (e.g., Cohen, 1998; Piaget, 1936/1952), a minimally conscious infant cannot represent these schemata in minimal consciousness (the infant is aware only of the stimuli that trigger them). In the absence of recursion the contents of minimal consciousness are continually replaced by new intero- and exteroceptor stimulation and cannot be deposited into working memory.

Implications for awareness of the self in time. It follows from the LOC model that infants are present-oriented prior to the end of the first year of life. Infants exhibit learning and memory from birth or before (e.g., DeCasper & Fifer, 1980), and may well perceive aspects of their current state (e.g., Neisser's, 1988, ecological and interpersonal selves) implicitly. Moreover, because perception and behavior must occur in time, learning necessarily entails some registration of event sequences. However, minimally conscious infants have no means by which they can consciously represent past experiences or states or by which they can entertain future-oriented representations; that is, they cannot engage in conscious recollection, although they provide clear behavioral evidence of memory, and they cannot entertain conscious expectations or plans, although their behavior is often future oriented (e.g., Haith et al., 1988; see Reznick, 1994, for a discussion of different interpretations of future-oriented behavior). Indeed, even their experience of current intero- and exteroceptor stimulation is limited (it is not in any way reflected on). Figure 12.2a captures the suggestion that the contents of minimal consciousness are restricted to present stimulation.

Onset of Recursive Consciousness at the End of the First Year of Life

At the end of the first year (9–12 months) a large number of new abilities appear with high-interval synchrony, which suggests some sort of underlying central, and probably maturational, determinant, as Kagan (1972) and others (e.g., Moore & Corkum, 1994; Tomasello, 1999; P. R. Zelazo, 1982; P. R. Zelazo & Leonard, 1983) have pointed out. Within the span of a few months, infants speak their first words; point proto-declaratively; search for hidden objects; use objects in a functional way; and display deferred imitation, social referencing, and joint attention, among many other major behavioral milestones. According to the LOC model the synchronous emergence of these behaviors can be explained parsimoniously by the onset of recursive consciousness, which is just minimal consciousness when the contents of minimal consciousness are re-entered into minimal consciousness so that they can be combined with other contents of minimal consciousness by means of an identity ("is" or "is a") relation (abbreviated Rel1 in Fig. 12.1).

Naming (or labeling) can be used to illustrate this recursive process. When a 12-month-old looks at his or her father and says, "Daddy," he or she says (effectively) that her perceptual experience of the man *is* "Daddy." That is, his or her perceptual experience is associated with a description from memory, and this description is brought to bear on the perceptual experience. Indeed, according to the LOC model, there *must* be two things, the perception and the label, in order for one of them, the perception interpreted in terms of the label, to become an object of conscious experience.

In the absence of a label or description the contents of consciousness are fleeting and unrecoverable; they are immediately replaced by new

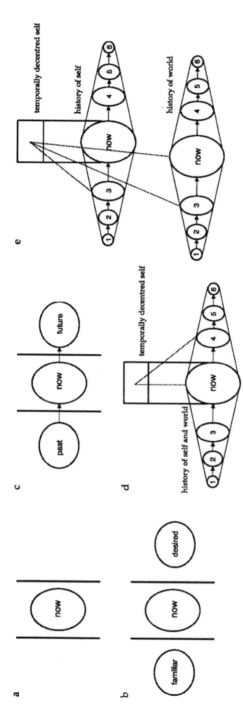

FIG. 12.2. Levels of consciousness of events in time. Panel a: Birth–12 months (m). The contents of minimal consciousness are restricted to present intero- and exteroreceptor stimulation (now). Panel b: 12 m–18 m. When descriptions of past experiences become the contents of recursive consciousness, they will feel familiar. Future-oriented states (goals) will generally be accompanied by a feeling of desire or fear. Panel c: 18 m–36 m. From the perspective of now, children can consider descriptions of past- or future-oriented events in relation to a present experience. For example, while conscious of their current state (now), 2-year-olds can appreciate that yesterday they went to the zoo. This creates the conditions for a subjective experience of self-continuity in time, but it does not allow simultaneous consideration of events occurring at two different times. Panel d: 36 m–48 m. From a temporally decentered perspective, children can consider two events occurring at two different times, including an event occurring in the present. For example, against the backdrop of now, they can consider that now, Event A is occurring, but yesterday Event B occurred. At this point, the history of self and the history of the world are confounded. Panel e: From a temporally decentered perspective, children can coordinate two series: the history of the self and the history of the world.

stimulation. However, because a label can be "decoupled" (cf. Leslie, 1987) from the experience that is labeled, the label provides a potentially enduring trace of that experience. This description can then be deposited into LTM so that the experience can subsequently be remembered under that description, as in deferred imitation (Barnat, Klein, & Meltzoff, 1996; Carver & Bauer, 1999; Mandler & McDonough, 1995; Meltzoff, 1988, 1995). In addition, the description can be deposited into WM, which is understood here simply to be a short-term buffer for maintaining contents of consciousness in an activated state (e.g., Goldman-Rakic, 1990).

Once a description is deposited into WM, it can then serve as a goal to trigger action programs indirectly so that the infant is not restricted to responses that are triggered directly, or "suggested" (Baldwin, 1891), by the (minimally conscious) perception of an immediately present (intero- or exteroceptive) stimulus. Consequently, when the infant is presented with a stimulus, such as a rattle or an object hidden at a new location (as in an A-not-B task; Piaget, 1936/1952), he or she is able to act mediately, in light of a description of the stimulus, rather than immediately, according to a prepotent, default action program that is triggered directly by a superficial, perceptual experience. For example, the recursively conscious infant may see a rattle, describe it *as a rattle*, and respond to it under that description, shaking it appropriately (functional play; P. R. Zelazo & Kearsley, 1980). Or, in the case of the A-not-B task, the recursively conscious infant may search successfully at location B on the basis of a representation of the hidden object (in WM), rather than respond directly and perseveratively to the perception of location A (see Marcovitch & Zelazo, 1999, for further discussion).

In terms of the LOC model (see Fig. 12.1), an object in the environment (objA) triggers an intentional object (IobjA), which then becomes the content of minimal consciousness (minC). However, instead of triggering an associated action program directly (as in a minimally conscious infant), the IobjA is fed back into MinC (which is called *recursive consciousness*, RecC, after one degree of recursion) where it is related by means of an identity relation (Rel1) to a description (descA) from semantic LTM. This descA can be decoupled from the IobjA and deposited into WM, where it can serve as a goal (G1) and can elicit an action program even in the absence of objA, and even if the IobjA would otherwise trigger a different, prepotent action program.

Implications for awareness of the self in time. Recursive consciousness allows a description of an experience to be related to the experience itself. This description can then be decoupled from the experience and deposited into LTM or WM. As a result, past experiences can subsequently be remembered under that description, or the description can be maintained in WM, where it can serve as a future-oriented state (i.e., a goal) to guide future-oriented behavior. When descriptions of past experiences become the contents of recursive consciousness, they will feel familiar. In contrast, future-oriented states (goals) will generally be accompanied by a feeling of desire (cf. Baldwin, 1891) or fear.

However, the limitations on recursive consciousness are such that only one description of an experience can occupy recursive consciousness at any one time. Thus, recursively conscious infants cannot consider past- or future-oriented representations from the perspective of the present (i.e., from the perspective of an experience of the present, or Now), because this would require an additional element (namely, a description of Now). Therefore, it is impossible for these infants to appreciate past or future representations *as such*, because the concepts of both past and future are meaningful only when considered in relation to a perception of the present circumstances. This situation is depicted in Fig. 12.2b. As shown in the figure, recursively conscious infants are no longer present oriented (i.e., they are no longer restricted to Now, as in Fig. 12.2a), but they cannot explicitly consider events as occurring in the future from the perspective of the present. Similarly, they cannot explicitly consider past events as occurring in the past from the perspective of the present.

Emergence of Self-Consciousness

Between 18 months and 2 years, an additional degree of recursion in consciousness yields a new level of consciousness, referred to as self-consciousness (cf. Kagan, 1981). It is this further reflection on the contents of recursive consciousness that allows children to relate a description of an experience not only to the experience described but also to another description. One major consequence of this new level of consciousness is that children can take as an object of consciousness a conditionally specified self-description of their behavioral potential (i.e., what they can do, conditions permitting). This self-description can then be maintained in WM as a single explicit action-oriented rule, considered against the background of the goal that occasions it (i.e., the goal that provides a motive for doing what they can do, conditions permitting). Note that an explicit rule is itself intrinsically relational because it relates an antecedent or enabling condition to an action to be taken.

To assess the emergence of rule use in children's behavior, P. D. Zelazo, Reznick, and Pinon (1995) presented 2.5- to 3-year-old children with a pair of rules for sorting pictures (i.e., "If I show you something that goes outside the house, put it here; things that go inside the house go over here"). When asked to sort test cards according to these rules, 2.5-year-olds started to use these rules but then perseverated on one of them, suggesting that they were able to represent and use a single rule but could not consider two rules in contradistinction.

In terms of Fig. 12.1, the conscious DescA of a goal established at the level of RecC is fed back into consciousness, which is called *self-consciousness* (SelfC) after two degrees of recursion. In SelfC, the DescA is related to a self-description (SdescA) of a rule (R1) linking an antecedent condition to an action (i.e., R1 = C1 —> A1). This rule can then be deposited into WM together with the DescA of the goal (G1), and the rule can then be used to control behavior systematically despite changing perceptual input.

Implications for awareness of the self in time. Unlike recursively conscious infants, self-conscious children can consider descriptions of events as past or future oriented, relative to a present experience (see Fig. 12.2d). For example, while conscious of their current state (now), 2-year-olds can appreciate that yesterday they went to the zoo (Friedman, 1993).

The concepts *"yesterday"* and *"tomorrow"* are intrinsically relational because they are indexed with respect to *"today."* Thus, in order for children to comprehend that an event occurred yesterday (or will occur tomorrow), children must be conscious of Now and consider two linked descriptions: a description of the event and a further description of the event as occurring yesterday (or tomorrow). Doing so corresponds in complexity to the use of a single rule considered against the backdrop of a goal that occasions its use. That is, G1; C1 —> A1 is instantiated as follows: Now; Tomorrow —> Event A.

When children can consider past or future events *as such,* they will have a subjective experience of self-continuity in time. This experience of self-continuity yields a feeling of personal concern about past and future states and corresponds to an important developmental advance in children's experience of the self in time. Despite the importance of this advance, however, there continues to be considerable room for development. For example, an additional degree of recursion will be required for children to consider two different events occurring at two different times (e.g., Event A, further described as occurring Now, considered in contradistinction to Event B, further described as occurring Tomorrow).

Reflective Consciousness 1

By about 3 years of age children acquire a higher level of consciousness, referred to as *reflective consciousness 1* (see Fig. 12.1). This additional degree of recursion enables children to reflect on a self-description of a rule from a relatively detached or psychologically distant perspective and consider this rule in relation to another self-description of another rule. Both of these rules can then be deposited into WM where they can be used contrastively (against the backdrop of a goal) to control the elicitation of action programs.

The ability to consider two rules in contradistinction brings about an increase in behavioral flexibility, and children at age 3 years no longer perseverate on a single rule when presented with a pair of rules (P. D. Zelazo & Reznick, 1991). However, there are still limitations on children's self-control. For example, 3-year-olds have difficulty switching between two incompatible pairs of rules in rule-use tasks such as the dimensional change card sort (DCCS; Frye, Zelazo, & Palfai, 1995; P. D. Zelazo, Frye, & Rapus, 1996). In the DCCS children are shown two target cards, each of which is affixed to a sorting tray, and they are asked to sort a series of test cards into the trays according to one dimension (e.g., for color, they are told, "If it's blue, put it here; if it's red, it goes there"). Then, after sorting several cards, they are told to stop playing the first game and switch to another game (e.g., shape, for which they are told, "Put the flowers here; put the boats there"). Regardless of which dimension is presented first, 3-year-olds typically continue to sort the cards by that dimension despite being told the new rules on every trial and despite having sorted cards by the new dimension on other occasions.

Nonetheless, 3-year-olds can state where the cards should be sorted under both pairs of rules, suggesting that they can represent both pairs of rules consciously at one level of consciousness (viz., reflective consciousness 1). The problem seems to be that they cannot further reflect on their conscious representations of the two pairs of rules, which would allow them to make a deliberate decision to use the postswitch rules as against the preswitch rules (which are now prepotent because they have been invoked and used in this context); that is, they cannot attain a level of consciousness that would allow them to formulate a higher order rule that integrates both pairs of rules into a single rule system.

Implications for awareness of the self in time. At 3 years of age children are able to consider two rules in contradistinction (i.e., they can consider a single pair of rules) from a relatively distanced perspective. From this perspective, which corresponds to a direct experience of Now, they are able to consider two events occurring at two different times. For example, against the backdrop of Now, they can consider that Now, Event A is occurring, but Yesterday, Event B occurred. Note that in this case children's direct experience of Now must occur from a temporally decentered perspective (McCormack & Hoerl, 1999, chap. 11, this volume), from which they conceptualize Now (see Fig. 12.2d).

This important developmental advance allows children to make judgments about history (e.g., now vs. before). For example, in a control task used by Gopnik and Astington (1988, Experiment 1), most 3-year-olds were able to judge that now there was a doll in a closed toy house, but before there was an apple. At this level of consciousness, however, children cannot differentiate between the history of the world and the history of the self—that is, the objective series and the subjective series remain undifferentiated; the two series are conflated in a single dimension. As a result, 3-year-olds typically failed Gopnik and Astington's representational change task, in which they must appreciate that they themselves changed from thinking Smarties to thinking sticks, even while the contents of the box did not change. According to the LOC model, this failure to differentiate between the history of the world and the history of the self occurs because children who are limited to reflective consciousness 1 are able to use only a single pair of rules, which allows them to make a discrimination *within* a single dimension but prevents them from making comparisons between dimensions (e.g., between shape and color in the DCCS).

The current account is broadly compatible with McCormack and Hoerl's (1999, chap. 11, this volume) account of the development of temporal understanding in this age range (i.e., at around 3 years of age), and, as they have noted, children's initial level of temporal decentering, although corresponding to an important developmental advance, is limited. According to McCormack and Hoerl, children first acquire the ability to switch temporal perspectives before they are able to reason about the relation between perspectives. We agree with McCormack and Hoerl on this point, although in our account the emergence of temporal decentering is a consequence of the more general psychological distancing that is made possible by an increase in children's highest level of consciousness. Children's initial level of decentering is limited on our account, because reflective consciousness 1 allows children to make discriminations only within a single temporal series. As a result, children not only fail to reason about the relation between different temporal perspectives, as McCormack and Hoerl pointed out, but they also fail to differentiate (and coordinate) objective and subjective temporal series, as in Gopnik and Astington's (1988) representational change task.

Reflective Consciousness 2

By 4 or 5 years of age an additional degree of recursion allows children to consider the entire contents of reflective consciousness 1 in relation to a self-description of comparable complexity. This enables children to appreciate that they know two incompatible pairs of rules for responding to the same situation and integrate these rule pairs into a single hierarchical system of rules (Frye, Zelazo, & Burack, 1998; P. D. Zelazo & Frye, 1998). As shown in Fig. 12.3, a rule such as A, which links antecedent 1 (a1) to consequent 1 (c1), stands in a contrastive (exclusive-

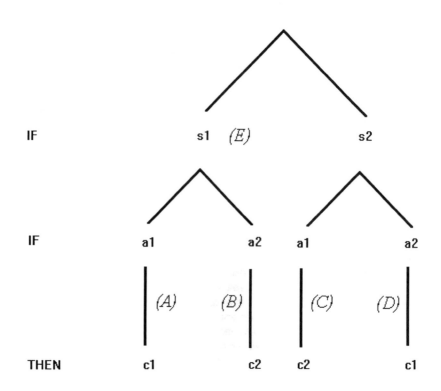

FIG 12.3. Hierarchical tree structure showing how one rule can
be embedded under another and controlled by it (adapted
from Frye et al., 1995). s1 and s2 = setting conditions; a1 and
a2 = antecedent conditions; c1 and c2 = consequences.

or, V_x) relation with Rule B, which links antecedent 2 (a2) to consequent 2
(c2). These rules are incompatible with Rules C and D, because the
relations between antecedents and consequents are reversed. With
reflective consciousness 2, children can formulate the higher order rule
that allows them to integrate both rule pairs into a single universe of
discourse. Only when the rule pairs are considered in relation to one
another can the appropriate rule pair be selected to control action.
Otherwise, a rule pair will be selected on the basis of relatively local
considerations (i.e., children will select whichever rule pair is most
strongly associated with the situation). Indeed, whereas most 3-year-olds
perseverate on the DCCS, 4- or 5-year-olds typically switch flexibly
between the two dimensions (e.g., color and shape).

    Implications for awareness of the self in time. Children with reflective
consciousness 2 can reflect on their ability to use two incompatible pairs
of rules, such as those for making discriminations within two different

dimensions (e.g., color and shape) in the DCCS. P. D. Zelazo and Frye (1997) suggested that it is only by distancing themselves from discriminations *within* a dimension and considering two or more dimensions in contradistinction that children are able to conceptualize dimensions *qua* dimensions (see also Smith, 1989). In terms of their understanding of the self in time, this ability to consider dimensions *qua* dimensions (or series *qua* series) allows children to differentiate and coordinate two series—the history of the self and the history of the world—from a temporally decentered perspective (see Fig. 12.2e). As Bieri (1986) noted, in order to have a genuine temporal awareness one must differentiate the progression of the self from the progression of events in the world and then understand the former relative to the latter. (The latter corresponds to the objective series, which ultimately serves as the unifying temporal framework.)

Behavioral evidence of children's ability to differentiate and yet coordinate the history of the self and the history of the world can be seen in 4- and 5-year-olds' success on Gopnik and Astington's (1988) representational change task. In this task, children appreciate that they themselves changed from thinking Smarties to thinking sticks but that the contents of the box did not change. Thus, against the backdrop of Now, children appreciate the history of the world, on the one hand: That is, they appreciate that in the past, Event A (sticks in the box) occurred; and now, Event A is still occurring. However, they also appreciate the history of the self, on the other hand: In the past, Event A (believed Smarties in the box) occurred; and now, Event B is occurring (believe sticks in the box). As was the case at the previous level of understanding, children must occupy a temporally decentered perspective from which they conceptualize Now.

Because reflective consciousness 2 allows children to integrate two incompatible pairs of rules within a single system of rules it allows them to understand that they can conceptualize a single thing in two distinct ways. For example, they can conceptualize a red rabbit as a red thing and as a rabbit in the DCCS, and they can acknowledge that a sponge rock looks like a rock even though it is really a sponge (Flavell, Flavell, & Green, 1983). When applied to time, this understanding permits children potentially to appreciate multiple temporal perspectives on the same event (e.g., that time present is time past in time future; cf. Eliot's, 1943, poem, *Burnt Norton*). This acquisition, at about 4 or 5 years of age, corresponds to the major developmental change identified in McCormack and Hoerl's (1999, chap. 11, this volume) account of temporal understanding: At a higher level of temporal decentering, children appreciate that multiple temporal perspectives are perspectives onto the same temporal reality, and they acquire the concept of particular times (i.e., that events occur at unique, particular times).

Children's ability to conceptualize a single thing in multiple ways can also be applied to *the self in time*, where it allows children potentially to conceptualize *themselves* from multiple temporal perspectives—to understand themselves as exhibiting both continuity and change in time. Müller and Overton (1998) discussed this understanding in terms of Stern's (1934/1938) notion of *mnemic continuity*: "I am the *same one* who *now* remembers what I *then* experienced" (p. 250), and they noted that Stern described this understanding as emerging around the fourth year of life. As in the current proposal, Müller and Overton explained this emergence with reference to a more general theory of cognitive development (in their case, however, the theory is essentially Piagetian).

COMPARISON WITH ANOTHER PROPOSAL

The LOC model of the development of the self in time differs in crucial respects from another recent approach to this topic (Povinelli, 1995), and a comparison of the two proposals will perhaps clarify some of the unique contributions made by the LOC model. According to Povinelli (1995), although children between 18 and 24 months of age can pass mirror self-recognition tasks (e.g., Amsterdam, 1972; Lewis & Brooks-Gunn, 1979), they do not yet possess an objective and enduring self-concept. Instead, Povinelli (1995) suggested that children at this age maintain a succession of present-oriented representations of self (termed *present selves*; Povinelli, 1995, p. 165), and they cannot compare these representations or "integrate previous mental or physical states with current ones" (p. 166). Consequently, their sense of self continuity in time is temporally restricted and they might be said to live in the present, depicted as "now" in Figs. 12.4a and 12.4b. Although Povinelli (1995) followed James (1890/1950) in noting that children must "recognize a time corridor into the immediate past and into the immediate future" (p. 166), he hypothesized that the temporal breadth of the present self is "very narrow" (p. 185)—perhaps on the order of 1 or 2 seconds (Povinelli & Simon, 1998, p. 190). Children may access representations of past selves beyond this narrow window (e.g., they may recall things they did), but they cannot understand the temporal–causal connection between these past selves and their present self; instead these past selves are dissociated from the present self. Indeed, it is not until about 3.5 years that children acquire a sense of themselves as temporally extended, which Povinelli (1995, p. 167) referred to as "the proper self."

According to Povinelli (1995), this acquisition is made possible by domain-general changes in children's capacity for representation. Here, Povinelli (1995) followed Olson's (1993; Olson & Campbell, 1993) model of the development of mental representations (see P. D. Zelazo, 2000a,

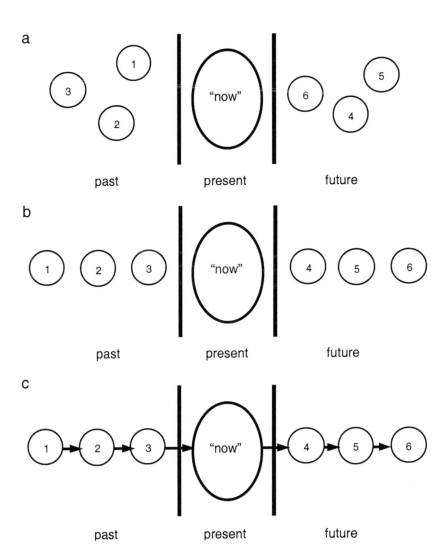

FIG 12.4. Povinelli's model of children's understanding of the temporal–causal arrow of time. From "Development of Young Children's Understanding That the Recent Past Is Causally Bound to the Present" (p. 1427) by D. J. Povinelli, A. M. Landry, L. A. Theall, B. R. Clark, and C. M. Castille, 1999, *Developmental Psychology, 35,* 1426–1439. Copyright 1999 by the American Psychological Association. Reprinted by permission.

for discussion). According to Olson, infants do not actually have mental states. Instead, their behavior is mediated by "perceptual" schemata, which Olson (1993) characterized as "simply causal functions" (p. 292). During the second year, however, children acquire the ability to form propositions that relate an idea to something perceived; that is, they acquire the ability to *predicate* something (i.e., a schema held in mind) about something else (i.e., a perceptual schema). For Olson, predication is the first step toward the formulation of beliefs, but not the last. The second, constitutive step occurs when children are able to consider this predicative relation between two schemata (i.e., a proposition) relative to a third (perceptual) schema. It is only at this third stage, which occurs at about 4 years of age, that mind emerges on Olson's account: "Beliefs, we recall, are the mental structures identified with Mind. No beliefs, no mind. So how do beliefs arise? Beliefs arise when the child becomes capable of relating the propositions constructed at stage 2 with the perceptual schemata constructed at stage 1" (Olson, 1989, pp. 623–624). Olson (1989) further suggested that with the emergence of mind at 4 years of age, "children come to specify the Self—the self-conscious self" (p. 624).

Working from Olson's (e.g., 1993) framework, Povinelli (1995) proposed that prior, to 18 months of age, children are unable to hold a representation of the self in mind. By 18–24 months the ability to form propositions allows them to represent the present self (which can then be related to a self-description or an image in a mirror). Finally, between 3 and 4 years of age, children acquire the ability to relate a proposition to a perceptual schema, and this allows them to construct the proper self. The *proper self* is defined as a higher order concept of self that integrates past and future states of self into a temporal progression. This proper self allows children to understand how current states of self are causally determined by previous states of self (Povinelli, 1995, p. 168; see Fig. 12.4c).

Support for Povinelli's (1995) proposal comes from several studies using a delayed self-recognition (DSR) paradigm (see Povinelli, chap. 5, this volume, for a review). In one study (Povinelli, Landau, & Perilloux, 1996, Experiment 1), children played a game during which an experimenter surreptitiously placed a sticker on their heads. About 3 minutes later, children were presented with a video image of the marking event. Whereas the majority of older children (4-year-olds) reached up to touch the sticker, few of the younger children (2- and 3-year-olds) did so.

Povinelli and Simon (1998) extended these results by examining whether 3-, 4-, and 5-year-olds act as if events that happened in the recent past (briefly delayed video condition) are relevant to current states of self but that those that occurred in the distant past (extremely delayed video condition) are not. As predicted, 3-year-olds were about equally likely to reach up to the sticker in both conditions, but the older children were more likely to reach up in the briefly delayed condition.

Finally, in a more recent series of studies, Povinelli, Landry, Theall, Clark, and Castille (1999) explored whether children in this age range could more generally appreciate "the causal arrow of time that binds each state of the world to each succeeding one" (Povinelli et al., 1999, p. 1428). In Study 1, 3- and 4-year-old children were videotaped playing a board game while an experimenter secretly hid a puppet in one of two boxes. After playing the game, children were shown two videotapes, one of which showed them playing the game while the experimenter hid the puppet behind them, and the other of which showed a different child playing the game while the experimenter hid the puppet in the other location. Povinelli et al. (1999) found that older 3-year-olds and 4-year-olds searched for the puppet in the correct location at above-chance levels. In contrast, younger 3-year-olds generally searched at the location indicated by the videotape that they had seen most recently.

Povinelli's (e.g., 1995) model provides a cogent account of his empirical findings. However, the results of our own recent research (P. D. Zelazo, Sommerville, & Nichols, 1999) call into question several key aspects of his model and the evidence on which it is based. In particular, these results call into question the claim that 3-year-olds' sense of self is temporally restricted, and they undermine the validity of DSR as a measure of self-concept development.

In an initial experiment, P. D. Zelazo et al. (1999, Experiment 1) attempted to gauge the span of young children's sense of self, as assessed by the DSR paradigm, by using two levels of delay (5 sec vs. 3 min) between the media-recording event and the presentation of the self-image. In contrast to the 3-minute delay used by Povinelli et al (1996), 5 seconds might be expected to fall within the span of the present self if 3-year-olds are truly present oriented. However, the results revealed that dramatically decreasing the length of the delay did not improve 3-year-olds' performance. If one assumes that DSR provides a measure of the temporal span of children's self, then the results suggest that 3-year-olds cannot conceive of themselves as extending beyond a few seconds in the past and/or future. Is this plausible?

Although 3-year-olds are notoriously poor at long-term planning (e.g., Thompson, Barresi, & Moore, 1997), and it is at least conceivable that they do not yet engage in genuine episodic recollection (Perner & Ruffman, 1995; but see Howe & Courage, 1997; Wheeler, 2000), they do seem actively concerned about events that will occur more than a few seconds in the future. Indeed, research on planning, deliberate reasoning, delayed responding, and intentional action in the second and third years of life (see P. D. Zelazo, Carter, Reznick, & Frye, 1997, for a review), provides *prima facie* evidence that children's sense of themselves is not so severely temporally restricted as Povinelli and Simon (1998) suggested. In contrast, this evidence is consistent with the LOC account, which holds that children at this age not only have a subjective experience of self continuity in time but also are able to adopt a temporally decentered perspective from which they can consider two events occurring at different times.

In a second experiment, P. D. Zelazo et al. (1999, Experiment 2) sought to assess whether DSR is a valid measure of the temporal extension of children's self-concept. We found that 3-year-olds exhibited as much difficulty on an "other" version of the delayed-video mark test as they did on a closely matched self version. In the other version children were required to use delayed video to locate a sticker on the head of a stuffed animal. Their failure to do so indicates that children's difficulty using delayed-media representations to guide behavior is not specific to tasks involving the self and hence that children may fail the task for reasons unrelated to their level of self-understanding. Indeed, we hypothesized that in the DSR paradigm children may have a strong expectation that they do *not* have a sticker on their head (because they do not see it placed there and cannot see it directly at the time of testing), and we further proposed that when children are provided with conflicting information via a dimly understood representational medium (e.g., video; Flavell, Flavell, Green, & Korfmacher, 1990) the new, conflicting information may be ignored or treated as somehow irrelevant to the situation.

To test this hypothesis, P. D. Zelazo et al. (1999, Experiment 3) conducted a third experiment that revealed that 3-year-olds can, in fact, use delayed-video (and delayed-verbal) representations to guide their search for a hidden object in the absence of a conflicting expectation about the object's location but have difficulty doing so in the presence of a conflicting expectation. In the conflict condition, 3- and 4-year-olds helped an experimenter hide an object at one location in a room. Then they were informed that the experimenter was going to move the object to a different location, and they either watched this movement on video or were told the object's new location verbally. In the no-conflict trials, children were simply presented with the verbal or video information.

Results showed that 3-year-olds were more likely to err in the conflict condition than in the no-conflict condition, and in most cases when they erred, children searched where the object had been hidden initially. This finding suggests that the presence or absence of conflict in assessment procedures will affect estimates of children's understanding. Conflicting expectations may be especially difficult for children to ignore when they are based on direct experience but, more generally, the influence of information on children's behavior may vary with children's understanding of the medium by which it is presented. However, the main point for the present purpose is this: Because children have difficulty using conflicting delayed representations in general, poor performance on tests of delayed self-recognition does not necessarily indicate an immature self-concept.

These findings generally support the LOC model, which differs from Povinelli's (e.g., 1995) proposal in several important ways. First, our account suggests that performance on the DSR task is mediated by a number of variables—mainly, children's ability to reason about conflicting representations, but also children's understanding of various media. Therefore, DSR performance is not a good indicator of the temporal continuity of self. Whereas this paradigm led Povinelli and Simon (1998) to propose that the children's sense of themselves is temporally restricted to a specious present that spans mere seconds, on our account children appreciate the continuity of the self in time (see Figs. 12.2c and 12.2d) even while failing the DSR task.

Second, our model stipulates that changes in children's ability to reason about the self in time are brought about by changes in children's level of consciousness. These changes in level of consciousness have consequences for the complexity of children's reasoning—not just for the capacity of working memory—and the LOC model provides a detailed, functional alternative to Olson's (e.g., 1993) suggestion that mind first emerges (out of merely "causal" processes) in the developing child at 4 years of age.

Third, and most important, we identify several key distinctions in the gradual development of the self in time. These include the distinction between past and future orientation in behavior and a subjective experience of self-continuity in time, which we believe emerges at about 2 years of age. In addition, on our account an experience of self-continuity yields a feeling of personal concern about past and future states but does not require children to consider themselves from a temporal decentered perspective (e.g., to compare now vs. later). Finally, we make a further distinction between two different ways of conceptualizing history. At the level of reflective consciousness 1, 3-year-old children fail to differentiate between the history of the world and the history of the self (i.e., the subjective series and the objective series remain undifferentiated). As a result, they typically pass Gopnik and Astington's (1988) control task but fail the representational change task. In contrast, 5-year-old children with reflective consciousness 2 can distance themselves from a single dimension, which allows them to differentiate and coordinate two series—the history of the self and the history of the world—from a temporally decentered perspective.

CONCLUSION

The current proposal characterizes the development of the self in time and explains this development in terms of the LOC model of the role of consciousness in reasoning and intentional action. The LOC model describes four age-related increases in the highest level of consciousness that children can attain in response to situational demands. These increases come about through the functional process of recursion whereby the contents of consciousness are fed back into consciousness, making them available to consciousness at a higher level.

With respect to the experience of time and the self in time, these changes can be summarized as follows. Initially, consciousness is restricted to the here and now: Past experiences cannot be consciously recalled, and future states cannot be consciously anticipated—although behavior is both past and future oriented. By the end of the first year of life recursive consciousness allows for the conscious representation of (descriptions of) past experiences and future-oriented representations, although these states cannot be related to the present state. Between 18 months and 2 years, another level of consciousness, called *self-consciousness*, emerges. This additional degree of recursion allows children to consider descriptions of past- or future-oriented events in relation to a present experience, resulting in a subjective experience of self-continuity in time.

Reflective consciousness 1 develops by about 3 years of age, enabling children to adopt a temporally decentered perspective from which they are able to consider two events occurring at two different times (although the progression of their own subjective experiences remains undifferentiated from the unfolding history of events in the world). Finally, by about 4 or 5 years of age, recursive consciousness 2 allows children to differentiate and coordinate the history of the self and the history of the world from a temporally decentered perspective. As Bieri (1986) noted, such coordination is required for genuine temporal awareness. According to the current proposal, it is also required for children to understand themselves as exhibiting both continuity and change—essential aspects of the self in time.

ACKOWLEDGMENTS

Preparation of this chapter was supported in part by a grant from the Natural Sciences and Engineering Research Council of Canada to Philip David Zelazo. We thank Ulrich Müller for introducing us to Bieri's (1986) work and for translating it from the German and for discussion of the ideas contained in this chapter and a critical reading of an earlier draft. Virginia Boquiren kindly prepared Fig. 12.2.

REFERENCES

Amsterdam, B. (1972). Mirror self-image reactions before age two. *Developmental Psychobiology, 5*, 297–305.

Armstrong, D. M. (1980). *The nature of mind and other essays*. Ithaca, NY: Cornell University Press.

Baldwin, J. M. (1891, Nov). Origin of volition in childhood. *Science, 20*, 286–288.

Barnat, S. B., Klein, P. J., & Meltzoff, A. N. (1996). Deferred imitation across changes in context and object: Memory and generalization in 14-month-old infants. *Infant Behavior and Development, 19*, 241–251.

Bieri, P. (1986). Zeiterfahrung und Personalität [Temporal experience and personality]. In H. Burger (Ed.), *Zeit, Natur und Mensch [Time, Nature, and Human Being]* (pp. 261–281). Berlin: Arno Spitz Verlag.

Brentano, F. (1973). *Psychology from an empirical standpoint*. (D. Kraus, Ed.; A. C. Rancurello, D. B. Terrell, & L. L. McAlister, Trans.). London: Routledge.

Carver, L. J., & Bauer, P. J. (1999). When the event is more than the sum of its parts: 9-month-olds' long-term ordered recall. *Memory, 7*, 147–174.

Cohen, L. B. (1998). An information processing approach to infant perception and cognition. In G. Butterworth & F. Simion (Eds.), *Development of sensory, motor, and cognitive capabilities in early infancy: From sensation to cognition* (pp. 277–300). Sussex, England: Taylor & Francis.

Craik, F. I. M., & Lockhart, R. S. (1972). Levels of processing: A framework for memory research. *Journal of Verbal Learning and Verbal Behavior, 11*, 671–684.

Craik, F. I. M., & Tulving, E. (1975). Depth of processing and the retention of words in episodic memory. *Journal of Experimental Psychology: General, 104*, 268–294.

DeCasper, A., & Fifer, W. P. (1980, June). Of human bonding: Newborns prefer their mothers' voice. *Science, 208*, 1174–1176.

DeLoache, J. (1993). Distancing and dual representation. In R. R. Cocking & K. A. Renninger (Eds.), *The development and meaning of psychological distance* (pp. 91–107). Hillsdale, NJ: Lawrence Erlbaum Associates.

Dewey, J. (1985). Context and thought. In J. A. Boydston (Ed.) & A. Sharpe (Textual Ed.), *John Dewey: The later works, 1925–1953* (Vol. 6, pp. 3–21). Carbondale: Southern Illinois University Press. (Original work published 1931)

Eliot, T. S. (1943). *Four quartets*. London: Faber and Faber.

Flavell, J. H., Flavell, E. R., & Green, F. L. (1983). Development of the appearance–reality distinction. *Cognitive Psychology, 15,* 95–120.

Flavell, J. H., Flavell, E. R., Green, F. L., & Korfmacher, J. F. (1990). Do young children think of television images as pictures or real objects? *Journal of Broadcasting and Electronic Media, 34*, 399–419.

Fraisse, P. (1982). The adaptation of the child to time. In W. J. Friedman (Ed.), *The developmental psychology of time* (pp. 113–140). New York: Academic.

Friedman, W. J. (1993). Memory for the time of past events. *Psychological Bulletin, 113*, 44–66.

Frye, D., Zelazo, P. D., & Burack, J. A. (1998). I. Cognitive complexity and control: Implications for theory of mind in typical and atypical development. *Current Directions in Psychological Science, 7*, 116–121.

Frye, D., Zelazo, P. D., & Palfai, T. (1995). Theory of mind and rule-based reasoning. *Cognitive Development, 10*, 483–527.

Goldman-Rakic, P. S. (1990). The prefrontal contribution to working memory and conscious experience. In J. C. Eccles & O. Creutzfeldt (Eds.), *The principles of design and operation of the brain* (pp. 389–407). New York: Springer-Verlag.

Gopnik, A., & Astington, J. W. (1988). Children's understanding of representational change and its relation to the understanding of false belief and the appearance–reality distinction. *Child Development, 59,* 26–37.

Haith, M. M., Hazan, C., & Goodman, G. S. (1988). Expectation and anticipation of dynamic visual events by 3.5-month-old babies. *Child Development, 59,* 467–479.

Howe, M. L., & Courage, M. L. (1997). The emergence and early development of autobiographical memory. *Psychological Review, 104,* 499–535.

James, W. (1950). *The principles of psychology.* New York: Dover. (Original work published 1890)

Kagan, J. (1972). Do infants think? *Scientific American, 226,* 74–82.

Kagan, J. (1981). *The second year.* Cambridge, MA: Harvard University Press.

Leslie, A. M. (1987). Pretense and representation: The origins of "theory of mind". *Psychological Review, 94,* 412–426.

Lewis, M., & Brooks-Gunn, J. (1979). *Social cognition and the acquisition of the self.* New York: Plenum.

Mandler, J. M., & McDonough, L. (1995). Long-term recall of event sequences in infancy. *Journal of Experimental Child Psychology, 59,* 457–474.

Marcovitch, S., & Zelazo, P. D. (1999) The A-not-B error: Results from a logistic meta-analysis. *Child Development, 70,* 1297–1313.

McCormack, T., & Hoerl, C. (1999). Memory and temporal perspective: The role of temporal frameworks in memory development. *Developmental Review, 19,* 154–182.

Meltzoff, A. N. (1988). Infant imitation and memory: Nine-month-olds in immediate and deferred tests. *Child Development, 59,* 217–225.

Meltzoff, A. N. (1995). What infant memory tells us about infantile amnesia: Long-term recall and deferred imitation. *Journal of Experimental Child Psychology, 59,* 497–515.

Moore, C., & Corkum, V. (1994). Social understanding at the end of the first year of life. *Developmental Review, 14,* 349–372.

Müller, U., & Overton, W. F. (1998). How to grow a baby: A reevaluation of image-schema and Piagetian action approaches to representation. *Human Development, 41,* 71–111.

Neisser, U. (1988). Five kinds of self knowledge. *Philosophical Psychology, 1,* 35–59.

Olson, D. R. (1989). Making up your mind. *Canadian Psychology, 30,* 617–627.

Olson, D. R. (1993). The development of representations: The origins of mental life. *Canadian Psychology, 34,* 293–304.

Olson, D. R., & Campbell, R. (1993). Constructing representations. In C. Pratt & A Garton (Eds.), *The development and use of systems of representation* (pp. 11–26). New York: Wiley.

Perner, J., & Ruffman, T. (1995). Episodic memory and autonoetic consciousness: Developmental evidence and a theory of childhood amnesia. *Journal of Experimental Child Psychology, 59,* 516–548.

Piaget, J. (1946). *The child's conception of time.* New York: Ballantine.

Piaget, J. (1952). *The origins of intelligence in children* (M. Cook, Trans.). New York: Vintage. (Original work published 1936)

Povinelli, D. J. (1995). The unduplicated self. In P. Rochat (Ed.), *The self in infancy: Theory and research* (pp. 161–192). New York: Elsevier.

Povinelli, D. J., Landau, K. R., & Perilloux, H. K. (1996). Self-recognition in young children using delayed versus live feedback: Evidence for developmental asynchrony. *Child Development, 67,* 1540–1554.

Povinelli, D. J., Landry, A. M., Theall, L. A., Clark, B. R, & Castille, C. M. (1999). Development of young children's understanding that the recent past is causally bound to the present. *Developmental Psychology, 35,* 1426–1439.

Povinelli, D. J., & Simon, B. B. (1998). Young children's understanding of briefly versus extremely delayed images of self: Emergence of an autobiographical stance. *Developmental Psychology, 34,* 188–194.

Reznick, J. S. (1994). In search of infant expectation. In M. M. Haith, J. B. Benson, R. J. Roberts, Jr., & B. F. Pennington (Eds.), *The development of future-oriented processes* (pp. 39–59). Chicago: University of Chicago Press.

Sigel, I. (1993). The centrality of a distancing model for the development of representational competence. In R. R. Cocking & K. A. Renninger (Eds.), *The development and meaning of psychological distance* (pp. 91–107). Hillsdale, NJ: Lawrence Erlbaum Associates.

Smith, L. B. (1989). From global similarities to kinds of similarities: The construction of dimensions in development. In S. Voisiadou & A. Ortony (Eds.), *Similarity and analogical reasoning* (pp. 146–178). New York: Cambridge University Press.

Stern, W. (1938). *General psychology from the personalistic standpoint.* New York: Macmillan. (Original work published 1934)

Thompson, C., Barresi, J., & Moore, C. (1997). The development of future-oriented prudence and altruism in preschoolers. *Cognitive Development, 12,* 199–212.

Tomasello, M. (1999) *The cultural origins of human cognition.* Cambridge, MA: Harvard University Press.

Wheeler, M. (2000). Varieties of consciousness and memory in the developing child. In E. Tulving (Ed.), *Memory, consciousness, and the brain: The Tallinn Conference* (pp. 188–199). Philadelphia: Psychology Press.

Zelazo, P. D. (1996). Towards a characterization of minimal consciousness. *New Ideas in Psychology, 14,* 63–80.

Zelazo, P. D. (1999). Language, levels of consciousness, and the development of intentional action. In P. D. Zelazo, J. W. Astington, & D. R. Olson (Eds.), *Developing theories of intention: Social understanding and self-control* (pp. 95–117). Mahwah, NJ: Lawrence Erlbaum Associates.

Zelazo, P. D. (2000a). Minds in the (re-)Making: Imitation and the dialectic of representation. In J. W. Astington (Ed.), *Minds in the making: Essays in honour of David R. Olson* (pp. 143–164). Oxford, England: Basil Blackwell.

Zelazo, P. D. (2000b). Self-reflection and the development of consciously controlled processing. In P. Mitchell & K. Riggs (Eds.), *Children's reasoning and the mind* (pp. 169–189). Hove, England: Psychology Press.

Zelazo, P. D., Carter, A., Reznick, J. S., & Frye, D. (1997). Early development of executive function: A problem-solving framework. *Review of General Psychology, 1,* 198–226.

Zelazo, P. D., & Frye, D. (1997). Cognitive complexity and control: A theory of the development of deliberate reasoning and intentional action. In M.

Stamenov (Ed.), *Language structure, discourse, and the access to consciousness* (pp. 113–153). Philadelphia: John Benjamins.

Zelazo, P. D., & Frye, D. (1998). Cognitive complexity and control: II. The development of executive function in childhood. *Current Directions in Psychological Science, 7,* 121–126.

Zelazo, P. D., Frye, D., & Rapus, T. (1996). An age-related dissociation between knowing rules and using them. *Cognitive Development, 11,* 37–63.

Zelazo, P. D., & Reznick, J. S. (1991). Age-related asynchrony of knowledge and action. *Child Development, 62,* 719–735.

Zelazo, P. D., Reznick, J. S., & Pinon, D. E. (1995). Response control and the execution of verbal rules. *Developmental Psychology, 31,* 508–517.

Zelazo, P. D., Sommerville, J. A., & Nichols, S. (1999). Age-related changes in children's use of external representations. *Developmental Psychology, 35,* 1059–1071.

Zelazo, P. R. (1982). The year-old infant: A period of major cognitive change. In T. Bever (Ed.), *Regressions in mental development: Basic phenomena and theoretical alternatives* (pp. 47–79). Hillsdale, NJ: Lawrence Erlbaum Associates.

Zelazo, P. R., & Kearsley, R. B. (1980). The emergence of functional play in infants: Evidence for a major cognitive transition. *Journal of Applied Developmental Psychology, 2,* 95–117.

Zelazo, P. R., & Leonard, E. L. (1983). The dawn of active thought. In K. Fischer (Ed.), *Levels and transitions in children's development: New directions in child development* (Vol. 21, pp. 37–50). San Francisco: Jossey-Bass.

Zelazo, P. R., & Zelazo, P. D. (1998). The emergence of consciousness. In H. H. Jasper, L. Descarries, V. F. Castellucci, & S. Rossignol (Eds.), *Consciousness: At the frontiers of neuroscience: Advances in neurology,* (Vol. 77, pp. 149–165). New York: Lippincott–Raven.

Author Index

Subject Index

Contributors

Cristina M. Atance, Department of Psychology, University of Waterloo. E-mail: cmatance@watarts.uwaterloo.ca

John Barresi, Department of Psychology, Dalhousie University. E-mail: jbarresi@is.dal.ca

Robyn Fivush, Department of Psychology, Emory University. E-mail: psyrf@emory.edu

Christoph Hoerl, Department of Philosophy, University of Warwick. E-mail: C.Hoerl@warwick.ac.uk

Judith A. Hudson, Department of Psychology, Rutgers University. E-mail: jahudson@home.com

Karen Lemmon, Department of Psychology, Dalhousie University. E-mail: kmlskene@is2.dal.ca

Teresa McCormack, Department of Psychology, University of Warwick. E-mail: Teresa.McCormack@csv.warwick.ac.uk

Chris Moore, Department of Psychology, Dalhousie University. E-mail: moorec@is.dal.ca

Katherine Nelson, CUNY Graduate School, New York. E-mail: knelson@gc.cuny.edu

Daniela K. O'Neill, Department of Psychology, University of Waterloo. E-mail: doneill@watarts.uwaterloo.ca

Josef Perner, Department of Psychology, University of Salzburg. E-mail: josef.perner@mh.sbg.ac.at

Daniel J. Povinelli, Cognitive Evolution Group, University of Louisiana at Lafayette. E-mail: ceg@louisiana.edu

Jessica A. Sommerville, Department of Psychology, University of Chicago. E-mail: jsomm@ccp.uchicago.edu

Melissa Welch-Ross, National Institute on Early Childhood Development and Education, U.S. Department of Education, Washington DC. E-mail: Melissa_Welch-Ross@ed.gov

Philip David Zelazo, Department of Psychology, University of Toronto. E-mail: zelazo@psych.utoronto.ca